Government for the People

Reflections of a White House Counsel to Presidents Kennedy and Johnson

Lee C. White

Foreword by Bill Moyers

Hamilton Books
A member of
The Rowman & Littlefield Publishing Group
Lanham • Boulder • New York • Toronto • Plymouth, UK

Copyright © 2008 by
Hamilton Books
4501 Forbes Boulevard
Suite 200
Lanham, Maryland 20706
Hamilton Books Acquisitions Department (301) 459-3366

Estover Road
Plymouth PL6 7PY
United Kingdom

Library of Congress Control Number: 2007932835
ISBN-13: 978-0-7618-3905-7 (clothbound : alk. paper)
ISBN-10: 0-7618-3905-4 (clothbound : alk. paper)
ISBN-13: 978-0-7618-3872-2 (paperback : alk. paper)
ISBN-10: 0-7618-3872-4 (paperback : alk. paper)

Cover photo: Lee C. White at a pensive moment during a meeting in the Oval
Office with President Lyndon Johnson and Dr. Robert Weaver, Administrator of
the Housing and Home Finance Agency (not pictured), on January 24, 1964.
Photo Credit: Yoichi R. Okamoto. (Personal Collection of Lee C. White)

∞™ The paper used in this publication meets the minimum
requirements of American National Standard for Information
Sciences—Permanence of Paper for Printed Library Materials,
ANSI Z39.48—1992

Dedication

I, like almost everyone, am indebted to my parents for the gifts that I inherited. I dedicate this book to their memory.

My mother, Ann Ruth Ackerman White, and my father, Herman Henry White, were Russian immigrants: my dad at age fourteen; and my mother at age one-and-a-half. Both wound up in Omaha, Nebraska, where they established themselves as solid members of the community. My father was a natural for the retail grocery business, and he provided for the family until the depression of the thirties shoved his business into bankruptcy. But he got back on his feet and did well.

As a big bug on genetics, I would have preferred to have been given my mother's genes, which my sister inherited, that would have made me tall and given me a full head of black hair that would stay black into my nineties, instead of my dad's short, dumpy, and bald genes. But I wound up with a sense of optimism, a strong urge to play poker, and a sense of humor that came from both sides. What family do you know who played three-handed Pitch—high, low, jack, and the game—where the winner was excused and the remaining two played another hand with the loser having to do the dinner dishes?

Contents

List of Photographs

Foreword

In the governance of this great nation, God and the Devil are in the details. It is the more-or-less anonymous White House staff—and the so called "faceless bureaucrats" spread throughout the government—who keep the ship of state afloat and, more often than the public ever guesses, away from the icebergs. No one ever served this country or its President (in this case, two Presidents) better than Lee White. Wise as a hedgehog, cagy as a groundhog, witty, and utterly selfless, Lee made things happen, large and small, earning the admiration of JFK and LBJ, and the awe of those who served with him.

This book is an invaluable addition to understanding the way Washington works.

Bill Moyers
New York, New York
March 2007

Preface

If one lives long enough, the inclination to recount one's life experiences in conversations with family or friends or in written form emerges. In my case, I first acquired this habit from the conversations a few of us had with my great-uncle Morris White. Every year, Uncle Morris would come from his home in Omaha to Chevy Chase, Maryland, for the Passover holiday. During these visits, his son Bernie, his son-in-law Bud Polsky, and I would question him about the history of our family while recording his conversations on audio tape. He was a sharp article and blessed with a great memory and a delightful sing-song voice. He reported what he knew personally and what had been told to him by his elders, going back about one hundred fifty years. It was a delight to listen to him and gain a sense of the family into which I was born. Unfortunately, the tapes were destroyed in a house fire.

My next encounter with recording personal history was through the John Fitzgerald Kennedy Library's oral history program organized after his assassination. Milton Gwirtzman, a Washington lawyer who floated in and out of the Kennedy administration, interviewed me extensively; but Milt had to keep reminding me that this was the oral history of John Kennedy, and not Lee White. I, in turn, had the opportunity to interview then Governor Luis Munoz-Marin of Puerto Rico. So I learned how useful contemporaneous recollections are in developing an historical record, even if a discount factor had to be applied because of the tendency to build one's own importance into the interviews.

Subsequently, I spent additional hours in interviews with University of Texas researchers preparing President Johnson's oral history project for the Lyndon Baines Johnson Library, as well as with University of Kentucky historians conducting Senator John Sherman Cooper's oral history project.

Through this process, I developed a greater appreciation for the nuances of recorded history.

There was no great clamor for my story to be told; but over time, some who knew of the experiences I had gone through raised the idea with me. As I thought about it, it occurred to me that it was true that I had something to pass on, especially to my children and grandchildren, and, rather naturally, I started putting words on paper.

Writing one's memoirs is an intricate process. Presumably, the author reflects upon his or her experiences with the intention to write honestly and straightforwardly about them, relating the ups and downs and the turning points. Sometimes the memoirist wants to be (or at least appear to be) modest and maybe even a little humble. But there's a problem. As time passes, one's focus shifts: In one's memory, the positive events in one's life grow larger and assume greater importance while the negative ones tend to recede and sometimes disappear from view. Congenital optimists and jokesters like me are at particular risk for this transformation. With this caveat in mind, I began writing this memoir a little over five years ago.

My story-telling ability may not match that of my Uncle Morris, but that would never deter me, as I am blessed with as good a memory. In writing my story, as opposed to telling it, I have used quotation marks to convey the tenor of a conversation as I recalled it. These conversations, recalled after forty years, may not be verbatim. However, most of the instances that I have recounted with dialogue relate to the previously recorded JFK or LBJ oral histories or were of importance to me personally; thus, my recollection of them remains strong. The episodes I recall reflect my particular role and perspective, and the conversations as I have recorded them in writing are intended to provide context and texture to my story. I believe including these dialogues, despite any lack of precision, lends a more authentic flavor to the account of my experiences.

Upon joining the White House staff in January 1961, I considered whether I should keep a diary. I had never been in the habit of doing so and decided against the idea of recording daily notes of what I was engaged in doing. However, on rare occasion, I wrote a memorandum to my personal files summarizing an issue. In preparing the manuscript for this book, I occasionally referred to letters, memoranda, and a collection of presidential speeches from my personal collection to refresh my memory or to confirm dates. I also referred to the photographs in my personal collection, a few of which are included in this book.

In the course of writing the manuscript, I gave a radio interview based on my experiences working in the White House during the Kennedy administration, which was featured on *The Bob Edwards Show* in January 2006 and later rebroadcast. In the case of the Johnson Presidency, the critical examination of his legacy has undergone a re-evaluation with the passage of time. In a review of *Judgment Day* by Nick Kotz, published in the June 6, 2005 edition of *The Legal Times*, I described the relationship between President Johnson and Dr. Martin Luther King, Jr., and provided some insight into the mix of their personalities. Many of the events I relate here in the two chapters on civil rights during the Kennedy and Johnson administrations have been described by me in a chapter on civil rights in *Lyndon Johnson Remembered: An Intimate Portrait of a Presidency*, edited by Thomas W. Cowger and Sherwin J. Markman.

Finally, the most important people in one's life and the major events and milestones in one's personal life and career intersect in ways that can be difficult to describe in a linear narrative. Thus, I have appended a "Chronology of My Life, Work, and Times," which presents a timeline of selected events in my life to date. I have also included a chapter on some of my favorite gleanings or "Reflections" as a White House counsel and devoted a chapter to my "Family, Friends and Heritage," both of which appear near the end of the book. The order in which they appear departs from the chronological organization of the previous chapters; however, they are intended to convey the fruits of my experience and the gentle winds that carried me in fortuitous ways.

Despite the frailty of memory, I hope this brief discussion provides a sense of how I proceeded to write these memoirs.

NOTES ON THE PHOTOGRAPHS

Both President Kennedy and President Johnson presented their staffs with photographs on various occasions. In selecting the photographs for this book, I found far fewer photos from the Kennedy Presidency than the Johnson Presidency in my personal collection. The difference in the number of photos, as far as I can tell, was based on the changing role of White House photographers. It seemed as though, in the case of JFK, the photographer, notably Cecil Stoughton, was called to photograph certain events and occasions. LBJ, on the other hand, appointed Yoichi R. Okamoto as the first official White House photographer, and Okamoto was shadowing President Johnson a great deal of the time. The photos I have chosen to include are intended to provide a visual background for those remarkable times.

Nearly all of the photographs included in this book are from my personal collection. With notable exceptions, most were taken by White House photographer Yoichi R. Okamoto, and are within the public domain. Photo 7.1 was published with the permission of Getty Images, and Photo 10.1 was published with the permission of the Associated Press. Where known, I have identified the photographer by name in the caption to the photograph, and I acknowledge their role in providing a permanent record of the events depicted.

As an example of the phenomenon noted above where happier memories often prevail over the darker moments, as well as my particular use of direct quotes, one of the two photographs depicting scenes from the Kennedy Presidency requires comment. Photo 7.1, taken outside of the Cabinet Room of the White House on October 24, 1963, was taken extemporaneously by the highly regarded photographer Arnold Newman, who had been commissioned by *Holiday* magazine to take a group portrait of the key JFK staff. Newman was on the scene preparing to take a group photograph that was subsequently published by *Esquire* magazine in November 1965, when President Kennedy stepped outside the Cabinet Room and quipped, "Isn't anybody doing any work around here?"

I also wish to call the reader's attention to details reflecting the passage of time in two of the photographs from the Johnson Presidency. In Photo 13.1, depicting the January 18, 1964 meeting with civil rights leaders, the absence of décor on the walls of the Oval Office is a stark reminder that this photo was taken less than two months after the assassination of President Kennedy. In Photo 13.2, taken September 22, 1965, both the photograph of First Lady "Lady Bird" Johnson on the table to the right and the photograph of the President and First Lady's daughter Luci Baines Johnson on the left side table are in full view from the President's rocking chair.

Finally, the photograph of me on the cover was taken in the Oval Office a few days after the January 18, 1964 meeting with civil rights leaders. President Johnson and Dr. Robert Weaver, then Administrator of the Housing and Home Finance Agency, and later the first Secretary of the Department of Housing and Urban Development, were present but do not appear in the photo. I include it with these memoirs because my mother said it made me look "thoughtful." It was her favorite picture of me.

Acknowledgements

I assume full responsibility for the contents of this book, but wish to acknowledge and thank the many fine folks who have helped (or tried to help) as the manuscript went through many iterations. I suppose one could write one's life story and publish it exactly as written; but I wouldn't count on it. Like many individuals who fancy themselves to be good editors but are incapable of editing their own manuscripts, I eventually realized I couldn't edit my own deathless prose.

Fortunately, my manuscript was rescued from oblivion in the spring of 2006 and revived by an experienced editor of memoirs, Zabelle Zakarian, who had listened to excerpts from the presidential tapes. I am indebted to Zabelle for her tenacious research, writing, and editorial skills and her dogged pursuit of historical accuracy. I also owe her a special debt for her persistence in urging me to seek documentation of the photographs from my personal collection and for her fine insights into them, particularly the photos by Arnold Newman and Yoichi R. Okamoto.

Were it not for Tom Puff, my manuscript might not have come to life as a book. Tom is a distinguished lawyer (most lawyers are "distinguished" when they're on your side) from Minneapolis who heads the law firm of Venture Law Resources. I have known Tom since he was a law student at American University, and a legal intern with White, Fine & Verville. When a few very nice rejection notices had me willing to scrap the entire project, Tom took over and with his indefatigable persistence, his shrewd salesmanship, and his natural Irish charm, found a willing publisher; and we were on our way.

University Press of America and, especially, its agreeable and helpful contact point Patti Belcher have made the publishing part of the process smooth and free of turbulence.

Chief Archivist Allan Goodrich of the John F. Kennedy Presidential Library in Boston was most helpful in providing information about photo materials at the Library. Colleen Cooney, also of the JFK Library, supplied important details on the photo of White House staff by Arnold Newman.

Margaret Harman and Elizabeth Hansen of the Lyndon Baines Johnson Library in Austin were also very obliging in providing information on photos from their collection. Elizabeth's efforts in corroborating the notations on the photographs from my personal collection with the President's daily diary were most helpful for preparing the captions to the photographs depicting scenes from the Johnson years.

A special debt of gratitude goes to the law firm of Spiegel & McDiarmid where I am Of Counsel. This collection of extremely bright and congenial, public interest lawyers and staff has tolerated and assisted me in numerous ways. Partner Frances Francis, who was one of my contemporaries at the Federal Power Commission, thoroughly polished the chapter dealing with the Federal Power Commission. Computer guru Lee Ausley, along with former "Spiegelites" Jean Donaldson and Jessica White, took this computer novice by the hand in the manuscript preparation process, while Marilyn Smith, my on-the-ball secretary, was helpful in every little and big way. Partner Scott Strauss encouraged this project in quiet ways, and Carol Gloss, the firm's Executive Director, kept a watchful eye on the enterprise. Finally, Bob McDiarmid, co-founder of the firm and long-time friend, graciously encouraged my efforts.

My old friends Ann and Don Farber and Murray Comarow took cracks at reviewing early drafts. Former Kennedy administration colleague and publishing maven Ron Goldfarb was most helpful and generous with advice and guidance.

Finally, I am indebted to the two senators—John F. Kennedy and John Sherman Cooper—and the two presidents—John F. Kennedy and Lyndon Baines Johnson—whom I served and who gave me the opportunity to participate in their offices and administrations during this remarkable period in our nation's history.

Lee C. White
Washington, DC
May 2007

And so, my fellow Americans:
ask not what your country can do for you—
ask what you can do for your country.
My fellow citizens of the world:
ask not what America will do for you,
but what together we can do for the freedom of man.

John Fitzgerald Kennedy
January 20, 1961

. . . The time has come for Americans of all races and creeds and political beliefs
to understand and to respect one another. So let us put an end
to the teaching and the preaching of hate and evil and violence.
Let us turn away from the fanatics of the far left and the far right,
from the apostles of bitterness and bigotry, from those defiant of law,
and those who pour venom into our Nation's bloodstream.

Lyndon Baines Johnson
November 27, 1963

Introduction

One day during my first year of law school at the University of Nebraska, a member of the class told the professor that the lesson about cause and effect that the professor had just described was called the "Queen Mary Syndrome." When the professor looked mystified and pressed him, the student explained, "Well, it's like this: A fellow tells his wife that he had leaned against the Queen Mary at the pier in New York harbor, and the Queen Mary went out to sea. The ship didn't go out to sea because he was leaning against it, but because three tugs were pulling it." That student was Theodore C. "Ted" Sorensen. He and I became good friends, and we studied together in his father's law office close to the campus. I explained some fine points to Ted, and Ted did a little explaining, too; but his grades were always a little better than mine, partly because he typed his answers, but mostly because, as the world found out, the fellow wrote quickly and beautifully.

Ted's father, C. A. Sorensen, had played the dominant role in getting the various public, electric power groups together to take over the ownership of all facilities in the State of Nebraska, which was a remarkable feat.—Nebraska was and is the only all public power state in the Union.—C. A. was a Republican who had been elected Attorney General of Nebraska, and he was a close colleague of Nebraska's Senator George W. Norris, a fellow Republican who later became an Independent. When President Franklin Roosevelt, following the recommendation of Norris, nominated C. A. to a federal district judgeship in Nebraska, the state's Democratic leadership went berserk. FDR withdrew the nomination, but not before Martindale-Hubbell, the national legal directory, included C. A. Sorensen in its list of judges, even though he had not been confirmed and never would be.

Within the political landscape of Nebraska, Senator Norris became one my boyhood heroes. His concern for the public and public policy issues resonated with me and seemed to touch my latent liberal instincts, even though he was then a Republican. My subsequent career choices—the people with whom I have chosen to work and the paths I have followed—reflect this initial bent.

Thus, after graduation in 1950, I went to work in the legal division of the Tennessee Valley Authority in Knoxville, Tennessee, and kept in touch with Ted Sorensen. In early 1953, Ted reported that he had wound up as a legislative assistant to the newly elected young senator from Massachusetts, John Kennedy. In May, Ted called to say the senator's other legislative assistant was leaving and that when Sorensen told Senator Kennedy about me, the senator told him to ask me to come to Washington, DC to meet him.

So, it was off to see the senator. I met his secretary, Evelyn Lincoln, whose maiden name was Norton. I had known her brother Bill at the University of Nebraska, and her father had been a one-term Democratic Congressman from western Nebraska. When Evelyn ushered me into the senator's office, I was surprised to find Senator Kennedy not wearing any trousers. He must have thought some explanation was necessary, saying, "I spilled some ink on my pants, and Mrs. Lincoln is trying to get the spots out."

After a brief conversation, and donning trousers, Senator Kennedy took Ted and me to the senate dining room for lunch. As we were talking, Senator Estes Kefauver of Tennessee ambled by. JFK said, "Estes, here's one of your guys from TVA." Kefauver said to me, "I hope you're telling him about all the good things TVA is doing down in the Valley." I said, "Senator, I keep trying, but he keeps telling me about the problems of New England."

After Kefauver moved on, Senator Kennedy said, "I don't know whether you fellows know it, but we have some law schools in Massachusetts." Indeed, we did; and I left Washington with the understanding that it had been a pleasant meeting and that the senator would hire a Massachusetts lawyer.

Back in Knoxville, I read about the senator's marriage to Jacqueline "Jackie" Bouvier in September. About a week into his honeymoon in Acapulco, the senator called his office to check on things. After talking to Timothy J. "Ted" Reardon, his Administrative Assistant, he talked to the other "Ted"—Sorensen. After discussing some legislative items, the senator asked, "When is that kid from Tennessee going to join us?" Without batting an eye, Ted (Sorensen) said, "He'll be here the first of the year."—Later, as President, Kennedy playfully griped that he thought he had hired more Nebraskans than had voted for him: Nebraska gave him the smallest percentage vote of any state in the country.

In November, Sorensen called to say that the senator was going to speak to a Rotary Club (it might have been Kiwanis) meeting in Chattanooga, arranged by Charlie Bartlett, a Washington newspaperman who was a native of Chattanooga, and an old friend of the senator who had introduced JFK to

Jackie. I got in touch with Bartlett, who gave me the details of the meeting, and I arranged to meet the two of them at the hotel where the meeting was to take place.

When I entered the senator's hotel room, Kennedy was in the bathtub soaking his back. This was my second meeting with him and, remember, the first time he was not wearing trousers. The senator asked me what the law in Tennessee was dealing with company-labor union contracts. I hadn't the slightest idea. A few weeks earlier, I had talked to a Nashville lawyer about a business issue; so, quickly and luckily, I got him on the telephone and he spouted out the answer. I proudly reported the information to the senator. JFK muttered "OK," and kept reviewing and making notes on the text of his speech. Later, I learned that he had become accustomed to staff pulling minor miracles out of hats.

It was now time for the senator's luncheon speech, his first in the South. His theme was a warning to Southern jurisdictions that were offering tax and other inducements to textile companies to leave New England and relocate in the South. He made the point, among others, that after a while the same company could well receive another attractive offer from a different location that it could not refuse and be long gone. Two elderly gentlemen sat opposite me. After listening, one fellow said to his friend, "That young guy's pretty smart—I like the way he laid it out."

Next came preparations for the move to Washington, DC. My wife was pregnant with our third child. Her obstetrician, Dr. Diddle, said the baby was due on December 18th. When my wife asked him if it was all right for her to drive in her eighth month, the very careful doctor said, "I don't know. Do you have a driver's license?"—Dr. Diddle, who charged twenty-five dollars more than the other obstetricians in town, enjoyed a fine reputation but was a cautious man.—The 18th came and went and Murray White did not emerge until January 4, 1954.

I arrived in Washington, DC on January 8, 1954, and checked into the senator's office enthusiastic about my new job. A few weeks later, my wife, Dorothy, and our three children—Bruce, Rosalyn, and Murray—moved from Knoxville to our new home in West Hyattsville, Maryland.

Part One

MY EARLY CAREER

Chapter One

An Ideal First Job

My family and I arrived in Washington, DC by way of Tennessee. In 1950, having passed the Nebraska bar exam, I headed to Knoxville for an interview at the Tennessee Valley Authority Division of Law. My interview with then General Counsel Joseph Swidler and his top three lawyers went quite well. After asking if I had any more questions, he said I would do well to talk to the young lawyers in the office because they could better tell me how it was to work there in terms of the legal work and in terms of the personnel, especially the top dogs. Swidler knew what he was doing because these lawyers — Sol Edidin, John Murray, and Richard M. "Dick" Freeman — were great pitchmen for the legal division. They were sharp fellows who were very satisfied with the nature of the work assignments they had, and they praised the quality of the leadership of the Division of Law.

When I asked if there were any negatives about the place, the response I got was that I probably thought I would be the General Counsel in a few years (I did have something like that in mind) and that I could forget about it, because the top lawyers were highly competent, happy and healthy. Swidler had come to TVA as the protégé of David Lillienthal, the first TVA Chairman appointed by President Roosevelt in 1933. Tom Griffin, the Solicitor, was an incredible contract draftsman who could dictate a complex contract for an hour at a time with practically no need for revision. Charlie McCarthy, the Assistant General Counsel for Litigation, was such a strong personality that it didn't occur to me or anyone else for that matter to mention Edgar Bergen. Bob Marquis, a deceptively brilliant lawyer, was the Assistant General Counsel for Legislation.

The next day, Swidler offered me a job. I told him that I was very interested, but I was going on to Washington, DC, and then had to complete thirty days of service in the Army Reserve at Fort Monmouth, New Jersey. He suggested that I skip the military assignment. I told him that I couldn't. His response was that he'd try to keep the job open, but no promises. Later, I learned that he was a world-class negotiator and he just couldn't help himself.

To illustrate the point, fast forward to 1962, when he and I were part of a United States delegation to the Soviet Union to inspect hydroelectric plants that was headed by then Secretary of the Interior Stewart Udall. Our Moscow hosts had told us we could take all the pictures we wanted to take. There was no problem until we got to the Bratsk Dam site in Siberia. There, the project manager said, "No pictures." Udall protested, informing him that we had been advised otherwise in Moscow. After wrangling for a few minutes, Udall decided it was not worth an international incident and acquiesced in the decision. That did not stop Swidler. He started all over and finally wore down the project manager until he gave up. The best part was that Swidler had run out of film at the last dam we had visited, so he just pretended to be taking pictures with his empty camera.

"A BAD MISTAKE"

When I arrived in Washington, I made the rounds of the agencies that interested me as potential employers, but I also called a number of individuals whose names had been given me by my Nebraska law school faculty. I was absolutely astounded at the time and attention they gave me and the calls they made to arrange meetings for me. I resolved then and there that if I ever was in a position to lend a helping hand to a young graduate, I would do so.

The most exciting prospect came out of one of those meetings. It was with a personnel officer at the State Department who was working on staffing the new Point Four section of the European Recovery Program (the Marshall Plan). This was the technical assistance part of the program that had just been authorized by Congress. He was struck by the fact that I had both engineering and law degrees, and he asked me if I'd be available to do a great deal of traveling as special assistant to the director of Point Four. I assured him that I would not only be able to but also would love to do so. He told me to come back the next day for another interview. I was plenty excited and showed up at the appointed hour. He told me that he was very sorry, but because of the heavy round of reductions in force (the federal job market was in fact very tight), I was being bumped by an employee with bumping rights. That was the end of my diplomatic career.

I received an offer from the Department of Labor, but working at TVA was far more attractive to me. I went on to Fort Monmouth, for my active duty training and, while there, got in touch with an old engineering school buddy,

Gus Douvas of Hastings, Nebraska, who had a job as a junior patent attorney with AT&T in New York. He introduced me to his boss who said he would recommend that I be added to the staff. Even though the salary was $5,100 per year compared to the $3,900 offered by TVA (which was one level above starting salaries owing to my military service), I believed the work was more engineering than law. Besides, I wanted to work in the federal government; so another career ended before it started.

When I returned to Lincoln to pack up, I happened to see Judge Harry Spencer, a probate judge who had taught a course in wills at the law school. I told him I was leaving Nebraska to work for the federal government. The staunch Republican said I was making "a bad mistake." Then I told him I was going to TVA, and he said that was the worst agency of all—"almost pure socialism." I replied that I'd better hurry up and get down there and straighten things out. When I visited Judge Spencer a couple of years later (he was then on the Nebraska Supreme Court), he said "You know, you haven't done a damn bit of good."

A 21-MAN LAW FIRM

In Knoxville, I joined what was basically a 21-man law firm, there being no women lawyers, or black lawyers, during the three and a half years I was at TVA. The Division of Law was, in part, a governmental agency legal shop; but because TVA could sue and be sued, by virtue of the statute creating the agency, it was also handling claims by and against TVA, as any private firm would. For me, it was an ideal "first job." The lawyers were excellent, the work was interesting and diverse, and the camaraderie made the daily routine most enjoyable and comfortable.

Swidler was a strong personality. I had a terrible time calling him "Joe," although every one else did. It appeared he had persuaded the agency leaders that they had better check with the Division of Law before they even went to the men's room.—Speaking of the men's room, when we happened to be standing next to each other in the men's room one day, he said to me, "See, we both do it the same way, and I think you should call me Joe." And, of course, I did.

Within weeks, I was going to internal TVA meetings representing the Division of Law. I returned from a meeting of the Division of Reservoir Properties, which had responsibility for the areas surrounding the reservoirs created by TVA dams, and the Division of Water Control, which regulated the flow of water into and out of the reservoirs. I told Joe that I thought they had reached the wrong result in what they planned to do. So, he said to his secretary, Dewdrop

Rule, (honest), "Get Ed Campbell and Jim Bowman on the phone." Although I only heard one end of the conversation, it was obvious that one of them had asked, as long as I was at the meeting, why hadn't I said anything? Swidler said, "He's new here and made the erroneous assumption that you fellows must know what you're talking about." That was the last time I sat quietly at a meeting.

Because of the unique character of TVA as a government corporation, and because the headquarters was five hundred miles from Washington, DC, we had the feeling that we were "us" and the federal government was "them." The standard running gag was that Bob Marquis, the TVA legislative guru, had a great big rubber stamp that said "Except TVA," and every legislative bill that came to TVA for review and comment got the rubber stamp treatment. There was a sense of competence and even superiority that permeated the agency, and that was especially true of the legal division.

Every new employee heard the story of the confrontation between the first TVA Chairman, David Lilienthal, and Tennessee's senior senator, Kenneth McKellar. Senator McKellar, who was a member of the Senate Appropriations Committee, phoned the new chairman and told him of a nephew who the senator thought would be a fine assistant general counsel. Lilienthal said, "Fine, have him send me a resume and we'll be glad to consider him." McKellar explained, "I don't think you understand; he's going to be an assistant general counsel." Lilienthal and his other board members discussed the situation and concluded that if they gave in to the senator at the outset, they would have crossed a great divide and would for evermore be vulnerable to political pressure. They screwed up their courage and rejected the senator's nephew.

MY LEGAL ASSIGNMENTS

One Swidler innovation was to appoint each new young lawyer as an Assistant Secretary of the corporation to serve in that capacity for a year or so. Swidler, the Corporate Secretary, simply used that designation as a teaching device so each new lawyer could grasp the big picture by attending board meetings and be better prepared to know how and where our day-to-day work fit into the overall scheme of things. The one specific assignment of the Assistant Secretary was to sit next to the General Manager, and as the board finished each item on the agenda, the GM would hand the file to the Assistant Secretary, who would place the completed file in a neat pile. Once during my service, the file for the first agenda item handed to me was not stapled correctly. As I pulled the by now heavy pile off the beautiful table at the end of the meeting, I heard a sickening sound and looked down to see two deep scratches, which would prompt me later to note that I had left my mark at TVA.

One item discussed was the agency's response to a proposal by Bowaters Paper Company to come into the valley and enter the forestry and paper business. It was an old British company which had operated in Canada for decades. The power division people thought it would be great because of the enormous power load they would need. The navigation folks saw the company as using the waterway for commercial transportation. The economists saw it as developing the economies of the valley states. But how impressed I was when the Chairman of the Board, Gordon Clapp, said that he didn't disagree with what he had heard, but the most significant aspect of the proposal was the fact that the company operated on a 75-year plan of planting, caring for and harvesting, unlike the standard valley practice of cutting and maybe re-seeding. He believed that the example of proper forestry practices with the economic benefits of those practices would be a boon to the valley.

One of the assignments I had was to enforce the agency's flowage easements. TVA purchased or, if necessary, condemned the right to flood areas surrounding the reservoirs. The language of the easements was very clear that no permanent buildings could be erected on the flowage areas without specific written consent of TVA. When our people saw any violation of the easement, it was reported to the legal division, and we were very tough in demanding the removal. TVA had the benefit of a sad experience of the U.S. Corps of Engineers. The Corps had acquired flowage rights on a tributary of the Mississippi River, and when it sought to exercise those rights because of flood conditions, it was faced with the fact that hundreds of homes and facilities had been built on the land and would be ruined. It decided to protect the facilities that shouldn't have been there in the first place. TVA did not want to repeat that mistake.

One of the more offbeat matters I was involved in had to do with a budding television employees' union, a local in New York City, called the Television Agency or the Television Authority. Someone from New York had sent us a copy of *Variety,* the entertainment industry's daily newspaper, with the headline, "TvA Threatens Shutdown." This prompted a quick study of trade name law. The conclusion: We could threaten legal action, but the chances of success were not strong. We doubted that many readers of *Variety* would confuse TvA with TVA; even the initials were not identical because of the capitalization. Moreover, the culture within the legal division required that its resources be used prudently; so why flail away when there was no need to do so?

Although many of the lawyers were engaged in formulating policy, commenting on legislative proposals, drafting contracts with TVA power distributors or pleadings for condemnation, one lawyer, for whom I would occasionally substitute, handled claims against TVA. Charles "Red" Mynatt handled negligence and personal injury cases and knew the tricks of the trade. In a particularly horrible accident in which two women employees of TVA were killed, Red investigated and interviewed potential witnesses. After taking notes on what each witness had to say, Red would dictate a statement covering the relevant points but would be certain to have one or two obvious misstatements in the copy submitted to the prospective witness, such as "I turned left" when Red knew he had said "I turned right." As the witness read over the statement in Red's presence, he or she would say, "You didn't get that right." And Red would say, "Sorry, would you please strike out "left," write in "right," and put your initials beside the change." Although a witness could claim that the statement was inaccurate or that he hadn't read it, those little initials made it a lot tougher to dispute it.

Because there was a high volume of these items, most not nearly as significant as the automobile accident, I would use the dictabelt (a fairly primitive device in the early 1950s) for my drafts when substituting for Red. Since the law librarian transcribed those belts, I wanted mine to be done first. I came up with the idea of interspersing a few gags and jokes between drafts, so I got pretty good service.

A major activity at the time was acquiring rights-of-way for power transmission lines. The vast majority of rights-of-ways were negotiated between TVA real estate people and the landowners. Where agreement could not be reached, Congress had provided a special procedure for determining the value of the rights taken from landowners, namely a three-person panel appointed by a United States District Court Judge, which would take testimony from TVA witnesses and the landowners and their experts, if they offered any. Our most colorful litigator, Tom Pedersen, would tell the tribunal that those one hundred fifty-feet towers dotting the countryside were "sleek symbols of progress," and the TVA side prevailed more often than not. But one old country lawyer used to beat TVA pretty regularly by his homespun drawl saying, "Y'all know these TVA lawyers are a very smart bunch from some of the big time law schools and my client is represented by 'little ole me' and I know I don't know all that those other fellers do." The commission would sympathize with the poor landowner and frequently come down on his side. John Murray and I wrote an article for the *Tennessee Law Review* detailing the procedures and the related case law, but I assume that country lawyer was still racking them up.

I worked on a case in which Sullivan County, Tennessee, had sued TVA because it had failed to provide a direct route to the main commercial center of the area for the folks who lived in a community that was cut off by a new TVA reservoir, so they had to drive forty miles around the reservoir to reach the center. As TVA's railroad engineer bluntly put it, "Those folks didn't have any political clout, so the negotiators for the County had not insisted that TVA provide them access." It was not a very bright decision by TVA people, and following a recommendation by the Division of Law, we agreed to provide access.

THE QUALITY OF LIFE

As a young lawyer with an electrical engineering degree and the motivation to work in the government for the betterment of society and people, I enjoyed my work and coworkers.—My best compliment came from Charlie Mc-Carthy, the Assistant General Counsel for Litigation, who wrote on a draft of a brief I had written on removing a case from a state court to the federal district court, "Not bad for you. Cut it by a third."—When 11:30 a.m. came each workday, every lawyer dropped what he was doing and marched in a bloc to the S&W Cafeteria on Gay Street, where we would sit around a couple of large round tables and discuss the state of the nation and some local matters. It provided an opportunity for those who had attended Congressional hearings involving TVA to inform the rest of us about how things had gone.

Tom Pedersen was a great jokester, and one Saturday he set up a golf game that included two fellows who did not know each other. He separately told each one that the other was really hard of hearing and that he would have to shout to be understood; so the guys practically screamed at each other for eighteen holes.

That reminds me of George Baker, a very big guy and the head of TVA's real estate acquisition unit. He was stopped at a red light on one of Knoxville's busiest streets. When the light turned green, the car behind George immediately honked. George got out of his car, walked back slowly, and said, "Did you want me?" When he got the answer that the fellow only wanted him to move on, George sauntered back to his car, got in and by then the light had turned red again.

One evening in late 1950, my wife and I went to a TVA employees' dance and happened to share a table with a young couple, an engineer named S. David "Dave" Freeman, and his wife, Marianne. Later, while visiting the engineering division, I saw Dave at an engineering drawing desk and stopped to chat. He was working on the drawings for the footings (the base structures supporting the facility) for a new coal-burning steam plant for generating electricity to be built in Johnsonville, Tennessee. When I had to return about six weeks later, Dave was still working diligently on those same footings. I told him about the varied and interesting problems I had worked on since I had last visited the Engineering Division. He was impressed and promptly enrolled in the University of Tennessee Law School, arranging to work halftime for TVA. He graduated first in his class and joined the Division of Law. By that time, I had left TVA, but our lives and careers were to cross many, many times. In the late 1970s, President Carter appointed Dave Freeman as Chairman of the TVA Board. After fifty years, our friendship has remained strong.

Speaking of the UT law school, Dick Freeman (no relation to Dave), one of the "young lawyers" mentioned above, taught a course in contracts. On occasion when he was out of town or otherwise unavailable, I would sit in for him. Dick was later appointed as a TVA board member by President Carter.

I was quite happy and we led a fairly active social life. The presence of friends at the University of Tennessee and at the Atomic Energy Commission's complex in Oak Ridge added to the quality of life. We had bought a house in a modest part of town (price: $8,300) and welcomed a second child, Rosalyn.

The political life of the area was also interesting. The two Eastern Congressional districts of Tennessee were Union during the Civil War, and were solidly Republican. The Second District was represented by Howard Baker, Sr. (the father of the Senator and Minority Leader). In 1952, he was opposed by a first-rate Democrat, Frank Wilson (who later became a U.S. District Court Judge). I voted for Wilson, who lost even though he had run a respectable race. The next time, the Democrats had a lousy candidate and since Baker had been good on TVA issues, I voted for him, thereby losing my virginity. Also in 1954, Congressman Albert Gore (the Vice President's father) ran in the Democratic primary against the incumbent, Senator Kenneth McKellar, the Chairman of the Senate Appropriations Committee. I recall seeing telephone poles all over the area with posters reading, "A Thinking Feller Votes for McKellar." The next day each pole had another poster reading, "Think Some More and Vote for Gore." Gore won, and with the colorful Estes Kefauver, Tennessee had two very good senators.

I regarded my position at the TVA legal division as a superb first job. In addition to the high quality of the staff and the work products, there was a good feeling about the agency and the high regard in which it was held in the region. As a congenital do-gooder, I was happy in an agency that was doing a lot of good. The river was tamed; the barge traffic on the river was helping the economy of an area that needed it badly; the areas surrounding the reservoirs were well managed and were producing great recreational and economic benefits; and the power operations were going quite well.

At the time, the only disquieting note was a hushed reference occasionally to air pollution problems created by the massive coal-burning steam generating plants. When the pollution problem emerged nationally after I let TVA, I recalled those hints of some difficulty and realized that, at least in one respect, TVA was not much different about that subject than the investor-owned segment of the industry.

After three years at TVA, the itch to leave was getting strong. In 1953, when I told Joe Swidler that I was leaving to go to Washington, DC to be a legislative assistant to a United States senator, he asked me which one. When I told him, he said, "That young fellow is a dilettante who'll never amount to anything."—I reminded Joe of that observation in later years.—He had thrown cold water on other prospects I had mentioned to him, but his remark helped me understand why every job prospect I brought to him wasn't good enough for me: He simply didn't want to go through the hassle of finding another lawyer.

Chapter Two

Legislative Assistant to Senator Kennedy

Senator Kennedy's office consisted of three large rooms in the Senate Office Building (now the Russell Senate Office Building). One room was the senator's office. The middle room was a reception area, with only one chair for visitors, and was shared by five casework staff who handled constituent requests for assistance, the senator's personal secretary, and the receptionist. The third room had six desks: one for Ted Reardon, the Administrative Assistant; one for Ted Sorensen; one for me; and one for each of our secretaries. The seven women in the middle room, who back then were called "girls," reflected the diverse population of Massachusetts: the Irish, Italians, Scotch, and Jews. The three women in our room represented the Portuguese, Irish, and a Boston Republican wasp (my secretary, Elva Benting). The atmosphere was congenial, but noisy, with relatively few personal difficulties.

The senator was on the Labor and Education Committee and the Government Operations Committee. Ted Sorensen worked with the senator on the labor committee assignments; I staffed the government operations committee. But everybody did a bit of everything. The hours were long, including time on Saturdays, but the work was stimulating with a sense of 'This is where things are getting done.'

LEGISLATION

We worked closely with the office of Republican Senator Leverett Saltonstall, the senior Massachusetts senator. He was a reserved Brahmin New Englander whose family probably came over on the first Mayflower voyage. The Saltonstall office had some people who later went on to very big assignments: Elliott Richardson gained great fame when he resigned as Attorney General, rather than follow President Nixon's order to fire Archie Cox, the Watergate Special Prosecutor; Chuck Colson who went to prison as a result of his Watergate activities; Bradford Morse, who was elected to Congress from the Lowell Massachusetts district and who subsequently became the Deputy Secretary General of the United Nations; and Tom Winship, who followed in the family tradition and became Editor and Publisher of the Boston Globe.

Many bills affecting New England were introduced jointly. Oddly enough, in our office, they were referred to as the Kennedy-Saltonstall bills, and in their office, as the Saltonstall-Kennedy bills. But, truly, Senator Kennedy was the sparkplug; and Ted Sorensen was at his right hand in creating a New England conference of senators who didn't always agree on a common goal but did so frequently enough that it became an effective and viable caucus. It became the model for many similar regional groups that were subsequently established.

From my perspective, the Kennedy-Saltonstall Fisheries Research bill had special significance. It was the first bill on which I had done the staff work, and it fit nicely with Senator Kennedy's efforts to strengthen the New England economy. Additionally, it would be the first time I would sit next to the senator on the Senate floor as he made the presentation in support of the bill and handled questions and any opposition (there really wasn't any). At my desk prior to the scheduled consideration of the bill, I was going over my notes while trying to pry the lid off of a cup of coffee. In my haste, and probably nervousness, I managed to spill coffee all over my suit. As the senator and I headed to the Senate floor, he looked at me and said, "What the hell happened to you?" When I told him what had happened, he grinned and we went on with the business at hand. The bill passed easily and proved effective.

Another important piece of legislation I worked on would provide assistance to individuals and communities that were adversely affected by imported products. In Massachusetts, the textile industry was especially hard hit by imports. Although Senator Kennedy was not opposed to international trade, he believed that if there were specific damage to individuals and communities because of a national policy to promote international trade, those so harmed should be assisted. There were provisions in his bill for retraining workers and for economic assistance to communities. The senator sought a Republican co-sponsor; so he and I called on Senator John Sherman Cooper of Kentucky, who was a good friend of Senator Kennedy and was generally in tune with Kennedy's positions on issues. The meeting was inconclusive, and I consulted with Senator Cooper's administrative assistant Bill Macomber off-and-on for weeks before we concluded that Cooper was not going to co-sponsor. (I had occasion to recall that experience when I went to work for Senator Cooper three years later.)

We found a House co-sponsor in Democratic Congressman Harrison "Pete" Williams of New Jersey, a friend of Kennedy's from his House days, who, subsequently, was elected to the Senate from New Jersey. The companion bills (Senate and House) were introduced the same day with a bit of fanfare: Williams touted it as a means of promoting international trade, while Kennedy trumpeted it as a means of aiding those harmed by our nation's trade policies. It did not become law. In the 1970s, the cause was taken up by Senator Hubert Humphrey of Minnesota, and a later version became law.

In an undertaking of that nature, help comes from all over. Some from the Senate Labor Committee staff; some from the Senate Legislative Counsel's Office; some from interest groups, such as labor organizations, and some from interested parties in the state. Frequently, name changes in legislation can make a difference. Back in the 1950s, the bill was lodged in a subcommittee called Aid to Depressed Areas, a title that would not move too well in today's legislative world. One day, Senator Kennedy chaired the subcommittee in the absence of the chairman, Senator Paul Douglas of Illinois. When the meeting had gone on for an hour and a half, Senator Ralph Flanders, Republican of Vermont, rose and said "Mr. Chairman, I appreciate your having let me sit in on this meeting, but I must leave to attend a meeting of the Armed Services Committee. If it's all right with you, I'd like for my assistant—I can never remember whether his name is Haywood Carleton or Carleton Haywood—to remain in the meeting." Without missing a beat, Senator Kennedy replied, "Senator, both Mr. Haywood and Mr. Carleton can remain."—Incidentally, Flanders was the Casey Stengel (the major league baseball manager who was notorious for forgetting names) of the Senate who was alleged to have asked one of his daughters who visited his office what her name was. He also figured in the censure of Senator Joe McCarthy of Wisconsin, who, in turn, is alleged to have said somebody should nab Flanders with a butterfly net.

Subcommittee Legislation

Senator Kennedy was the chairman of the Reorganization Subcommittee of the Government Operations Committee, which was regarded as a fairly inconsequential assignment at the time. But two matters brought some attention to it. The first involved a proposal to amend the retirement program for Members of Congress. On retirement, Executive Branch employees received one and a half percent for each year of service multiplied by the average of their last three years' salary. The bill that passed the House raised that amount to two and a half percent for members and, to provide a shield, included congressional staff in the upgraded plan. Kennedy dug into the matter, securing actuarial experts from the Social Security Administration, and determined that the plan, considering what the members would contribute from their salaries, was not actuarially sound. It was a little raid on the Treasury. But his buddies from the House said, "Even though money doesn't mean much to you, we have heavy financial obligations, and because there is no way politically we can raise our salaries ($10,000 at the time), you've got to let this go through. With some relatively minor modifications, it became law.

By far the most significant matter to come to the subcommittee was the regulation of lobbying. I was looking into possible changes and maybe even hearings when the issue exploded in the Senate. A highly controversial bill was being fought over in the Senate that would have reversed a Supreme Court decision finding that the Federal Power Commission had jurisdiction over the price of natural gas at the wellhead.—Little did I know the impact of that issue on my future activities.—As the time for the vote on the bill neared, lobbying efforts had grown in intensity. Senator Francis Case, a conservative Republican from South Dakota, took the senate floor and dramatically announced that a lobbyist for Pure Oil Company in Wyoming had come to his office and told him that if he did not support the bill which would reverse the Court's decision, he would no longer receive campaign contributions from the company. The senator then told his colleagues that in light of that threat, he had no alternative but to vote against the bill; so he did.

The bill passed and was sent to President Eisenhower for his signature. His administration had strongly supported the bill, but the President said that, in light of the Case scandal, he was compelled to veto the bill. As one wag noted, there were tear drop stains all over the veto message and the veto was not overridden. The great irony in the whole incident is that there is no way that Senator Case would have not voted for the bill. For me, there was a personal twist: it turned out that the inept lobbyist was from Lexington, Nebraska, and was a graduate of the University of Nebraska Law School. Senator Lyndon Johnson of Texas, who was then Senate Majority Leader, was another very sad participant, because he saw his work in support of the bill go down the drain.

This was very explosive and, naturally, every representative and senator wanted to get in on the act. Because Kennedy's Subcommittee had jurisdiction over lobbying, we started hustling around. I heard about Joe Dolan, a Denver lawyer, who had worked on some lobbying issues while an attorney in the Department of Justice. When I reached him by phone and explained that the Kennedy subcommittee was going to go into the natural gas fiasco, Dolan was not only interested, but said he would pack up his car and leave for Washington, DC the next morning. By the time he got to Washington, the Senate had established a Select Committee to explore the gas deal, with Senator John McClellan of Arkansas, the chairman of the full Government Operations

Committee, as Chairman of the Select Committee. At least Senator Kennedy was on the new committee, and Dolan could work for the new group. There was a full report and recommendations to tighten the reporting requirements, but there have been precious few cases, if any, enforcing the reporting requirements.

The Bricker Amendment

Another hot issue at that time was what was known as the Bricker Amendment, named for the Republican senator from Ohio. It would amend the Constitution to expand the requirement that the Senate approve treaties to include lesser international agreements. To start the process for amending the Constitution, the vote in the initiating body in Congress requires a two-thirds majority. The forecasts were for a very close vote.

In preparing his position opposing the amendment, Senator Kennedy knew he would be in a minority and wanted a strong statement to buttress his position; so he told Ted Sorensen to call the Library of Congress and get the name of the British Member of Parliament who said, "When it is not necessary to change, it is necessary not to change." Sorensen asked the Library for the citation. A few days later, the Library reported that no one had said that. Sorensen dutifully reported this, to which Kennedy said, with a few expletives, "Don't tell me nobody ever said that.—I read it in college; I didn't make it up." So Sorensen told the Library they better find it. A couple of days later, the answer came back.—It wasn't a Brit who said it, but a French statesman.

Another Senate device was stalling while a vote was being conducted. Members would rise and address the reading clerk, asking how the senator was recorded. As preposterous and transparent as it was, it was used often for as long as twenty minutes. In this particular vote on the Bricker Amendment, the ayes were about to prevail, but one senator who had made it clear he would vote against had not shown up. In fact, he was across the street from the Senate Office Building at the Carroll Arms Hotel (which no longer exists) in the bar. At long last, he was helped into the senate chamber somewhat unsteady on his feet. The Clerk recognized him and intoned, "Mr. Kilgore," who shouted, "No!" That was the end of the Bricker Amendment.

The Atomic Energy Act

The handling of mail on legislative matters was not a major time consumer, but did require some knowledge of the senator's positions. Senator Kennedy was accessible and would quickly review drafts and make any necessary changes, especially for those issues that were prominent in the news and controversial. One major vote was on amendments to the Atomic Energy Act in 1954. Because of my TVA background, this fell in my bailiwick. The issue was whether the Atomic Energy Commission should be authorized to construct prototype nuclear power generators, as distinguished from only approving and licensing utilities to construct and own such facilities. The unions and generally liberal Democrats supported giving AEC the authority. After discussing it at length, Senator Kennedy said he'd go along with my recommendation to support AEC's authority. On his way to the senate floor to vote, while riding in the little trolley-like cars connecting the Senate Office Building and the Capitol, he happened to sit next to Senator Spessard Holland, a conservative Democrat from Florida. By the time he reached the senate floor, Kennedy had changed his mind and voted against the amendment.

When the bells rang in the Senate Office Building to signal a roll call vote, senators would head for the senate floor. Clearly, not all of them got there right on the minute. As the late comers entered the chamber, the reading clerk who had finished the reading of the roll, would recognize the senator who had just entered the chamber and would call out the senator's name so he or she could vote and be recorded. Frequently, those senators who had not heard the debate and were not even aware of the substance of the issue being voted on would turn to a colleague from the same party with whom he normally voted and say, "How are we voting?" As it happened, Senator Tom Burke, Democrat from Cleveland, Ohio, asked Kennedy, "How are we voting?" Kennedy replied, "I'm voting No." So Senator Burke voted "No." The amendment was defeated.

The unions from Ohio jumped all over Senator Burke, who the next day did something highly unusual. He told the Senate that he had misunderstood the issue and had made a mistake and intended to vote "Yes." The vote could not be changed, but Burke, at least, had set the record straight. Subsequently, when Senator Kennedy was seeking the Democratic nomination for the presidency, the issue of his vote was raised and he received a bit of static about it, but not enough to do him in.

THE ROLE OF STAFF

The staff director of the Government Operations Committee was considerably older than Senator Kennedy. He had been staff director longer than Kennedy had been in Congress, and had come to believe he was pretty important. Occasionally, this posed a problem. As mentioned earlier, the bill to enhance the Congressional Retirement program was drafted to include congressional staff as a protective device. So this old bull of a staff director tried to push around the young senator, who was only the chairman of a subcommittee; but the senator was not about to be bullied by a member of the staff and that insurrection was quickly put to rest.

Another staff member told me that the staff never made any policy decisions but only did what the committee or the subcommittee leadership told them to do. Of course, that's pure nonsense. As I told him, when you get to the office in the morning and look at your desk and decide which item you're going to work on that day, that's a major policy decision insofar as we are concerned. Even more to the point, a staff member generally prepares the first draft of a bill, a report on the bill, analysis of sections of the bill, and statements to be used by the senator or congressman in introducing and in advocating the bill. It was fairly obvious to me that whoever prepared the first draft had a great advantage, because that was the starting point. Thus, whenever I could swing it, I volunteered to do the first draft.

Legislative Mail

I was generally in charge of seeing that mail dealing with legislative issues got answered. One incident concerning legislative mail involved the secretary who was responsible for getting the responses to legislative mail reproduced and mailed out. A fellow from Springfield, Massachusetts, reached me on the telephone one day and said he had been trying for a few weeks to get someone from Senator Kennedy's office to talk to him about some correspondence he had sent the senator, which had not been answered or acknowledged. He had always previously received a fairly prompt reply. He was not a happy constituent. In the evening after this secretary had left, I did something I wasn't proud of, but I thought I had no alternative. I searched her desk and found it stuffed with unanswered mail. Every drawer in her desk was filled as well as the large opening which housed the typewriter.

The next morning I confronted her and she acknowledged that she had fallen far behind and was afraid to tell me because she was sure she would be fired. In the senator's office next to his desk was the desk his father had used as Ambassador to Great Britain. We piled all of the unanswered mail on that desk so the senator could see the magnitude of our problem. Clearly, he was not happy about it but told me to hire some extra help to come in the office after hours to answer every letter and postcard that was in the pile. We used a letter from the senator explaining that one of his staff people had had a problem and that he was sorry but was pleased that the mail had been discovered and would be answered at last. The reaction was totally positive: some saying they were puzzled when they had no response, but were happy to get the explanation; others told about comparable experiences they had or had heard about. Of course, I phoned the whistleblower from Springfield to thank him profusely.

SECURITY THEN AND NOW

Compared with today's requirements, security on the senate floor in the 1950s was lax. It was only necessary for me to appear at the entrance to the lobby behind the presiding officer's rostrum, announce "I'm from Senator Kennedy's office" to an attendant, who was probably a law student with political aspirations, and walk onto the floor. Clearly, that was entirely too casual and relaxed, even though it had proved satisfactory since the Senate began operating a long time ago. Only after a group of Puerto Rican supporters of independence for Puerto Rico shot up the House of Representatives chamber from the gallery in 1954, injuring a number of House members, did security begin to tighten. Today, the Capitol looks like an armed fortress, and access to the floor is carefully controlled.

Another sharp contrast was in the number of staff and the parking facilities. In 1954, I parked across the street from the Senate Office Building (there was only one—now called the Russell Office Building after Senator Richard Russell, Democrat from Georgia) on an empty lot taking up half a city square. That space now holds the Dirksen Office Building, named after the late Republican senator and Senate Minority Leader from Illinois. Although it is not taught in most collegiate political science courses, it was obvious to senate staffers that there was no chance that Alaska or Hawaii would be admitted to statehood until the second Senate Office Building was completed.—There simply wasn't any more room in the building for any more senators.—Sure enough, when the building was finished, two more states were admitted to the Union.

"SECRETARIES FOR KENNEDY"

Another matter involving the Library of Congress arose out of the senator's desire to inform a group known as "Secretaries for Kennedy" of his activities in the Senate. Senator Kennedy was not very enthusiastic about the Democratic Party apparatus in Massachusetts, so he chose to form his own statewide network after deciding to run in 1952 for the senate seat held by Henry Cabot Lodge. He enlisted interested and enthusiastic people in his cause by designating one or more individuals from each community in the state as a "Secretary for Kennedy." If I recall correctly, there were about 10,000 Secretaries.

Today, virtually every member of Congress issues a newsletter; but in those days, it was quite rare. We were preparing a newsletter reporting on his activities; and in an effort to justify it being sent as regular franked mail (that is, paid out of senate funds), I wanted the first one to be framed in a manner that would pass muster. I called the Library of Congress and asked for the name of any Congressional member, past or present, who had said that there was an obligation on the part of legislators to give an accounting of their stewardship of office to their constituents. In a few days, came the reply that there wasn't anybody who had said that. Because I was certain that someone would have said something like that, the opening paragraph of the senator's report stated that the report was being sent in accordance with the admonition laid down by "one of our founding fathers" that legislators should periodically give an accounting of their stewardship.

A favorite campaign story passed on by Ted Reardon took place at the entrance gate of the Gillette Razor Blade Company at the 7:00 a.m. change in shifts. The candidate was trying to shake every hand, muttering something like, "I'm John Kennedy and would appreciate your support." An old guy asked if he was the Kennedy kid. When he acknowledged that he was, the old geezer said "Have you ever done an honest day's work in your life?" JFK was prepared for almost any question but not that one. While he was fumbling for an answer, the fellow said, "Don't worry, you haven't missed a Goddam thing."

A VISIT FROM VICE PRESIDENT NIXON

The Kennedy office was immediately across the hall from that of Vice President Richard Nixon. The Vice President had a more formal, but smaller, office in the Capitol building, but his staff operation was right there and we'd occasionally see him in the hallway. When President Eisenhower was in the hospital, I believe with ileitis, the Vice President gave a brief report on Eisenhower's hospitalization to the news media in the hearing room of the Senate Banking and Currency Committee, which was a few feet down the hall from our office. I stepped in to watch. Nixon looked at the TV cameras and gave a five-minute statement without notes explaining that he, Nixon, would stay in close touch with the White House staff and report on the President's progress. A few reporters arrived late and asked if the Vice President would repeat his statement. I was flabbergasted to hear him go through it again. As far as I could tell, it was word-for-word identical to the first time. He had memorized the entire statement but wanted it to appear spontaneous. It was simply amazing.

A better story about Nixon occurred while Senator Kennedy was in Florida, convalescing from his back operation. In January 1955, following the 1954 elections, there was speculation that the newly elected senator from Ohio, Frank Lausche, a very conservative Democrat, was considering voting with the Republicans in electing the new Senate leaders, which would result in a vote of 47 to 47. (This was before the second senate office building was built.) For some reason, there was a Democratic vote other than Kennedy's that would not be available. Thus, the Vice President would be able to vote to break the tie and turn control of the Senate over to the Republicans, if Senator Kennedy was not present to vote. The speculation was that Kennedy would come to the senate floor on a stretcher to be able to cast his vote.

Without any formal communication or publicity, Nixon strolled across the hall into the Kennedy office and told Ted Reardon that it would be ludicrous for Senator Kennedy to take any risks just to vote. If it came to that, his Republican colleague Senator Saltonstall would simply withhold his vote. It was a small gesture, but a thoughtful one.

SENATE PERSONALITIES

The Senate has many traditions and one of the oldest is that of the existing senator from a state escorting the newly elected senator from that state to the well of the senate where the new senator is formally sworn into office. On one such occasion, the newly elected Democratic senator from Ohio, Stephen Young, created a bit of a stir. When the very liberal and crusty Young was about to walk to the senate well, Senator Lausche attempted to take his arm to escort him. Young said with a whisper that was heard throughout the chamber, "You didn't do a damned thing to help me get here and I can make it to the swearing-in without your assistance." Young was along in years when he got elected to the Senate, and said he only planned to serve one term; but he changed his mind and was re-elected.

Once, when he received a very rough and insulting letter from a constituent who was unhappy with a Young vote, he wrote back and said, "I thought I ought to let you know that some idiot got a hold of your stationery with your letterhead on it and is sending stupid letters and signing your name to them." To a veteran who wrote complaining about a vote, he wrote back, "Listen Buster, I was in uniform in World War I when you were in knee pants, and I don't need any advice from the likes of you."

Another senate story involved Senator Pat McNamara, a Michigan Democrat, with a gravelly voice. He walked into the almost empty senate chamber and found two senators engaged in heated debate. Wayne Morse, of Oregon, and Bill Proxmire, of Wisconsin, were both liberals who were very bright and very talkative, and not especially favorites of their colleagues. So McNamara said with that voice that carried to every far corner of the room, "It looks like there's trouble in the leper colony today," a line that was bruited about by staff for quite a while.

Then there was Senator Theodore Frances Green, Democrat from Rhode Island, who was a very wealthy octogenarian bachelor. He lived at the University Club, a couple of miles from the Capitol, and used to tip his cab driver a dime and cheerfully say, "Vote Republican." While pausing at the doorway to an elaborate reception room at the State Department, Senator Green, who was chairman of the Senate Foreign Relations Committee, reached into his jacket pocket and took out a 3- by 5-inch card on which his schedule was written. He was examining it when a young man trying to make conversation said, "Senator, are you figuring out where you're going next?" Green replied, "Hell, no.—I'm trying to figure out where I am now."

OFFICE CAPERS

Ted Reardon, the administrative assistant, was a special guy. He had been a Harvard classmate of Joe Kennedy, Jr., the senator's older brother who was killed during World War II, and was a close friend of the family. He served as Kennedy's administrative assistant during his three terms in the House of Representatives and moved with him to the Senate. He was not a policy man, but ran the office and had an easy relationship with the senator and with the staff. His best line came when a Massachusetts Congressman from Lowell was indicted and convicted of failing to pay federal income taxes on fees he received as a member of the board of directors of a Savings and Loan association. Reardon said, "That's the first time I heard of someone being put in prison for failing to show the proper interest."

But far and away, the worst thing he did—and I was worse than he was—involved an intern by the name of Roger Morgan from Amherst College. Roger was a gregarious football jock who was spending a couple of summer months in the office and, incidentally, was staying at my house during the tail end of his assignment while my family was away. He had been working on a variety of projects but was nearing the end of his internship. I knew he had been out carousing one Friday night until early in the morning with some of his fellow interns and told him he didn't have to come into the office the next day.

But when Reardon and I started talking about what a great fellow Roger was, an idea sprang into Reardon's head. Ted was able to put on a fine British accent and, with my connivance, called Roger at my house and said to the sleepy young man that he was the press officer for the British Embassy, and that he had called Senator Kennedy's office to inquire about the senator's position on the controversy surrounding Cyprus, and had been told that Mr. Morgan was the person handling the matter for the senator. Well, Roger had done a little work on the topic, but said he'd have to dig a bit deeper and would call back on Monday. Reardon gave him the telephone number of the Metropolitan Police Department and told him to ask for "the Chief" since he was the chief of the press section of the embassy. Pretty soon Roger showed up and worked all Saturday afternoon and part of Sunday, boning up on Cyprus. On Monday morning, Roger dialed the police department and asked for the Chief.

At that point, I put my finger on the telephone cradle and cut off the call. We all then laughed because the office was in on the dastardly thing we had done to the likeable Roger. I believed this big guy was going to knock my brains out, but he took the outrageous prank better than anyone, especially me, would have. He admitted he was a little relieved because he wasn't very comfortable making the report to the "Chief." Roger went on to marry his college sweetheart and become a prominent lawyer in Hartford, Connecticut, and raised a raft of kids.

THE SALARY AND PERKS

By the time I left TVA, my annual salary had risen to $6,300; thus, the jump to my new $8,000 level was healthy, although the cost of living was also higher in Washington, DC. Because the senator had used up most of the money for staff allotted by the Senate, he arranged for $4,000 of my salary to come from the Senate and $4,000 from his own personal funds, administered by his father's office in New York City. The arrangement was agreeable, but I did not realize until the next April, when tax time came, that each was withholding on the assumption that $4,000 was the full salary. All of a sudden there was some scurrying around.

Shortly after I joined the staff, we were invited to a reception at the Kennedy's home in Georgetown. I can't recall any of the guests other than Supreme Court Justice William O. Douglas and his wife. There I was talking to a Justice of the Supreme Court.

One special benefit that came my way was Senator Kennedy's decision to skip the inaugural ceremony of President Eisenhower's second term at the beginning of 1957. I casually asked Evelyn Lincoln whether the senator was planning to attend. She said he wasn't and asked if I wanted to use his two tickets. Thus, eight-year-old Bruce White and I were in the VIP section. It was a cold day, but nothing like the day four years later when John Kennedy took the oath of office.

Chapter Three

The Hoover Commission

One day in November 1954, I returned to the office from a lunchtime stroll with Ted Sorensen and was told that Ambassador Kennedy had called me. Sorensen said he must have meant him or Ted Reardon, rather than me; but it was clear that Ambassador Kennedy wanted to talk to me and I hadn't the slightest idea why. Joseph P. Kennedy was a member of the Hoover Commission (a bi-partisan group of twelve distinguished men that was established to review the operations of the Executive Branch of government, and to make recommendations for improvements to the President (then, Eisenhower) and the Congress. Mr. Kennedy wanted me to be his assistant. Wow!

His son Bobby, who had been his assistant for eight or nine months, had told the old man that he was taking a job with the Senate Subcommittee on Investigations, which was chaired by Senator John McClellan of Arkansas, who was also a member of the Hoover Commission. When Mr. Kennedy asked his son John, the senator, to recommend someone, the senator replied that his office would be at less than full force during his convalescence from the operation on his back and that I could be spared until he returned. With a pay raise from $8,000 to $9,300 annually, I embarked on yet another happy interlude in my young (I was thirty-one) life.

Sorensen had advised me that there was some suggestion that Mr. Kennedy might harbor some anti-Semitic views. When I mentioned to Bobby that I was Jewish, despite a name like White, he said there was absolutely no problem— and there wasn't.

THE MEMBERS

Former President Herbert Hoover had been appointed to and named Chairman of the first Hoover Commission in 1948 by President Truman. One of President Truman's first actions after succeeding President Roosevelt to the presidency was to call Mr. Hoover and invite him to the White House to gain his perspective on issues and to benefit from his experiences. The first Hoover Commission, on which Mr. Kennedy also served, had done a fine job in examining Executive Branch operations; and a large percentage of its recommendations, which dealt primarily with logistical and procedural operations, were enacted into law.

Congress authorized the 1954 commission, and President Eisenhower approved the legislation and again designated Mr. Hoover as the Chairman. In addition to former President Hoover, there were from the Eisenhower administration Attorney General Herbert Brownell, and the Director of the Bureau of the Budget, Arthur Fleming (who subsequently served as Secretary of the Department of Health Education and Welfare). From the United States Senate came John McClellan, Democrat of Arkansas, and Chairman of the Senate Government Operations Committee; and Homer Ferguson, Republican of Michigan. From the House of Representatives came Chet Hollifield, Democrat of California, the only liberal on the commission; and Clarence Brown, Republican of Ohio, and a crusty old curmudgeon. There were two Hollisters (not related)—one a lawyer from Cincinnati and part of the Taft law firm and political apparatus; the other was the Dean of the Cornell Engineering School. Along with Mr. Kennedy, the other prominent Democrat was James Farley, the former Postmaster General and political ally of President Franklin Roosevelt. Another conservative Democrat was Dean Robert Storey of the Southern Methodist University Law School. The final member was Sidney Z. Mitchell, a New York financier who was the son of the founder of Electric Bond and Share Company, a major investment house and consulting company for electric utilities, who had been the staff director of the first Hoover Commission.

The commission was housed in a new building at Fourth and G Streets, N.W. Its offices on the third floor were known as the Gold Coast, because they were spacious and nicely furnished in executive style government issue. Two members, each with private offices, shared a large common reception area with room enough for a desk for each member's assistant and secretary. Because most of the members showed up only for meetings, the member's assistant could occupy the member's private office, which was quite a treat for a fellow who had shared an office with five others in the Senate Office Building.

INNER WORKINGS

I had the good fortune to start at exactly the time when the commission began its work. It had operated initially through task forces set up to examine the operations of the Executive Branch, and now the task force reports including their recommendations were to be reviewed and acted on by the members of the commission. The first meeting at which the commission was going to consider task force recommendations provided me with the opportunity to analyze the recommendations in considerable detail and to include my own thoughts on what the commission ought to do with recommendations. I prepared a four or five page single-spaced memo which Mr. Kennedy glanced at and proceeded to ignore. From then on, any memos were very brief. For the most part, I'd discuss any thoughts orally, either by phone or just before commission meetings.

The most interesting conversation I had with Mr. Kennedy came during a phone call from Florida prior to a commission meeting. In what was obviously a thought connected with his son's operation and convalescence, he said, "You know, American doctors don't know a Goddam thing about backs. Prepare a recommendation for me to offer at the meeting increasing funds for back research." I said, "Mr. Kennedy, wouldn't it make more sense to make it apply to all medical research?" "Sure," he said. So, the Hoover Commission that wanted to cut appropriations for virtually every federal program had one recommendation calling for a significant increase in funding for medical research.

While the commission was addressing health matters, Mr. Hoover told the group that one of the accomplishments of his administration of which he was proudest was the arrangements made with every Central and South American country. If the country would institute a public health program following U.S. guidelines, the United States would fund the first year at one hundred percent; if it continued, the United States would fund seventy-five percent the second year; and so on down to zero percent. He was pleased to note that every country had stuck with its program.

Mr. Hoover, who was then in his eighties, was alert, patient, and skillful. He had also read the material and was a very fair presiding officer. Although it was not necessarily true on every discussion of issues, there developed a pattern in which Mr. Hoover would go to the next item on the agenda and say, "What do you think, Joe?" Mr. Kennedy would then say to Mr. Fleming, who would generally have a well thought out response, "What do you think, Arthur?" The discussion would go from there, with Congressman Hollifield, acting through his very bright assistant Herb Roback, generally dissenting.

One incident was especially challenging. Congressman Brown had a health condition and on one afternoon he was not feeling particularly well. He was expounding on some issue when Dean Hollister, the mildest and most gentle member, asked Brown what he meant by a statement he had made. Brown repeated it, but Hollister was still confused, as was almost everyone else; so he asked Brown to say it one more time, whereupon Brown erupted, saying "I can explain it to you and I can explain it you again, but I can't give you the ability to understand." Mr. Hoover judiciously intervened by saying, "Meeting adjourned.—We'll meet tomorrow morning."

KEEPING THINGS STRAIGHT

Mr. Kennedy was very breezy and had a ton of charm, even if he didn't take all this stuff too seriously. He had a great smile and lots of warmth. He was everyone's favorite. One day, he told me, "I'm going to have to leave early. I'm buying half interest in a big oil company this afternoon." Another time, he said, "Give me a call at Hialeah race track tomorrow." When I asked how he could be located at the track, he said, "Don't worry, they know where my box is."

My biggest thrill came one beautiful Monday morning in November when the small committee focusing on foreign economic assistance (consisting of Mr. Hoover, Sidney Mitchell, and Mr. Kennedy) was to meet. The special deal was that the meeting was to be in Mr. Hoover's suite at the Waldorf Astoria Hotel in New York City. I flew up on the Eastern Airlines shuttle and proceeded to Mr. Kennedy's office at 230 Park Avenue, where I was to meet him and accompany him to the meeting. It happened that Jackie Kennedy was at his office, and I recall her asking me in that breathless way of hers, "How do you keep all these different things straight?" I don't recall the answer I gave.

As Mr. Kennedy and I started the six or seven block walk to the Waldorf Astoria, we must have walked past at least ten people, including doormen, cops and trades people who said, "Good morning Mr. Ambassador," or "Good morning, Mr. Kennedy." I thought to myself, the way he saunters up Park Avenue, you'd think he owned it; and then I thought, maybe he does.

Mr. Hoover's suite was at the top of the hotel and, frankly, was dark and dreary with an awful lot of old furniture.—One insignificant fact is that Mr. Hoover for some reason did not have confidence in paper clips. He always had a small glass container filled with straight pins, which he would use to pin pages together by bending over the upper left hand corner of the sheets and sticking a straight pin through the folded part.—The meeting wasn't particularly productive, but I could hardly believe my good luck to be the only staff person in Mr. Hoover's apartment.

Prior to the Monday meeting, Sidney Mitchell had asked me to come to his suite at the old Wardman Park Hotel on Sunday afternoon. Of course, I said, "Yes," and he sent Mr. Hoover's limousine to pick me up. As we settled in, he asked if I would like a martini; and there was no way I was going to refuse that offer. He clapped his hands and the cutest French-speaking maid appeared, who shortly returned with two absolutely lovely martinis. For a brief moment, I thought I could get used to that life.

THE COMMISSION'S RECOMMENDATIONS

In June 1955, the commission concluded its work and produced eight volumes of material for the Congress, the Executive Branch, and whoever else might be interested. The great bulk of the eight volumes were the task force reports. Basically, the commission wanted the government to do less, with the notable exception of funding for medical research, and, wherever possible, let private industry do the job. With the fairly high-powered members, one might have thought that the commission's analyses and recommendations would have been significant and useful to the Congress and the Executive Branch. But because this second commission focused on policy issues, rather than on the nuts and bolts of running the government, it was evident that this group was not likely to hold much sway with Congress; and it didn't. The commission accepted the task force ideas, but they went no where in Congress, with the noted exceptions of funding for medical research and one other commission recommendation related to medical research that clearly made a great deal of sense.

The other recommendation was to convert the Army's medical library, deemed to be the most extensive in the United States and probably the world, into a National Library of Medicine. The library was then housed in a decrepit building on Independence Avenue in Southwest Washington (now the site of the Air and Space Museum), and there was great fear that the materials in the library would be damaged, if not destroyed, by fire or water damage from leaky roofs.

COMINGS AND GOINGS

As the commission was winding down in June 1955, a reception for commission members, task force participants, staff and friends was held at the Anderson House on Massachusetts Avenue, a grand old beautiful building, the home of the Order of the Cincinnatus. My wife and I had difficulty finding a parking place and were a little late. As we were approaching the Anderson House, Mr. Hoover's car was just leaving the circular driveway in front of the building. When he saw us, he had the driver back up and gave me the opportunity to introduce my wife and to bid him good-bye.

The Hoover Commission experience had been a most unusual opportunity to study the workings of the Executive Branch, and to watch some important people function from up close. I had found Mr. Kennedy to be a delightful fellow to know and work for, and at the conclusion of our work, I received a nice letter of appreciation from him.

After an interlude of nearly eight months, I was now ready to return to the more invigorating pace of a senate office. Senator Kennedy had returned from Florida, and his office was getting back into full swing.

Chapter Four

Return to Senator Kennedy's Office

As interesting and educational as my work with the Hoover Commission had been, I felt a sense of relief being back in the hurly-burly of the Senate. Senator Kennedy had returned with his back operation an apparent success.— Later it was reported that on at least two occasions his condition was so precarious that a priest was called to his bedside to administer last rites.—He was, however, anything but a take-it-easy sort of fellow, and he embarked on a full schedule.

THE NATIONAL LIBRARY OF MEDICINE

Upon returning to Senator Kennedy's office, I told him that the Hoover Commission's recommendation to convert the Army's medical library into a National Library of Medicine was a natural for him, because he was the chairman of the Reorganization Subcommittee of the Senate Government Operations Committee. He told me to get Senator Lister Hill, Democrat of Alabama, to introduce it, and Kennedy would be a co-sponsor. Because Senator Hill was regarded as "Mr. Health Care" in the Senate, Senator Kennedy did not want Lister Hill to think he was trying to muscle in on Hill's territory. The bill was introduced, and Senator Kennedy even got Mr. Hoover to testify in favor of it at the hearings on the Commission's report. Former presidents did not usually testify before Congressional committees, but Mr. Hoover's main purpose in testifying was to support a recommendation (that went nowhere) that a position of Administrative Vice President be created.

It was smooth sailing for the national medical library bill except for one small wrinkle. Senator Paul Douglas, Democrat of Illinois, and probably the

most highly principled member of the Senate, said he had a two word amendment: "in Chicago." We thought that was just a stunt to gather some favorable
attention at home; but the senator, who had enlisted in the Marine Corps during World War II at about age fifty-one and had been wounded, was quite serious and determined. He argued that a national library should be centrally located; that Chicago is a superb medical center; and that the great collection of
medical literature would be safer in the mid-west. The military, the great majority of the Senate, including Senator Hill, were opposed.

Under senate procedures, one determined senator can cause much mis-
chief. Happily, Senator Douglas finally relented; and the National Library of
Medicine now is located on the campus of the National Institutes of Health,
across the street from the Bethesda Naval Hospital in Bethesda, Maryland.

THE MAKING OF A NEW POLITICAL FORCE

As *Profiles in Courage* hit the best sellers chart, the senator became very active.
There was—and continues to some extent to be—speculation as to whether Ted
Sorensen wrote the book. I remember Ted doing a great deal of research and
some outlining. And I would be surprised if he did not do a considerable
amount of drafting; but as my own limited experience demonstrated, if you had
a pretty good idea of what Senator Kennedy wanted, you could produce what
he would. On a subject like political heroes, I assume there was great interest
on the senator's part; and I have a hazy recollection of loads of books and excerpts being sent to the senator in Florida. Ted and the senator worked so
closely that their writing styles and their take on issues seemed to merge; but in
the final analysis, not a single thought got into the final version that was not
written by JFK, edited by him, or endorsed by him. It was his book.

The book won a Pulitzer Prize and helped Kennedy get a ton of publicity, almost all of it favorable. He had been paying a news clipping service to clip and
send him all newspaper and magazine articles mentioning his name. I don't
know when he realized that even he couldn't afford that service any longer.

On one occasion, the senator was dashing through the clips when he yelled
at Ted Reardon, "What's this business about my sending a telegram of con-
gratulations to Max Rabb at some testimonial dinner?" Reardon said he had
asked about it before the telegram was sent, and the senator had approved.
JFK replied, "I thought you told me that was for Max's father.—I sure as hell
wouldn't have congratulated Max." Max Rabb had been Administrative Assistant to Senator Henry Cabot Lodge, the incumbent Massachusetts Republican senator that Kennedy defeated in 1952, and had served as Lodge's campaign manager. So here was a clipping from an English-language, Jewish

weekly newspaper in Boston praising Kennedy for his "bigness" in congratulating Rabb, when he never intended to do so.

HANDLING DEFEAT

Former President Hoover's testimony on an important, but hardly block-busting, issue like the National Library of Medicine was small potatoes compared to the fiery hearings on Jimmy Hoffa and the Teamsters Union. Both the senator and Bobby Kennedy were in it up to their eyeballs. That attention didn't hurt as the Democrats assembled in Chicago in the summer of 1956 for the Democratic nominating convention. Illinois Governor Adlai Stevenson, who had run unsuccessfully against General Eisenhower in 1952, was a reluctant candidate but was willing to give it his best shot. Young Senator Kennedy gave one of the short seconding speeches for Stevenson to be the presidential nominee, which was well received. Then Stevenson shocked the convention by throwing the selection of his running mate open to the convention, something that had not been done prior to that time or subsequently.

I was in Washington, DC minding the store, while Ted Sorensen was with the senator and reported the excitement and mind boggling politicking that erupted. The favorite to win the contest was Senator Estes Kefauver of Tennessee; but Senator Kennedy was also nominated and the race began. Kefauver was ahead but, surprisingly, quite a few Southern states gave some support to Kennedy. All of a sudden, Kennedy was ahead and the apparent winner. He was called in his hotel room and told to hurry over to the convention to address it. Whatever had been prepared for his "victory" talk, I never saw, but as he was arriving at the convention hall, the tide turned and Kefauver won the race to be Stevenson's vice presidential running mate. Senator Kennedy got to the podium, quickly shifted gears, and gave a five- or six-minute speech that was a gem. He pledged support of the ticket, of course, but his words were graceful and impressive.

I started receiving calls in the Washington office from all sorts of people who had been taken by his wit and charm. But the best category of calls was from mothers who told their children that the senator had demonstrated good sportsmanship and the right way to handle defeat.

Many political pundits told Kennedy how lucky he was because he had received national attention but didn't have to be on a ticket certain to lose. Also, it wouldn't be helpful to his long-range aspirations if it were perceived that his being Catholic was responsible, even in part, for the defeat of the ticket.—Four years later, when Kennedy was considering seeking the presidential nomination, many of his friends told him that he was too young and that he should angle for a vice-presidential nomination and get over the Catholic hurdle that way. His answer was that if there were a political bank where one could deposit his political credits and withdraw them later when needed, that advice might be useful. But since there is no such bank, you move while you're hot.—In any event, it was obvious that a new political star was lighting up the sky.

THE SENATOR'S CHARM

The office was a relatively happy one, especially at Christmastime when the cartons of Haig & Haig Scotch whiskey showed up to be dispensed to staff, news people, and a list of JFK friends. The generally accepted story was that Ambassador Kennedy had nailed down an exclusive arrangement with the producers while he was Ambassador to Great Britain. Part of the charm—if you can call it that—of the office was Muggsy O'Leary. Muggsy was a general gofer who would make deliveries and place bets on races or on the numbers games that flourished before government lotteries. He moved with JFK to the White House, where he was assigned to the Secret Service and was a big pal to everyone.

Senator Kennedy's charm was always evident. One time he was driving north on 15th Street and made a left turn into a street next to the Treasury building despite two clear "No Left Turn" signs. A burly Irish cop walked off the sidewalk and motioned the car to pull over. He started to chew out the driver and had his ticket book in hand when he recognized Kennedy. He put his book away and said, "Senator, you must be more careful.— You could get hurt making turns like that."

Reardon knew the Capitol Police Chief, a friendly Irishman named Sullivan, and it was a special perk to have parking or moving violation tickets taken care of by Reardon. When a friend pointed out to me that there was something wrong with such an arrangement, I stopped asking Reardon to fix tickets. Of course, I got one within a month of having sworn off.

The senator's fortieth birthday was not a happy day. I thought he was putting on a bit of an act, as men will do. It soon became apparent that it was no act; he was truly depressed. I suppose it could have rested on his knowledge of how precarious his health actually was; but whatever the reason, he didn't go peacefully over that little hump.

SENATE STAFFERS

Senatorial staffs were quite a bit smaller then than they are now, and there was easy communication among staffers, particularly when we all sat in the same office. I learned how easy it was to begin to realize one's own "importance" when lobbyists wanted to get a bit of my time to help me help Senator Kennedy know "the right way" to vote on a particular bill. Imagine my surprise to learn that some fellow whom I had kept waiting for way too long turned out to be Charlie Murphy (a name I did not know at the time), who had been an assistant to President Truman and then Chairman of the Civil Aeronautics Board. All he wanted to do was tout some legislation, and I thought he certainly deserved more respect than I had accorded him.

My own name helped at least once. I called the Defense Department for some information regarding a project I was working on. There wasn't any particular urgency about it, but in twenty minutes it showed up hand-delivered by a soldier in uniform. It turns out that a recently resigned Eisenhower administration Assistant Secretary of the Air Force was named H. Lee White.

Compared to present day practices, lobbying then was relatively uncomplicated. Senate staff members were given modest gratuities. For example, the Airline Transportation Association would invite twenty or thirty staff members to a dinner and present a film about airlines and issues of interest to them. The owner of the DC Transit Company held a large reception in an old car barn in Georgetown that had been renovated and richly furnished. But even then, there was some concern. Senator Paul Douglas of Illinois told his staff they could not accept anything they could not carry in one hand or consume in three days.

Assistants to various blocs of senators would naturally flock together. The leader (I believe, self-appointed) of assistants to liberal Democratic senators was Julius C. C. Edelstein, assistant to Senator Herbert Lehman of New York. The group would occasionally have dinner meetings to discuss various legislative subjects. One evening when dinner was concluded, Julius got our attention and observed, "You know I'm an expert on Social Security." (I thought to myself, what an egomaniac.) He went on: "An expert on Social Security is anyone who happens to have Wilbur Cohen's telephone number." What followed was a treat: Wilbur was there to take us through the ins and outs of the statute. He was, indeed, the living authority on the subject, having participated in its drafting during the Roosevelt Administration. Wilbur later became Assistant Secretary of Health Education and Welfare under JFK, and Secretary under LBJ.

ITCHY FEET

As the year moved along, I got itchy feet about moving on. A number of factors came together to start me thinking about a change. First and foremost was the fact that with four young children (a fifth came later), prudence dictated that I try to move to the more lucrative private sector; and I seemed to have a biological clock that made me think about a change every three or three-and-a-half years. Sorensen was the top banana and deserved to be, and I wasn't nuts about being second banana. But the scrambling around the new political force, Kennedy, was unseemly and made me quite uncomfortable. His former House of Representatives buddies and his senate chums all reported how many votes they had secured for him in Chicago. When totaled, the sum was more than all the votes cast for him and Kefauver. Like salmon, I would be swimming upstream because everyone seemed to want to join his band-wagon. I figured that even if Kennedy made it to the White House, I could probably hook on somewhere.

Senator Kennedy had been named to the Senate Small Business Committee, in addition to his other committee assignments. Thus, when I approached him about leaving, I could suggest that he was entitled to name someone to that staff. That would be a comfortable perch from which I could explore outside possibilities. He accepted the idea of my leaving with an easy attitude. He didn't try to dissuade me because I had pretty good reasons to support my decision. What he did say was that it would be easier for him if I were to remain, but he understood my reasons for leaving, and the Small Business Committee arrangement would work out fine. Also, he'd be glad to help in my efforts to go out of the government. Although he didn't think I was goofy to be leaving his office, almost everyone else did.

Was it the right decision? I missed not being in the presidential campaign of 1960; but, even today, I'm satisfied it was the right move for me.

Chapter Five

The Senate Small
Business Committee

My transition to the Senate Small Business Committee staff in January 1957 was very smooth. Senator John Sparkman of Alabama (who had been Adlai Stevenson's running mate in 1952) was the chairman; the staff director was Walter Stults, a Republican, albeit a very moderate one, who had been appointed by Senator Robert Hendrickson of New Jersey. The ranking minority member was Senator Ed Thye of Minnesota. My title was Counsel to the committee, which made me feel a little important. Of course, all of the staff who were lawyers were called "counsel."

The committee offices were located in a World War II-era building about three blocks from the Senate Office Building. The building had a Siberia-like quality about it, so staff had a tendency to wander over to the Senate Office Building to check into the offices of their sponsors on the committee. The normal reaction of the Kennedy office was to suggest that I must have something better to do than bother them. And, generally, I did.

A "SPECIAL COMMITTEE"

The Senate Small Business Committee was a "Special Committee" that, at that time, was not authorized to report legislation to the floor of the senate. Instead, it was required to submit its recommendations for legislation to regular standing committees. This added to our inferiority complex. But the committee did issue reports on the conduct of the Small Business Administration, which itself suffered as an agency that, at that time, had to be re-authorized periodically.

At one committee hearing, the Small Business Administrator, Wendell Barnes, testified that an extremely high percentage of loans that the SBA had made the preceding year had been repaid on time. He was obviously proud of that fact and was bowled over when Senator Thye, a fellow Republican, chastised him, saying that the agency must be making only such solid loans that commercial banks could make and earn money on them. In short, the point was that if there were not a record of defaults, the agency wasn't making the type of loans it was set up to make. Sometimes you just can't win.

THE DAYTIME RADIO HEARINGS

The major project I worked on was a long-festering struggle by the relatively impecunious Daytime radio stations to have greater access to the airwaves. They were opposed by the so-called Clear Channel stations that operated on much more powerful signals. During daylight hours, the smaller local-oriented stations could broadcast without significantly interfering with the larger stations that were operating on the same frequencies even though hundreds or even thousands of miles away. In a nutshell, during summertime with longer hours of daylight, the Daytime stations could function profitably and meet the needs of the local communities they served. When the shorter winter daylight hours were in effect, the situation was different. This was the nub of the problem the committee sought to address.

The Daytime group had some impressive testimony about how their stations' inability to be on the air during early morning hours in the winter because of darkness deprived the people who listened to their stations from knowing whether there were school closings and what the weather forecasts were for the area; and local advertisers didn't like the idea that their stations had to cease broadcasting at dusk. The Clear Channel group said they had had their licenses for years and served vast areas of the country; and when the Daytime stations applied to the Federal Communications Commission (FCC) for their licenses, they knew the rules and what they were getting into. The FCC's response was that this was a tough technical problem which their engineers were trying to work on to see if some engineering solutions could offer help and comfort to the Daytime stations.

It was not an easily solvable problem. It had been going on for nearly thirty years and had gained a bit of notoriety for probably being the longest running regulatory issue. The subcommittee report of 1957 contained some exhortation to find an engineering solution and expressed sympathy for the Daytime stations and the communities and people they served. The last I heard, the problem was still unresolved.

What I got out of the Daytime radio hearings was the opportunity to explore a problem in great detail, to participate in the process, and to watch trade associations at work on legislators and their staffs. Sitting next to the chairman on the dais, questioning witnesses, and shaping a committee report was pretty heady stuff for this kid from Nebraska.

SENATOR WAYNE MORSE

The Chairman of the Subcommittee on Communications was Senator Wayne Morse of Oregon, and he chaired the Daytime radio hearings. He had been dean of the University of Oregon Law School, and had one of the best legal minds in the Senate. He had originally been elected to the Senate as a Republican, but switched to being an Independent, and then a Democrat. It was a privilege to work with Senator Morse. He was on time, sharp, courteous, and clearly listened intently to the witnesses, even if this issue was not the hottest item on the senate agenda.

To demonstrate Senator Morse's remarkable talent, he single-handedly threw a big monkey wrench in Senate Majority Leader Lyndon Johnson's carefully developed use of "unanimous consent" agreements to keep the Senate moving on track. A vote was scheduled for an afternoon when Morse had to be in Oregon, so he asked and then demanded of Johnson that the vote be postponed until Morse's return. Johnson said he couldn't do that because a unanimous consent agreement had been entered into with no senator objecting; thus, the schedule had to stand. Without notes, Senator Morse gave an extemporaneous, learned, detailed and sophisticated dissertation as to why the use of unanimous consent agreements was a corrupting influence in the processes of a deliberative body. As I recall, no significant change in Johnson's use of unanimous consent agreements occurred, but he was always careful to check with Morse when presenting such agreements.

THE "BURROS"

While serving with the committee, I had an unusual opportunity to introduce Senator Kennedy, who was scheduled to speak to a group of assistants to Democratic House members, known as the "Burros."—The Burros organization was created by Lyndon Johnson when he was an assistant to a Texas Congressman many years earlier.—I had arranged to attend the luncheon meeting and was minding my own business when the chairman of the group came over to me to report that Congressman Torbert "Torby" McDonald, a Massachusetts Democrat and, more importantly, a former Harvard College roommate and big buddy of Kennedy, had planned to introduce the senator. Unfortunately, his plane had been held up and he would not be able to get to the luncheon. Would I please do the honors? Of course, I agreed to do so.

It was undoubtedly one of the shortest introductions Senator Kennedy ever received, at least before he became President. I said that a bunch of political junkies such as the Burros obviously knew all about Senator Kennedy's background and I could skip all of that; but I did want to tell them about an extraordinary compliment that had been paid him by Frank McCulloch, the Administrative Assistant to Senator Paul Douglas of Illinois. He said that Senator Kennedy was bright enough to be an assistant to a senator. Those congressional assistants knew that was, indeed, high praise. Senator Kennedy responded by saying that he now had a better idea of why small business was having such a tough time in this country. Later, as President, Kennedy appointed Frank McColloch Chairman of the National Labor Relations Board.

BREAKING MY PATTERN

In December 1957, I was amazed to receive a telephone call from Lorraine Cooper, the wife of John Sherman Cooper, the Republican senator from Kentucky. She said her husband was looking for someone to serve as his Administrative Assistant because his current assistant was leaving the first of the year. She had been talking with some of the Kennedy people, who had suggested she contact me. Rather politely, I informed her that her husband was a Republican, and, unfortunately, I was a Democrat. She replied that, at least, I should talk to him. I realized that as a senate committee staff member, I probably should meet with him. After all, he was a member of the Senate.

I called his office and a meeting was set for six o'clock that evening. I explained that friends were coming to pick me up and that perhaps another day would be better. "No, this shouldn't take too long," said one of his assistants, Bailey Guard. I went to the office and Bailey greeted me and asked me to take a seat; the senator would be available shortly. The minutes ticked by slowly and, in my mind's eye, I could see our friends from Worcester, Massachusetts, Sip and Bernie Webman, with two or three of their kids and two or three of mine coming to pick me up at seven o'clock, as we had agreed. There was no way I could reach them (no cell phones in those days) to explain why I wouldn't be where I said I would be. It was now 6:40 p.m.; so I told Mr. Guard that I would have to leave, explaining why. He said I couldn't do that and went into the senator's personal office. In a moment, the senator came out and I explained the situation, saying that I couldn't possibly be comfortable in any discussion under those circumstances. Quite casually, he asked why didn't I come in tomorrow?

I had given some thought to the matter; so when we met the next day, I quickly set out what I saw as reasons why he shouldn't want me in that position. He listened attentively while I laid them out: he was a Republican; I was not from Kentucky; I couldn't make a long-term commitment since I had certain financial needs; I was Jewish; and Mrs. Cooper had been the one who had contacted me. He went down the list. There were more Democrats in Kentucky than Republicans. Because I wasn't from Kentucky, it would be easier to get rid of me if it didn't work out, and I could learn about the state. As for long-term commitment, that posed no problem for him since he might well like to move me out if things didn't work out. Next, he said, "I don't see how you're being Jewish is a problem or even relevant. And my wife does not get involved in the operation of my office." He summed it up saying, "These sound like questions for you, not for me." When he said he'd like me to join his staff, I told him I'd discuss it with my wife and promptly get back to him. Although I can't be certain, I believe I had given him the impression that I was only lukewarm about the position, which heightened his interest in me.

Walter Stults had told me the word around the Senate was that Senator Cooper was a tough fellow to work for and had gone through a few administrative assistants. Besides the fellow who had been the committee's Chief Counsel, Lou Odom, was leaving, and Stults said I could have that job.

I remembered how indecisive Cooper had been when Senator Kennedy and I tried to get him to co-sponsor the trade adjustments legislation; but he enjoyed a wonderful reputation for being a man of integrity and decency and was clearly in the liberal wing of his party. I certainly liked the idea of being the top dog; and, besides, I hadn't been successful in moving into private practice. I fully believed that if it did not go well, I'd somehow land on my feet.

After discussing it at home and receiving a green light there, I decided to check with Senator Kennedy. When I told him that I had the chance to be the Administrative Assistant to a Republican senator, Senator Kennedy wanted to know why I would want to do that. Then he asked who it was, and I told him it was Cooper. He said, "That's different.—You go work with him and when you're through, you can come back to work for me for as long as it takes to get rid of the stigma."

Breaking my pattern, in early January 1958, I headed to Senator Cooper's office, precisely one year after leaving the Kennedy office.

Chapter Six

Senator John Sherman Cooper

John Sherman Cooper was a Republican from the eastern Kentucky town of Somerset, in the Appalachian Mountains of Pulaski County. His grandfather, who had crossed the Cumberland Gap and settled in the small town of Somerset, was a businessman who got into politics. The senator's father was a businessman who was elected County Judge of Pulaski County, an administrative, not a judicial, position. When he died during the depression, John, who was then a student at Yale University, returned home to find things in a shambles. John was elected to succeed his father as County Judge, and began the struggle to bring some relief to the hard-hit area. Impressions from those depression years of families without money and food stayed with him his entire life and shaped many of his attitudes and priorities.

"MR. WHITE"

Once I made the decision to join Senator Cooper's staff, the senator had me go to his house in Georgetown to discuss his legislative hopes and plans. The house was on a beautiful double lot with a garage and garden in the rear, but inside it was very dark and even dreary. In the wood-burning fireplaces, coal was burning. He was, after all, a Kentuckian. It was December, so it was especially bleak. He had a lawyer's yellow pad and proceeded to tell me what he wanted to do in the Senate, while making notes at the same time. There was a change he wanted to achieve in how the Defense Department procured military items. He wanted to help lift the economy of the Appalachians, especially Eastern Kentucky, and he wanted to help the coal and burley tobacco industries. I do not recall that any part of his agenda involved international matters.

In January 1958, I began one of the most interesting chapters of my life. After about two weeks, I concluded that the book on him was pretty accurate: he was the most decent, compassionate and honorable human being, but was disorganized and indecisive. As I saw it, I had three choices: I could go back to the Small Business Committee; I could try to shape him into what I thought a United States Senator from Kentucky should be like; or I could work with him trying to help him do a somewhat better job of being a senator. I chose the last option. After all, he certainly had accomplished a great deal without me.

His procrastination could be a real problem, so I decided to let him know about deadlines and have the necessary documents or papers ready for him. If time was running out, I would make the decision and sign myself, use his initials, or on occasion sign his name. It was a bit of a risky policy because you couldn't make too many mistakes (meaning he would have gone the other way). Certainly, there were many decisions only he could make. When he realized what I was doing, he said to me, "Mr. White, you're a strange fellow." He called everybody else in the office by their first name.

I would put the letters he was to sign in an "in" box on his desk, but he tended to ignore them. I also noticed that he would stop frequently at my desk and browse through my "in" box. After all, everything in the office was his, so I had no complaint to make; but I decided to put the mail for him to sign at the top of my "in" box. Sure enough, he signed them. Then I moved that box to a stand just outside the door to his office and he would sign the mail. The next obvious move was to his desk; and, of course, it worked.

"THIS LITTLE BEAR"

Senator Cooper's staff was a varied crew including veterans from Capitol Hill offices and Kentuckians. Bailey Guard was a slight, somewhat jumpy former Air Force pilot who was absolutely devoted to the senator and worked on legislative matters arising out of the senator's Agriculture Committee assignment. He knew so much about burley tobacco that he was called Burley Guard. He served the senator as an assistant longer than any one else and was there when Senator Cooper finally retired from the Senate. Dick Gerrish was a heavyset, red-faced Kentucky pol who thought almost exclusively in terms of Rs and Ds. He never forgave Cooper for hiring a D like me.

Because Senator Cooper had become the ranking minority member of the Public Works Committee, we had the services of the minority staff director, Tom Jorling. Because of my background, I could help work that committee assignment. Most senators stayed on that committee for as short a time as they could manage, but Cooper liked it because the development of river projects in Kentucky was a very big deal. In fact, when the Bureau of the Budget (now the Office of Management and Budget) was considering the Rivers and Harbors Appropriations Bill, the entire Kentucky congressional delegation would pile into a couple of cars and go to the Executive Office Building to make sure none of the money they had put in the bill would be knocked out by the Bureau of the Budget. Generally, that committee did not have partisanship problems; everybody was in favor of public works projects, especially in their state.

Joan Haffler, of Lexington, Kentucky, was my secretary, and she had a cute little girl way about her. When the senator was not in his office, I would use his office for dictating, because it was much quieter. One day, while I was using the senator's office, Senator Cooper entered his office through a door from the outer corridor. We visited briefly and he decided to make a phone call. He buzzed on the intercom, and Joan, thinking I had buzzed, said in that cute way of hers, "And what does this little bear want?" The former ambassador to India, and distinguished United States Senator said in a deep voice, "This little bear would like to talk to Senator Bush." He was referring to another Yale friend of his, Prescott Bush of Connecticut, whose son and grandson each became President of the United States.

A CONSTRUCTIVE PLAYER

During the time I was with Senator Cooper, he did not sponsor many major bills that became law. Primarily, this was due to the fact that he was in the minority, and it's always tougher for a minority member to wind up a principal sponsor; but he was a constructive player with amendments. He was deeply involved in legislation, enacted in 1958, authorizing the TVA to secure its financing on Wall Street, rather than borrow from the U.S. Treasury, but imposing a "fence" around TVA's jurisdiction. He played an important role in passing coal mine safety legislation, which, with safeguards, exempted small coal mines. Although I never understood what it was all about, he managed to preserve the burley tobacco program for Kentucky farmers.

One piece of legislation that bore the senator's name dealt with a dispute over the underlying mineral rights in land the U.S. Government had taken for a national forest. A Kentucky landowner claimed that since the deed to the land was silent on the question, he was entitled to the oil and gas that could be removed without adversely affecting the surface rights. The Cooper bill made it clear that the former landowner was entitled to the mineral rights. It passed the Senate and the House and went to the President for signature.

The U.S. Department of Agriculture and the Bureau of the Budget opposed the bill, claiming it would establish a precedent and recommended that President Eisenhower veto it. I went to the White House with the senator to meet with General Wilton Persons, the President's counsel. Senator Cooper told Persons that if any other former landowner came to him with the same problem, he would introduce special legislation to correct a wrong. He said, "You can't oppose something because it might set a precedent; you have to say that it would set a bad precedent and here the government was overreaching." President Eisenhower signed the bill.

One piece of legislation that went through the Eisenhower administration more smoothly was a bill creating the Cumberland Gap National Monument. The gap is located at the juncture where Kentucky, Tennessee, and Virginia meet. A lovely park was created at that point on the Cumberland River. A brief ceremony was scheduled at the White House at which President Eisenhower would sign the legislation. Senator Cooper told me to come along because I had worked on the bill. Of all the senators and congressmen present, I was the only staff person to attend, again, demonstrating the senator's thoughtfulness. That was the first time I had set foot in the Oval Office.

The senator was a dependable supporter of the administration, but it didn't bother him to go a different direction if he believed the administration was headed in the wrong direction. When I would draft a letter or senate floor statement for the senator, I would use the softest phraseology in criticizing the President or his administration. Senator Cooper would say, "We can do better than that," and he would strengthen the language, saying that we don't have to beat around the bush. For me, this was my style. When using the boss's name, I would be very restrained and careful, because it was someone else's name and reputation that was at stake; when I got to the spot in my life where I was the principal, I got to say, "Let's strengthen that."

Senator Cooper was one of the most liberal members of the Senate, and after working for him for some time, I came to appreciate the intensity and public-spiritedness of his political views. One day, I asked him how he happened to be a Republican. He replied, "My grandfather was a very staunch Republican, my father was a staunch Republican, and I'm a Republican." Considering this diminishing pedigree, I replied by teasing him that his family was going in "the right direction."

THE SPIRIT OF JOHN SHERMAN COOPER

Senator Cooper was, by nature, mild-mannered. One day, however, he wasn't. He was sitting in the hearing room of a House committee waiting to testify in support of a mine safety bill, and I was seated next to him. A lobbyist for the Peabody Coal Company, a giant outfit headquartered in St. Louis, approached us and beckoned me to meet him outside of the hearing room. He told me that Peabody was strongly opposed to the bill and that Cooper would be in deep trouble if he supported it. I replied that he had co-sponsored the bill, and where had you been if you wanted the senator to know the coal industry's view? He replied that he simply had not been aware of the senator's position, and would I tell the senator Peabody's view? I returned to my seat and whispered the message to the senator. Senator Cooper had a hearing problem (although I'd swear that if you were whispering so he wouldn't hear you, he heard every word). I had to repeat and maybe a little too loud. When he understood the message, he said to me in a voice loud enough to be heard in the rear half of the hearing room, "You tell him he can go to hell."

The lobbyist was appropriately named Bill Blewitt. When the hearing ended, Senator Cooper told reporters, "I just got so mad, I blew up and shouted. After all, I've been working on this bill two years and this is the first time the coal people ever said anything to me about it. They have a right to present their views any time they want to; but they can't pressure me, they can't tell me when and what to testify." There were some pretty big coal companies in Kentucky.

When the senator was committed to make a major speech, he went through a strange process. First, he would ask half a dozen people to give him drafts or at least thoughts or speech sections. Normally he'd put the writing of it off until almost the last minute (he was a world class procrastinator), then he'd cut out some paragraphs or partial paragraphs of the various drafts to be inserted somewhere in the final text. He felt obliged to use at least some part of each draft he had asked others to submit. He would then assemble them with some transitional hand written material and paper clip the whole thing to a yellow lawyers' pad. Then his secretary would type it out. It would look like a speech written by a committee. He was not a great orator, but his integrity and his sincerity always showed through, and he could sway senators to vote his way. That was especially true of matters involving India, because of his highly successful service as ambassador to India.

The incident that beautifully captures the spirit of John Sherman Cooper involved a man from India that the senator had not previously known, but whom he met at a cocktail party one Friday night. The gentleman wanted to talk to the senator about some matter in India, so Cooper told him to come to his office Saturday morning at ten o'clock. Senator Cooper called me at the office and told me to make the fellow comfortable and let him know that he was on his way. The fellow arrived and I entertained him. Pretty soon it was 10:30 a.m.; soon it was 11:00 a.m.; and it only took about twenty minutes from Cooper's house to the office on Saturday morning. I was doing a slow burn and at about 11:30 a.m., the Indian fellow looked at his watch and told me he absolutely must leave to catch an airplane. Fifteen minutes later, the senator showed up. He wanted to know whether the fellow showed up and I reported what had happened. The senator said, "I'm sure you're put out with me, but I did leave when I said I was going to. While reading the paper in the cab, I noticed that John Murphy, the tall guy with the handlebar moustache who was a reading clerk on the senate floor for years and years had died, and I had just enough time to get to the funeral. I was the only senator there." (This was before cell phones and pagers.) Now how can you be mad at a decent compassionate man like that? Besides I worked for him; he didn't work for me. A few days later a very touching letter came to the senator from Murphy's family.

Senator Cooper did not want anyone to think that he'd gotten too big for his britches, particularly his old college chums, so he wanted me to be sure I got those letters and promptly prepared answers. One of his Yale buddies, Lionel "Hank" Harris, who was a live wire, sent him a short note with a clipping from the now defunct *New York Herald-Tribune,* suggesting the senator read it. So I drafted a one paragraph reply saying, "Dear Hank: Thanks for sending the clipping from the *Herald-Tribune.* I hadn't seen it and appreciate your thoughtfulness in sending it." Senator Cooper signed the letter with a large scrawling "John." Underneath he handwrote, "I did, too, read that article." Knowing Harris would understand, I sent it that way.

Once, when the senator agreed to give a speech at the annual meeting of the National Rural Electric Cooperatives Association in Dallas, I had made the arrangements with NRECA staff for the senator to receive a $400 honorarium and expenses. He went through the usual convulsions in preparing the speech and flew off to Texas, speech in hand. All went well, and I took the check made out to the senator for him to endorse. I planned to apply it to his account at the senate recording studio where he made tapes to be distributed to Kentucky television stations for showing as a public service. He said, "Send the check back." He, of course, was the boss; but I told him I had made the arrangements and that was exactly what we had agreed to, and, besides, I knew how much he owed the recording studio—in the thousands. He said, "I know, but I always vote with those folks, and I don't want to have to worry one day that I might have been swayed by accepting the $400."—Oh, how things change.

THE ROAD TO HAZARD

One memorable experience was a tour of East Kentucky by a team of executive branch personnel, headed by Bertha Adkins, the Undersecretary of Health

Education and Welfare. There were representatives from the Small Business Administration, the Corps of Engineers, the Department of Agriculture, the Economic Development Agency, the Federal Highway Program, and the Department of the Interior. A strong effort was being made by the administration for Senator Cooper, and he wanted the group to see how tough things were in that area of the country. The group started in Barbourville, and soon moved to Harlan, known to many as "Bloody Harlan" because of the frequent violence arising out of labor disputes in the coal fields.

The bus carrying the Washington group got stuck on a hairpin curve on a very high hill on the way to Hazard, which held us up for a very long time before help arrived to get us out of the jam. Even worse, lots and lots of cars and trucks also got held up. Subsequently, one of the key findings of the group was that the road system was totally inadequate. The only slightly good news was that the clinics that the United Mine Workers had funded provided some medical and health services and, in some cases, at a high level of quality and competence. Representatives of the various agencies pledged help and perhaps some actually provided assistance.

THE HEARINGS AT ROCK SPRINGS

Senator Cooper's concern for the impoverished resulted in the Senate creating a select committee in 1958 to look into the problems of the poor and the unemployed. In a somewhat unusual procedure, the committee had two co-chairmen: Senator Eugene McCarthy, Democrat of Minnesota, and Senator Cooper. In addition, there were an equal number of Democrats and Republicans. Hearings were held at various places in the country, but because a select committee cannot report legislation to the senate floor, its major contributions were reports, which so far as I recall never resulted in any legislative solutions. But one hearing is very clear in my memory.

Democratic Senator Gale McGee of Wyoming, asked the committee to hold a hearing in Rock Springs, Wyoming, in the southwest part of the state where unemployment was very high. Senators McCarthy and Cooper were scheduled to chair the hearing but some problem came up and Senator Cooper could not attend. I was designated to appear at the hearing in his place.

The best airline connections were from Washington, DC to Salt Lake City, and then to Rock Springs. I took advantage of the schedule to stop in Omaha and visit my mother. I took a very early plane to Salt Lake City to connect with a 7:00 a.m. flight to Rock Springs. There had been some snow overnight but not more than a few inches. When I appeared at the Frontier Airlines counter, the attendant told me the flight had been cancelled. The next flight was late that afternoon. I was not a happy traveler. There was a train I could take, but it wouldn't arrive until about an hour after the hearing was scheduled to start; so I called Larry Merthan, the staff director who had stayed in Rock Springs over night and told him of my problem and promised I'd get there as soon as I could. I got to the train station and settled in for the ride to Rock Springs.

As I walked off the train, two Wyoming state troopers whisked me into a police car and sped me to the federal building where the hearing was going on. I was acknowledged by Senator McCarthy, who explained my tardiness and I took my place at the dais. When the hearing concluded, Senator McGee thanked me profusely for coming. I was a bit mystified until Larry Merthan explained what had happened. Some state Republican leader had told the press that this wasn't a senate committee hearing, but a Democratic plot to help McGee who was up for reelection. As proof, there wasn't a single Republican present at the so-called hearing, that is, until I got there.

THE KENTUCKY DELEGATION

In 1958, the first year I was with Senator Cooper, his senate colleague was Earl Clements, a Democrat from the western part of the state, and Lyndon Johnson's number two in the senate leadership. It is a principle almost never proven incorrect that two senators from different parties get along beautifully, while there is friction if they're from the same party. If one is a Democrat and the other a Republican, each is very big in state party matters, and they can work together on matters of interest to their state. If they're from the same party, there is almost certain to be some rivalry, jealousy, and competition. Thus, Cooper got along famously with Clements; but when Thruston Morton, a Louisville Republican, defeated Clements, it was inevitable that there would be a little resentment on his part over the fuss that was always made over Senator Cooper. The fact that Cooper's strong support had been a crucial factor in Morton's election didn't matter.

A STOCK OF JOKES

Just about every politician has to have a stock of jokes, but John Cooper was no raconteur. As best as I can recall, he had three stories that he would tell again and again. The first was about two mice in a nose cone in an experimental rocket (this was in the late 1950s). The first mouse says, "This is really rough. It's awfully hot and then it's awfully cold and we keep banging around in here." The second mouse replies, "But it sure beats the hell out of cancer research."

The second story is about an old couple sitting on the front porch of a ramshackle house overlooking one of the hollers (a holler is a hollow or ravine or gully or ditch) of East Kentucky, rocking away. The old man says to the old woman, "Lucy, us mountain folk don't talk a lot, but I want you to know that after thirty-seven years, I'm proud of you." She says in a fairly loud voice, "Huh?" Now, he's talking louder and says, "I said after all these years, I'm proud of you." She practically yells, "What say?" He's near the top of his voice range and says, "I'm proud of you!" She yells back, "Yeah, I'm tired of you, too"

My favorite is about the campaign rally in front of the Courthouse steps of Pulaski County, Senator Cooper's home county, where the Republican Congressman from the district, Gene Siler, and Senator Cooper are running for re-election and are being introduced by the county Republican Chairman. He says, "We are mighty lucky to have one of the nation's outstanding legislators, one of the state's best speakers, and a man admired and respected where ever he goes." He pauses, turns around, and says to the two men seated at the top of the steps, "Which ah you fellas gonna talk first?"

At a ceremony honoring Senator Cooper in Somerset after his retirement, the indomitable Albert B. "Happy" Chandler, then in his nineties, showed his talent for down-home humor. He said, "John Cooper and I each had the good sense never to run against each other and I have to say that saying good things about John reminds me of the mosquito that flew into the nudist camp.—I just don't know where to begin."

THE 1960 ELECTIONS

Twice before the 1960 elections, John Sherman Cooper had been knocked off after completing partial terms; but this time would be different. The prior partial terms were for two years each, while this term had been for four years. Far more significant this time around was the respect and admiration that had developed for the senator. His stature within the Republican Party was such that he was among those considered by the kingmakers in the party to be Richard Nixon's running mate in 1960.

Although Senator Cooper, unlike the great majority of senators, did not have a regular press secretary, we decided that one would be helpful in the campaign. I don't recall how the senator found him, but he got a gem by the name of Jack Purcell. Purcell had been a reporter, and he seemed to know everybody in the field of congressional journalism. We were having a drink at

the Carroll Arms Hotel, across the street from the Senate Office Building, going over campaign strategy and tactics when a terrific idea emerged. We knew
how well liked and respected Senator Cooper was by congressional reporters.
The trick was how to capitalize on that fact. Well, the answer was to have reporters conduct a poll to determine the "best" legislators. If Cooper did well in
the poll, we could get some mileage out of that; if he didn't do so well, we
could forget about the poll. Jack approached a reporter for *Newsweek* whom
he knew and sold the idea. The poll of around fifty reporters who covered
Capitol Hill produced a fantastic result: the outstanding senate Democrat was
Senator Lyndon Johnson of Texas, the Majority Leader, and the number one
Republican was Senator Cooper. I believe Speaker Sam Rayburn of Texas was
the number one House member, and the House Minority Leader Gerald Ford
was the top Republican. That was potent stuff for the campaign. *Newsweek* ran
it on a single page, which we reproduced by the tens of thousands, and it became the most important piece of campaign literature.

The clear signal that Senator Cooper was going to sail to victory came in
the selection of his Democratic opponent. Keene Johnson had been Governor of Kentucky twenty years earlier, but had not held elective or appointive
office since leaving the governor's office. All of the Democratic prospects
who had name recognition and some following in the state refused to get in
the race. Keene was a nice enough fellow and wasn't sure how to run against
this living legend. His one attack backfired. Very early in the campaign he
charged that Senator Cooper was always late to everything and, of course,
there was something to the point. But it so stung the senator that he was almost always on time during the entire campaign. In fact, because most areas
of East Kentucky observed daylight savings time and a few did not, Senator
Cooper actually got to one meeting an hour early. The contest was never
close.

On election night in Republican Headquarters in Louisville, I was the only
truly happy individual. Cooper had won handily; and Kennedy was projected
to win, although the results were not firm until the next morning.

THE TRANSITION TEAM

Although I had clearly preserved my right to leave the senator on my own
schedule, I couldn't leave in 1960 without feeling that I would be letting him
down if I did not stick with him through the election. But that meant I
couldn't participate in Senator Kennedy's run for the presidency. I regretted
being in such a spot, but I didn't believe I had any alternative but to remain
with Senator Cooper. At the end of 1960, I would have been in his office three

years, so I told him regardless of how his race and the presidential race went, I would leave.

After the elections, I called Gloria Liftman, Ted Sorensen's secretary, to say that I wanted to talk to Ted. She said something about ESP, because Ted had just told her to get in touch with me. Ted was heading up the transition team on policy issues with the Eisenhower administration, and wanted to know whether I was I interested and available to participate. I cleared it with Senator Cooper and jumped into the assignment with enthusiasm.

As I recall, there were six of us on the team: Ted; me; Mike Feldman, a member of Senator Kennedy's staff; Dave Bell, who was to be Kennedy's Director of the Bureau of the Budget and who had served on the White House staff of President Truman; a fellow by the name of Adler whom I did not know; and I believe the sixth was Dick Goodwin, who had been deeply involved in the presidential campaign. The Eisenhower people were completely cooperative, the word having come from President Eisenhower, and we were informed of the issues coming up and given documents and briefings, with a lead role played by the Bureau of the Budget, in part because of its clearinghouse role in the executive branch.

While our group focused on policy matters, another team headed by R. Sargent Shriver, including Larry O'Brien, Kenny O'Donnell, Ralph Dungan and a few others, had the assignment of finding people to serve in the new administration. It was, of course, a very exciting time.

The time between election and inauguration went quickly. The evening before the inauguration, a Nebraska group sponsored a reception honoring Ted Sorensen. Ted had available to him a White House automobile with a military driver, which picked us up at the Senate Office Building. As we headed to the Sheraton Carlton Hotel at 16th and K Streets, one tremendous snow storm hit Washington, DC. The reception went well but there was a gigantic mess as the snow piled up—up to nineteen inches. Happily, our house was on Alaska Avenue, and there was a bus route that went straight up 16th Street and turned on Alaska; our house was only yards from the bus stop. The next day, the Baltimore & Ohio Railroad took us from Silver Spring, Maryland, to Union Station for the inaugural ceremony. Only four years before, my son Bruce and I had sat in Senator Kennedy's seats at the second Eisenhower inaugural ceremony.

THE COOPERS AND THE KENNEDYS

When I crossed the aisle to work for Senator Cooper, a lot of my Democratic buddies gave me a hard time. I had, however, developed an answer. I would say, "You know, just the other day I was on the senate floor whispering to my boss, who was sitting next to Clifford Case of New Jersey. In front of them was Jacob Javits of New York. (Case and Javits, both Republicans, were among the most liberal senators.) I looked over at you and you were talking to Jim Eastland of Mississippi, and Harry Byrd and Willis Robertson of Virginia (three Democrats who were among the most conservative senators); and I said to myself, 'How could I have left that side to come over here?'" That seemed to quiet the matter. It was not particularly noteworthy that Senators Case and Javits supported civil rights legislation; but it was that Senator Cooper, from a border state, did.

John Cooper and John Kennedy had an extraordinary relationship of mutual respect, as did Mrs. Cooper and Mrs. Kennedy. The bond between them was strong and longstanding, like that of father and son. As depicted in Photo 6.1,

Photo 6.1.   Senator John Sherman Cooper recorded a monthly television program on issues ranging from pending legislation, international activities, burley tobacco, and coal mine safety to rivers and harbors projects, which was paid for by the senator and distributed to television stations in Kentucky for broadcast to the public. Senators John Sherman Cooper (right) and John F. Kennedy (left) are pictured in the Senate Recording Studio, circa 1958. Photo Credit: Unidentified U.S. Senate photographer. (Personal Collection of Lee C. White)

they worked smoothly with one another across party lines. After President Kennedy's inauguration, the first Executive Order signed by the President on January 21, 1961 increased food stamp benefits for the area including eastern Kentucky; and the first quiet dinner for four that the newly elected President and First Lady attended was at the Cooper home. Probably the biggest boost to John Sherman Cooper's home state was when the Appalachian Regional Commission was established by legislative action during the Kennedy Administration.

Thus, John Sherman Cooper was one of Kentucky's outstanding political figures. His special qualities and his stature in the Senate were the basis for President Johnson appointing him, along with Senator Richard Russell of Georgia, as one of the two senators on the Warren Commission to investigate the assassination of President Kennedy in 1964.

Senator Cooper was not the type to say, "Quit while you're on top," or "Leave them smiling." He continued to serve with distinction until 1973, and prudently chose not to run when he thought a full six-year term may be longer than he could effectively perform at his age. The Kentucky Republicans begged him to reconsider because they contemplated losing the seat, but he resisted their pleas. Instead, having served as Ambassador to India earlier in his career, he accepted President Ford's appointment to become the first United States Ambassador to East Germany.

Part Two

THE KENNEDY WHITE HOUSE

Chapter Seven

Joining the White House Staff

The preparations for the first day were full of excitement and the anticipatory enthusiasm was substantial, but it was nothing like the real thing. I lived on Alaska Avenue about four and a half miles north on 16th Street, and figured it should be a straight shot to the White House in normal weather on a Saturday morning; but there was the residue of the snowstorm to contend with. I allowed plenty of time and started out with my 1950 Studebaker convertible and had a fairly easy trip feeling on top of the world.

I arrived at the southwest gate and told a uniformed officer that I was one of the new folks. He waved me in and told me to take any spot on the little street between the West Wing and the Executive Office Building (now the Eisenhower Executive Office Building). I parked and walked into the basement entrance to the West Wing, as I had been told to do. There was quite a bit of commotion and at the center of it was a uniformed White House Police sergeant seated at a desk talking on the telephone. As best as I can recall, his end of the conversation went something like, ". . . well, it's not our fault that Dutton's stuff got sent to the West Wing." As he finished, I said, "I'm Lee White, one of the new people," or something like that. He said, "Oh yeah," beckoned to a young fellow dressed in dungarees and said, "Show him where to go." The young man said, "Let's go, boss," and headed out the door with me behind him.—I'm thinking they really are organized.—As we're out in the cold (it's January 21, 1961) the young fellow said, "Where's the truck?" Having degrees in electrical engineering and law, I figured out there was some mistake. So I told the fellow I was going back in the building. Standing next to the sergeant's desk, I said to him, "I think there's been some mistake." He replied, "We didn't make the damned mistake—the delivery guys did." I responded, "I'm not a delivery man with a truck, I'm one of the new staff people in the new administration." Even after forty years, his response is very

57

clear in my mind: "Holy shit!" I got to know Sergeant Lanier very well because I worked with the Secret Service and the White House Police. He told me he went home that Saturday afternoon and told his wife that he was sure he had just lost his job. Of course, he didn't. To make matters worse, I believe I had on my best suit. So, my first few minutes in the White House were a little deflating.

THE EARLY DAYS

Around 9:30 or 10:00 a.m., about twenty of us were herded into the Fish Room (now called the Roosevelt Room in honor of President Franklin Roosevelt, whose aquariums prompted the "Fish" name) where we were sworn into office en masse by Bill Hopkins, a permanent White House staff member who had joined the staff during President Hoover's administration. Bill was a most valuable asset on procedures and precedents and as non-partisan as one could be. Now it was official—no more of this truck driver stuff. I told my wife that she would be amazed to learn how smart I had become in one day: Once I moved into the White House, everybody and his brother was calling me about one thing or another and seeking my advice or my help. I wondered whether it worked in reverse when you left.

The files were empty in accordance with tradition. Although the subject of presidential papers continues to be a controversial subject, we were starting over. First, we had to find an office. Kenny O'Donnell, the Appointments Secretary, and the building superintendent were in charge. I finally got a choice spot on the second floor of the West Wing, sharing a suite with Myer "Mike" Feldman. (Sorensen's office was on the first floor, and Goodwin just seemed to float around.) In the suite was Lorene Baier, who had worked with Roemer McPhee, an Eisenhower staff member. She became my secretary, eventually going with me to the Federal Power Commission and later to my private law practice. Lorene was highly competent and loyal; she served me well.

Early in February 1961, the President had a reception for members of the administration, and I remember being in awe of Edward R. Murrow, the head of the United States Information Agency, and Arthur Goldberg, the prominent labor lawyer and the new Secretary of Labor; and so on and on. It didn't hurt that the Eisenhower policy against hard liquor had been repealed. The reception was on a Sunday, and I was working with the Council of Economic Advisors on an economic message, when Walter Heller, the newly named Chairman of the Council came into our working room and said in a disappointed voice, "The new unemployment figures are out and they've gone down."

When I asked what was wrong with that, he answered that they went down before the new administration could do anything about it.

I was thrilled to be working in the White House, and I never got over the sense of excitement throughout my time there. It would have been exciting under any circumstances, but President and Mrs. Kennedy generated so much interest in and enthusiasm for government that the nation and, especially young people, were paying attention to what was going on in Washington. The Camelot analogy came later, but the sense of excitement was palpable. I believe presidents are more sharply compared with their immediate predecessor, and President Eisenhower was a relatively easy act to follow; it was partly generational, but mostly the phlegmatic was replaced by vigor and, as depicted in Photo 7.1, an abundance of talent.

Historical Preservation

One of the early stories that helped to set the new tone took place during a walk by the President and Mrs. Kennedy in the White House neighborhood. As they crossed Pennsylvania Avenue and walked through Lafayette Square, the President casually mentioned that all of the town houses on the west side of the square were to be torn down to permit construction of a new Executive Office Building, because the existing building was inadequate. Jackie responded by telling him that those town houses were beautiful examples of the Federal period, and it would be almost sacrilegious to destroy them. The President told her that the plans had been set for months and contracts had been let. Mrs. Kennedy's response was, "Jack, I thought you were the one elected President."

The town houses were preserved and renovated, and are in use today by various governmental agencies. Behind the row of town houses is a red brick eight-story building that is the New Executive Office Building facing Seventeenth Street.

THE SPOKES OF A WHEEL

Each president presides over the White House in the manner that he (or someday she) thinks best suits his particular needs and operating style. President Eisenhower, with his military background, preferred the chain of command with a chief of staff. A large beautiful office with full-length French windows at the Southwest corner of the West Wing had been occupied by former New Hampshire Governor Sherman Adams, Eisenhower's first chief of staff, and later by Adams' successor. President Kennedy wanted it to be clear that he did

Photo 7.1. As key White House staff were assembling outside the Cabinet Room for a formal group photograph on October 24, 1963, the noted photographer Arnold Newman snapped this impromptu photo when President Kennedy, who was conducting a meeting inside, stepped outside to observe the scene and quipped, "Isn't anybody doing any work around here?" L-R: Appointments Secretary Kenneth O'Donnell; Press Secretary Pierre Salinger; Science Advisor Jerome Weisner; Congressional Liaison Lawrence O'Brien; Director, Bureau of the Budget Kermit Gordon; Assistant Special Counsel Lee C. White; Administrative Assistant to the President Timothy Reardon; Special Assistant for District of Columbia Affairs Charles Horsky; President John F. Kennedy; Director, Office of Emergency Planning Edward McDermott; Chairman, Council of Economic Advisors Walter Heller (seated); Assistant to the President Ralph Dungan; Deputy Special Counsel Myer Feldman (partially obscured); unidentified; Military Aid Major General Chester Clifton; Special Counsel Theodore Sorensen; unidentified; unidentified; Food for Peace Assistant Richard Reuter; Staff Director, National Security Council Bromley Smith; National Security Advisor McGeorge Bundy. Photo Credit: Arnold Newman. Published with permission of Getty Images. (Personal Collection of Lee C. White)

not have a chief of staff. He purposely left the office vacant for about six months until Ralph Dungan, an assistant to the President, rather casually moved into the old Adams' office. The President's top staff included Ted Sorensen, Special Counsel; McGeorge Bundy, the National Security Advisor; Larry O'Brien, head of the Office of Congressional Liaison; and Kenny O'Donnell, the Appointments Secretary and the logistical boss in charge of running the place. Pierre Salinger was the Press Secretary.

JFK preferred the spokes of a wheel approach where quite a few staff had access to him. Being in that group gave me a good feeling; more important, it provided the opportunity to work directly with the President rather than through an intermediary. There were distinct levels of proximity to the President, especially on major problems. To illustrate, I didn't know about the Cuban missile crisis until half an hour before the President's announcement to the public; but I knew something big was going on when Kenny O'Donnell told me, "I don't know what you want to see the President about and it doesn't make any difference. Stay upstairs until I tell you to come down."

When the word was out about the crisis, Mike Feldman and I, after discussion with Ted Sorensen, asked the Bureau of the Budget and the Office of Civil Defense Mobilization people to give us all the material they had on responding to the threat of nuclear war. My recollection is that it was quite skimpy. We convened the cabinet officers who were not immediately involved in the crisis committee to start developing plans for emergency feeding and sheltering. The administration had not established a bomb shelter program and our efforts were chaotic. I had visited the secret location in the mountains of West Virginia where the governmental leadership was to assemble in the event of an attack on the United States. It was well stocked with food, water, and sleeping facilities, but somewhat small. The communications center was primitive compared with what is currently available. The instructions for government officials to assemble were clear enough, but the major deficiency was that there was no provision for families. Those rushing to the "Classified Location," as it was called, would have to abandon their families. What a grim thought. A great national sigh of relief was heard when the crisis ended satisfactorily.

PRESIDENTIAL APPOINTMENTS

During the transition, a team headed by R. Sargent Shriver, the President's brother-in-law, sifted through the voluminous pile of names and made recommendations to the President-elect. The general consensus was that a highly competent administration had been put together. After the Administration settled in, the key assistant for presidential appointments was Ralph Dungan, with John Macy, the Chairman of the Civil Service Commission, also participating.

President Kennedy had a general policy of not appointing to his administration members of Congress who had been defeated in elections. There may have been a few other exceptions, but the only one I was familiar with was the case of Frank Smith, of Mississippi. Because of re-districting, he and a

Democratic colleague were thrown into the same new district and Frank lost. He had been on the House Public Works Committee and was a highly regarded member. When a vacancy occurred on the Tennessee Valley Authority Board, I urged the president to appoint him. The fact that he was a Mississippian made it easier to deviate from the usual practice.

Frank Reeves, an active Democrat in Washington, DC, who had helped JFK in the 1960 campaign, was named an Assistant to the President, awaiting a vacancy on the three-member Board of Commissioners for the District of Columbia that ran District affairs (before partial Home Rule was authorized by Congress). He would have been the first black named to that position in a heavily black city. Unfortunately, Frank had been careless about paying his income taxes and was disqualified. (Until that time, taxes were not on the check list of matters to discuss with potential nominees. That practice was changed immediately.)

By far the slickest gambit was that adopted by Congressman Manny Celler, a Brooklyn Democrat and chairman of the House Judiciary Committee. He had an informal understanding with Larry O'Brien that the only letters of recommendation he sent for those seeking administration positions to be considered seriously, regardless of how forceful the language, were those he signed with green ink.

The Federal Power Commission

On occasion, I, too, would be involved with presidential appointments. I don't remember why the task fell to me, but I helped prepare Franklin D. Roosevelt, Jr. for his confirmation hearings as Undersecretary of Commerce. Later, in the Johnson Administration, I had the same job when he was named the first chairman of the Equal Employment Opportunity Commission. That name sure pumped up my interest level. Frank was a gregarious and affable fellow and I enjoyed my time with him.

When Speaker Sam Rayburn urged the President to appoint Larry O'Connor, then an Interior Department official, to the Federal Power Commission, an examination of O'Connor's record disclosed that he had been employed by oil companies as an accountant in Houston. We saw this as a potential problem. So Dungan and I grilled the would-be nominee, indicating forcefully that we were reluctant to endorse the Speaker's recommendation to President Kennedy, but we would do so if he assured us that he would be objective in considering the issues that came before the Commission. Later, when I got to the FPC, O'Connor told me that he developed a bad case of the hives as a result of the going-over he got from us. Although fairly conservative in his philosophy, he approached issues objectively and there was no criticism of his appointment.

The White House Mess

One of JFK's earliest actions was to ask Jim Landis to take a look at the various regulatory bodies in the Washington world. Landis had been dean of the Harvard Law School, but more significantly, the Chairman of the Securities and Exchange Commission and the brilliant adviser to Joseph P. Kennedy, who preceded Landis as the first SEC chairman (appointed by FDR). Landis's report didn't make a big splash; however, from my point of view, it was significant because it characterized the Federal Power Commission as the weakest and least effective of the whole range of agencies.

After the study was completed, Landis left the government, as did the rest of the staff, except for one of his associates in the study, Carlisle Bolton-Smith. Bolt, as we called him, hung on until one day many months after the report's completion, when he found something at the White House mess (the dining facility) that he thought needed correction and sent a memo to Kenny O'Donnell telling him about it. O'Donnell, in his cryptic way, said, "Is that SOB still here?" Bolt was gone the next day. I'm sure there's a moral to that story.

SPECIAL COUNSEL

Ted Sorensen, who had previously been involved in almost every phase of the senator's and the presidential candidate's activities, had to adjust to the new realities of White House life. I and others urged him to take the domestic policy portfolio. He agreed and asked to be named "Special Counsel to the President," I believe, in part, because Judge Sam Rosenman, one of FDR's key aides, had that title, and also because it is a good title for a lawyer. Later administrations had Domestic Affairs Councils and Domestic Affairs Advisors, but the Special Counsel's office was just that, with the addition of such legal duties as drafting executive orders, handling pardons and commutations, dealing with executive privilege issues, ethical issues, and the Secret Service and the White House Police. I still cringe when I see a reference to Ted Sorensen as "speechwriter to the President." Yes, he wrote speeches for President Kennedy, but Ted's portfolio initially was principal advisor on all domestic matters and, after the Bay of Pigs, on national security issues as well.

Mike Feldman, the Deputy Special Counsel, was an accomplished Philadelphia lawyer who came from humble origins. He had been on the staff of the Securities and Exchange Commission, moved to the staff of the Senate Banking and Currency Committee, and served on JFK's senate staff and on his presidential campaign.

Dick Goodwin and I were the two Assistant Special Counsels. Dick is a certified genius and graduated first in his class at Harvard Law School. Dick had earlier played a role in the 1959 congressional inquiry into the "$64,000 Question" television game show scandal, and had been involved in the 1960 presidential campaign. Like Sorensen, Dick is also a gifted writer; but unlike Mike and me, Dick found it difficult to be subordinate to Ted. He was a full-time rival and blithely breezed through the White House wherever he pleased. We four constituted the total group, but Goodwin didn't stick around too long.

With regard to titles, it isn't what White House staff members are called, but what the individuals do, that matters. In a general sense, it's what the President wants staff to do. As a lawyer, I, too, liked the "Counsel" designation, although a major portion of my time was devoted to domestic policies and programs. The list sounds impossibly long, but some of the programs and departments and agencies I worked with included: Civil Rights; Interior; Housing and Home Finance; Veterans Administration; the Small Business Administration; Agriculture (the National Forest Service); the Corps of Engineers (Department of the Army); the Foreign Economic Assistance Program; the Council of Economic Advisers; domestic economic assistance programs such as the Appalachian Regional Commission; the Interagency Task Force on Narcotics; TVA and other power issues; and the District of Columbia. I also reviewed Justice Department recommendations for clemency and commutation; drafted Executive Orders; handled Executive Privilege issues; and was involved in matters arising from international fisheries activities. I even had to get after commercial companies that used the Presidential seal and images of the President and Mrs. Kennedy without permission. Obviously, no one person could have done all that and done it well.

Another key assignment was to review and comment on proposed presidential approvals or vetoes of legislation. The prize winner in this category was the day Phillip "Sam" Hughes, the Assistant Budget Director for Legislation, told me that the Bureau of the Budget recommended that President Kennedy veto a bill increasing benefits for blind veterans on the grounds that the formula in the legislation was incorrect and could set a bad precedent. When I started laughing, he said, "You pols can do whatever you want, but we want to be on the record." Of course, the President signed the bill.

The Special Counsel's office was a mighty small group to handle as many programs as we did. We should have had more people but somehow we got by.—Nowadays, there probably are at least forty people working on the Domestic Council.—We managed, in part, because we all had worked for JFK at one time or another, and because we got tremendous assistance from the very talented people at the Bureau of the Budget (now the Office of Management and Budget) and from the departments and agencies.

A Bird's Eye View

The new President decided to set up a series of meetings with House and Senate Committee chairmen to establish a closer personal relationship with them. The chairmen were all Democrats, but they had spent years challenging Eisenhower proposals, and we wanted to remind them that a Democrat was now in the White House. I got the assignment to learn from cabinet officers and agency heads what was going on in those committees and summarize the findings in a memorandum to the President. It was an excellent way to get a bird's eye view of the vast government.

Occasionally, I sat in on breakfast meetings held on the morning of JFK's press conferences. About a week before a scheduled press conference, Press Secretary Pierre Salinger would tell the public information officer of each department and agency to provide him with a summary of questions the President might receive involving their agencies. He also wanted suggested answers. Woe be unto any information officer who failed to list an appropriate question that was asked of the President. What a terrific way for a president to learn what's going on in his government!

Of course, President Kennedy was the master of press conferences, and his charm and wit were well received. At one early press conference, he was asked a question that no one could have anticipated: "Mr. President, journalists and especially those covering the White House are in a very competitive business. Those of us who did not know you before you became President have noticed that you have continued your friendships with those you knew before you were elected. That puts us at a competitive disadvantage. Any comment?" The President paused about thirty seconds, turned on his spectacular smile and replied, "Well, I hadn't thought about that, but even though I've only been in this office a short time, I've learned that the presidency is not a very good place to make new friends. I think I better stick with my old ones." And that was the end of that.

Once, he was asked why he always managed to call on May Craig or Sarah McClendon, two reporters who seemed to specialize in off-the-wall questions. He said he couldn't explain it, because he intended not to recognize them; but somehow or other their raspy insistent voices proved to be irresistible!

Executive Privilege

One of the first matters that reached my desk involved executive privilege. The written word can't do justice to the Virginia drawl of the late conservative Democratic Congressman Porter Hardy, then chairman of a House Appropriations Subcommittee handling economic assistance to foreign governments. At

the Congressional receiving line immediately following the inaugural cere-
monies, the conversation went something like this: "Mister President, yore
folks at the State Department arh refusin' to give mah subcommittee information regardin arh aid program in Pee-roo, and I hope y'all can do somethin
'bout it." "Porter, for Chris' sake, I've been President for an hour and a half—
how could I have screwed up so fast?"

It turned out Porter was correct: the State Department was stonewalling. I
finally reached the fellow at the State Department who was handling the matter, Philander P. Claxton. That was a familiar and prominent East Tennessee
name, so we started off friendly enough. Phil explained to me that the new administration might as well start on the right foot. What he meant was: Don't
give them (Congress) any material deemed sensitive—if you give them an
inch, they'll want a mile.

Complicating the matter was information implicating the brother of the Peruvian President in some improper and probably illegal diversion of aid
funds. The Peruvian President was an ally of the United States, and we did
not want to break this story and embarrass him. President Kennedy listened
to what I had found out and had the following reaction: This was an Eisenhower administration problem, but now it's ours. If Porter is asking for what
the State Department has, chances are, he already has copies. Covering up
hardly ever works, and you get into more trouble over the cover up than if you
got whatever it is out in the public arena to begin with (Richard Nixon didn't
understand the principle). Adding that he didn't want somebody at the State
Department deciding what to give to Congress, he said, "See if you can't
work it out with Porter."

I called the Congressman and told him we had looked into the matter and,
indeed, we thought there were good reasons not to put the material in the public domain. We offered to bring the material to show him and the ranking Republican on the subcommittee so they could understand the administration's
position. He agreed and the meeting was held. As we had suspected, they
were as persuaded as we were that it should not be aired. They deemed the
Congressional Subcommittee to be a legitimate participant and didn't enjoy
being treated cavalierly. I'm sure this arrangement might not work in some
circumstances, but it worked that time.

Out of this experience, JFK concluded that executive privilege should not
be exercised by any one but the President. Democratic Congressman John
Moss of Sacramento, who chaired a subcommittee of the House Government
Operations Committee, had waged a personal war against governmental secrecy. He was so happy with the Kennedy approach that he and I worked out
a plan by which the President sent him a letter stating that only the President
was authorized to assert executive privilege in his administration. The letter

was framed and had a prominent position on his office wall. Later on, a comparable letter from President Johnson was on the same wall.

This worked. A few years later, when Senator Strom Thurmond of South Carolina, wanted to know what aide of Secretary of Defense McNamara wrote a speech that McNamara had delivered, NcNamara replied that it was his speech and he didn't believe it made any difference who had helped prepare it; and he wasn't about to provide that information. President Kennedy backed him and that was that. Admittedly, that was a pretty easy case. Subsequently, when President Nixon pushed the matter, the Supreme Court was forced to draw lines in what for nearly two hundred years had been a matter of comity between the executive and legislative branches.

Chapter Eight

The Legislative Agenda and the Legislative Process

The normal procedure for setting the legislative agenda for the Kennedy administration started with the President meeting with Special Counsel Ted Sorensen and Congressional Liaison Larry O'Brien. They would discuss a range of possible legislative items for the coming year, and the President would determine what the major items and programs would be for that year. (Obviously, everything was subject to change to meet unforeseen circumstances.) Ted would then assign one of us in the Special Counsel's office to shepherd the particular program through the government and end up with a draft of a Message to Congress, spelling out the elements of the program with accompanying legislative proposals.

The best part of the job was that we were able to work with the appropriate departments and agencies, with assistance from the Bureau of the Budget, to produce what we deemed to be the ideal package. It was up to Larry O'Brien and his congressional liaison people to recommend whatever adjustments were necessary to ensure serious consideration by committee chairmen and other political forces that had their roles to play in the overall legislative process. But we were the pure ones. Of course, the final word had to be the President's.

Larry O'Brien's group included Mike Manatos, who worked the senate side of the Congress. Mike had been administrative assistant to Senator Joe O'Mahoney of Wyoming, and was well liked on the Hill. Henry Hall Wilson was O'Brien's principal emissary to the House. He had been a member of the North Carolina Legislature and was a very bright cat who learned the ins and outs of the House procedures in record time. Also participating on the House team were Dick Donohue, of Lowell, Massachusetts; Chuck Daly, a former Marine with a laconic way about him; and Dan Fenn and David Bunn, a couple of low-keyed fellows.

68

THE LEGISLATIVE PROCESS

To illustrate the way the legislative process operated, the Natural Resources message would start with meetings with Interior Secretary Stewart Udall and his policy people to get their ideas about what should go into the President's package. After some tinkering on my part, the group of players would be broadened. The Corps of Engineers might be brought in, as well as the Forest Service from the Department of Agriculture. If taxes or fees might be involved, someone from Treasury and the Council of Economic Advisers would be asked to attend. Once, Treasury Secretary Douglas Dillon complained to Ted Sorensen that I had held a meeting involving taxes and he wasn't invited.—I told Ted someone from Treasury had been present, but Dillon was welcome to attend every meeting I held.

The Bureau of the Budget played a key role in coordinating agency reviews of proposed legislation and in drafting legislative language. When Stewart Udall proposed a visionary program to acquire land in a conservation program, almost every element of his department's proposal had to be modified in one way or another by the BOB experts. When polished up, it was a program that was sold to Congress and has proven to be hugely successful.

An example of the type of issue that would arise in developing an administration proposal was a message on urban matters. The administration had decided to propose establishing a mass transit program, quite a major development. When I was holding the meeting wrapping up the message, I made the call that the program should be lodged in the Housing and Home Finance Agency rather than the Department of Commerce. The decision could have gone either way: Commerce had a legitimate claim because of its jurisdiction over transportation; and HHFA because it would be a city-oriented program. I believed the HHFA group was more efficient and would push the program more effectively than the Undersecretary of Commerce would with his transportation portfolio. When the Secretary of Commerce, Luther Hodges, called to complain, I explained that a newer agency with less to do was the better choice, but obviously as a cabinet officer he had every right to appeal to the President. He grumbled a bit but never asked the President to reverse the decision. The Secretary of Commerce was not a major player in the Kennedy administration, and he had to use his appeals to the President sparingly. He would also have had to persuade Kenny O'Donnell to set up an appointment and must have concluded it wasn't worth it.

An example of an assignment that came my way was taking a JFK legislative proposal and tweaking it so it would be referred to a desired House Committee where the committee chairman was much more sympathetic to the program being proposed than a different chairman would be. The particular legislation had to do with providing economic assistance to distressed areas. This involved working with the House Parliamentarian who in the first instance decides which committee has jurisdiction over the subject matter. (Lew Deschler held the post for decades and was a mighty independent fellow.) Our strategy was to find the magic phrases that would permit the assignment to go where it had the best chance of receiving favorable consideration. It isn't possible to get it directed to a preferred committee if the jurisdiction is clear and unmistakable, but where the jurisdiction could go one way or another, a few word changes in the title and in some of the descriptive sections can make the difference. It is a delicate business because the chairman being avoided would not be pleased to learn that his committee had been manipulated.

THE DEPARTMENT OF THE INTERIOR

The Department of the Interior was in many ways my favorite. It had many diverse and great activities and Stewart Udall was especially colorful. Stewart Udall was and still is a warm and likeable character. One Udall story involved formal police charges that he shoplifted a five-pack of cigars from a Peoples Drug store in McLean, Virginia, where he lived. It was so improbable that no one believed the story. He apparently put the cigars in his jacket and forgot about them and was noticed by a security guard. I confess that I, at times, toyed with the idea of saying, "Stew, please run down to the corner and swipe me some cigars." He was easy to kid, but I wasn't certain how sensitive he was about the subject; so I refrained.

But I liked to kid the Interior gang by noting that when I first arrived at the White House, I had to decide whether I would keep a diary or a journal of some sort. Because I had never done that before, I instead placed a yellow lawyer's pad on the cover of the radiator behind my desk and every time Interior screwed up, I would make a note of it. I soon realized that activity took so much time I couldn't get the rest of my work done! It was always a sore point with the Udall gang when I mentioned the yellow pad, because they never knew whether I was kidding.

One of Interior's outstanding snafus involved the oft-proposed Passamaquoddy Tidal Project in Maine. It had been studied for years and was regarded as an efficient and natural source of electric energy because of the strong tidal action that occurs on the Bay of Fundy. The technology had not been mastered (and still hasn't been), but that didn't stop Stewart Udall from setting up a Presidential meeting with the Maine congressional delegation to announce the administration's support for the project. The only people who didn't know anything about the "commitment" were Larry O'Brien and his congressional liaison group; Jerry Weisner, the President's Science Advisor; the Bureau of the Budget; and me, the White House staff.

Almost as colossal a goof up as Passamaquoddy, but with limited local interest, was the Ice Age National Monument. One Special Message to Congress that the administration sent included a number of proposals to create some new national parks and monuments. The day after the message got to Capitol Hill, I received a phone call from a very irate congressman, Henry Reuss, Democrat of Wisconsin. I knew Henry fairly well. He was my sister's Congressman from suburban Milwaukee. I said, "Hold on, Henry, what are you talking about?" He said, "The people at Interior told me you had knocked out the Ice Age Monument." I replied, "Honest to God, Henry, I never heard those words—ice, age, and monument—put together and I have no idea what the hell it is. I can assure you I did not knock it out." It turned out that Bill Pozen, one of Udall's special assistants had told Reuss I had been the villain, even though, in fact, Interior had decided to eliminate it. I explained to Pozen that if somebody had to take the rap for bad news, it's the Department, not the White House. As I recall, the Ice Age Monument was restored to the list and to this day I have not the remotest idea of what and where it is.

The Wilderness Bill

A major goal of the administration was to enact a Wilderness Bill that would provide the procedures and legislative authorizations for designating parks, rivers, seashores and lakeshores as wilderness areas. This would be in lieu of individual legislative initiatives, which had been the prior practice. The proposal was controversial with ranchers, miners and other land users (especially on federally-owned land) in opposition. A key player, if not the key player, was Congressman Wayne Aspinall, Democrat of Colorado. He had a reputation for being a crusty old curmudgeon, and as Chairman of the House Committee on Interior and Insular Affairs, he had the clout to pass or block (at least temporarily) passage of the bill. Whether it was accurate or not, he was perceived to be less than enchanted with Secretary Udall. As a Congressman from Arizona, Udall was a very junior member of the House Interior Committee when President-elect Kennedy chose him to be the Secretary of the Interior. Udall had been especially helpful during the presidential campaign, a not insignificant fact.

Claude Desautels, now an assistant to Larry O'Brien, had been an assistant to Aspinall. Claude told Larry that in trying to persuade Aspinall, it would be better to send me and Elmer Staats, the Deputy Director of the Bureau of the Budget, to meet with him instead of Udall or any of his people. Both of us

had worked on the legislation, and Aspinall knew and got along well with
each of us. Incidentally, the decision to send me, even though I was not a part
of the Congressional Liaison Office, demonstrated how closely we all worked
together and how little struggling over turf took place. As luck would have it,
the day scheduled for our meeting with Aspinall in 1963 presented two big
negatives: *The Washington Post* carried an especially tough cartoon by
Herblock showing Aspinall in a most unflattering likeness blocking the
Wilderness Bill; and the night before, Mrs. Aspinall developed a heart problem that required her to be hospitalized. When we checked, his office told us
our meeting was still on. It went as smooth as a piece of silk. Aspinall told us
he didn't like everything in the bill but his committee would make some
changes and the bill, as modified, would pass that year. I was to tell the President, but he preferred that it be kept quiet. It was clear that the old goat liked
the young President. When I got back to the White House, I told the President
the good news. (As is well known, we all prefer to pass on good news). He
was pleased and called Aspinall on the phone to thank him, and I believe it
was the last time they talked. Chairman Aspinall kept his word and the bill
with some amendments became law after the President's assassination.

I should mention that Claude Desautels was a high-spirited French Canadian, who seemed to be in a constant state of excitement. One day when he
was in my office jumping up and down about something, I said, "Claude,
watch this." I picked up the telephone receiver and said to the White House
operator, "Please get me the frantic Frenchman," and without hesitation she
rang Claude's office.

Burn's Ditch

One of the most contentious projects of the 1960s was an area in Indiana on
the southern shore of Lake Michigan then known as Burn's Ditch. Adjacent
to it to the east was an Indiana State Park called the Indiana Dunes. It was
easy commuting distance from Chicago, and Senator Paul Douglas, Democrat
of Illinois, emerged as the great supporter of upgrading the state park and ex-
panding it into a National Lakeshore. Bethlehem Steel Corporation had a major plant at Burn's Ditch, and the two Democratic senators from Indiana were
not overly enthusiastic initially about a project that could adversely affect the
economy of the area. Although the point was not necessarily stressed, they
weren't wild about thousands of cars and buses bringing tens of thousands of
Illinois visitors over Indiana highways into a beach area. But Douglas was a
determined and formidable advocate.

I recall being in his office with Elmer Staats, the Deputy Director of the
Bureau of the Budget, and receiving the "treatment." The senator had maps

and photographs galore and they were impressive. But even more memorable was his peroration. He said, "When I first got to the United States Senate, I was determined to save the world. In my second term, I vowed to save the United States. In my third term, I was reduced to saving the Indiana Dunes, and I'll be damned if I'm going to lose that battle." With the cooperation of the Indiana senators, Birch Bayh and Vance Hartke, as well as the Democratic governor of the state, a compromise was hammered out. Today, the Indiana Dunes National Lakeshore is one of the most heavily attended units of the National Park Service.

The Bureau of Indian Affairs

An interesting piece of my Interior assignment involved the Bureau of Indian Affairs. The Assistant Secretary in charge was Phileo Nash, who had been the Lieutenant Governor of Wisconsin and a strong Kennedy supporter in the important 1960 Wisconsin democratic primary. Phileo arranged for me to take a trip to the Southwest where we visited the Navahos and the Hopis. The tribes were very different from each other and the opportunity to meet with tribal leaders demonstrated how different their problems were. The Navahos had fairly advanced industrial activity going on, while the Hopis seemed to be less sophisticated and, thus, more traditional. I would have to admit that the Kennedy administration was not as concerned and as helpful as it should have been. Unfortunately, it seems that limited attention continues to be paid to the legitimate problems of the American Indians.

On another occasion, I recall a large group of Native Americans gathered outside of the President's Oval Office. Knowing of JFK's aversion to hats, I told Phileo to be sure no Indian approached the President with an Indian headdress. As the President was addressing the group, I was standing a few feet to his side when I spotted an Indian making his way through the crowd with, yes, a headdress in his hand. As I was contemplating scalping Phileo, who incidentally was bald as a bowling ball, the Indian arrived in front and presented the headdress to JFK, who accepted it graciously. When I told him in his office how I had warned Phileo to keep that sort of thing away from the President, he said, "I don't mind receiving hats, I just don't want to have to put them on."

The Hydroelectric Project Delegation

A very happy and positive aspect of my relationship with Interior was participating in the 1962 delegation to the Soviet Union to examine and study hydroelectric projects. Secretary Udall was the leader. Among others in the group were Jim Carr, the Interior Undersecretary; Joe Swidler, my old boss at TVA and friend, then Chairman of the Federal Power Commission; Floyd Dominy, head of the Bureau of Reclamation; the poet Robert Frost, a personal friend of Udall; and Jim McNulty, an Arizona lawyer who was Mr. Personality and Mr. Congeniality all in one. We were the first Kennedy administration group to visit the Soviet Union and we were treated royally. We whipped around Moscow in fancy cars in a small caravan with police escorts. I believe every man has a little kid inside of him, and in this case, it was pretty exciting to tear through town with sirens blaring. I thoroughly enjoyed it. There was a reception in our honor with the Minister of Electricity, our ambassador, and other dignitaries. We attended the Bolshoi Ballet and saw a program depicting the might and the valor of the Red Army, a somewhat unsettling experience (this was before the Cuban missile crisis). We stayed in the Metropole Hotel and presumed our rooms were bugged. We arranged a little test by discussing something we wanted to see—probably the Gum Department Store—and sure enough Intourist (the Russian travel agency) had added it to our schedule the next day. While traveling in the country, we stayed at government houses which were plain but clean. There was always a lot of help available.

In Moscow, we were shown how the Soviet power grid was directed from a central office in Moscow. To the experts in our group, the equipment appeared pretty pedestrian. Our special treat was to be able to visit the construction site of the Bratsk dam in Siberia near the large city (300,000 to 400,000 people) of Irkutz. It would be the largest dam and reservoir in the world. It certainly was massive, and our technical people thought the Russians were doing a very good job, although many of their techniques were different from U.S. practices. We were there in August and could only guess at what difficulties they would experience in the Siberian winter.

Our Russian (although we were in the Soviet Union, this was a Russian undertaking all the way) hosts led us to one of the world's most remarkable natural wonders: Lake Baikal, which is close to Irkutz. It is by far the deepest lake in the world, apparently created by a great convulsion as the world was being formed. There was a museum by the side of the lake which exhibited sea animals that do not exist anywhere else in the world. I don't recall how it compared to our Great Lakes in surface area, but it was enormous. An extra delight was to speed along in a hydrofoil boat that literally flew above the surface of the lake. There was a considerable industrial complex on the shores of the lake, and recently I read where the lake is so polluted that extreme measures are being taken by the Russian government to bring it back to life.

McNulty had brought ball point pens and other trinkets that the kids loved. He couldn't speak five words of Russian, but he had the knack of getting the kids to laugh and have a great time with him. He had a football and, by golly, he organized two teams and had those little Siberian kids playing football. Each night at the government house where we stayed, the host group would start to drink vodka and before long it was song contest time. Frankly, we were no match for the Russians. We would sort of struggle through "I've been working on the railroad," and they would boom back with a powerful Russian song. Even though a few of them spoke English and none of us spoke Russian, a spirit of camaraderie developed easily and naturally. We did have interpreters.

On our return to Moscow, after we had visited projects in other areas such as Volgagrad, Udall was told that Khruschev, who was on vacation on the Crimean Sea, would like to talk to him. Initially, I was to accompany Udall, but alas, that was changed and I never got the chance to meet the Soviet leader. As we were leaving, Dennis (the English speaking person on our host committee) gave each of us about a pound and a half of caviar wrapped plainly in heavy butcher's paper which happily kept the caviar in great shape until we got home. It was a very interesting and exciting two weeks. Although I don't wear it, I still have my mink hat in the closet.

Five members of our group had arranged to stop in Paris on our return. The arrangements had been made by one of Udall's assistants. Imagine my surprise when I found we were staying at the George Sanc, one of the ritziest and most expensive hotels in Paris. I was not pleased. I always tried to handle other people's money, including the government's, as though it were my own. Even when I moved into the Chairman's office at the FPC, every piece of furniture and the paint on the walls remained untouched. At any rate, the high spot of our Paris stop was when my cousin Albert took us to his tiny neighborhood restaurant where we enjoyed one of the best meals any of us had ever experienced.

The Delaware River Basin Commission

Early in the Kennedy administration, a proposition arose which taxed our ability to "think outside the box." Water control officials from Pennsylvania, Delaware, New Jersey, and New York had developed a proposal for creating a Delaware River Basin Commission, which would formulate policies and practices for the fair and efficient use of the waters of the Delaware River. As proposed, the Commission would consist of the governors of the four states and the Secretary of the Interior. Preparatory to introducing legislation to authorize the proposed commission, the Congressional sponsors sought the administration's views. The Department of Justice and the Bureau of the Budget recommended against the basic idea, claiming that it would be untenable

to have the Secretary of the Interior on a commission where he could be out-
voted by state governors.

When word reached the Capitol about the administration opposition, Sena-
tor Joe Clark, a Democrat from Pennsylvania, called the White House Congressional Liaison Office and asked that the administration send spokesmen to
meet with senators from the four states (or their staffs) to discuss the matter.
Ramsey Clark, the Assistant Attorney General for the Lands Division; Elmer
Staats, the Deputy Director of the Bureau of the Budget; and I from the White
House were the designated team members to go to the Hill and tell them,
"No." Cordiality evaporated within a short time. Senator Clark, a bright and
aggressive fellow, said that provisions had been included in the draft that
granted the Secretary some safeguards protecting the federal interests, but that
he gathered that we were opposed, basically, because it had never been done
before. He said that the group's lawyers had found nothing in the Constitution
prohibiting such a joint federal-state instrumentality. He said he might have
understood if the Eisenhower administration were opposed, but he couldn't
understand the new dynamic Kennedy crowd being unwilling to consider the
idea because it had never been done before. That remark scored a direct hit on
me, and I told him we'd go back and review the proposal. We did and, with
some changes recommended by the administration, the legislation was enacted. Over forty years later, the Commission is still functioning.

Puerto Rico and The Virgin Islands

Among the many programs in Interior was the office that dealt with United
States Territories. Puerto Rico, designated as a commonwealth, had been a
"Territory" of the United States and as such, its government elected by the
people of Puerto Rico reported to the Interior Department, and at that, to a
fairly low level. The immensely popular and charismatic governor of Puerto
Rico, Luis Munoz-Marin, had supported JFK at the 1960 Democratic Convention. After the election, Munoz told the new President that it would be an
important psychological lift for Puerto Rico if it could report to the White
House, instead of to some low level office in Interior. The President readily
agreed, and I was the lucky fellow—lucky not only because my wife and I
were able to make a few trips to Puerto Rico where we were treated in a grand
style, but more so because of the opportunity to learn about the history, culture, problems, and especially the politics of the island.

Munoz was a poet-philosopher who had attended Georgetown University,
and was a master politician. His father had preceded him as governor, and
Munoz was a much beloved figure. However, there was a small but fanatical
element in Puerto Rico that wanted Puerto Rico to be independent of the

United States, and they were willing to use violence. In 1950, two Puerto Rican nationalists made an attempt on President Truman's life while he was living in the Blair House during restoration of the White House, and a White House policeman was killed in the assault. In 1954, the U.S. House of Representatives was thrown into panic as Independistas shot up the House floor from a visitor's gallery—there were some injuries, but fortunately no deaths. So, when the governor and his wife, Inez, were at our house for dinner one night, our neighbors got the once-over from the governor's security forces. They were pretty tough looking hombres.

Munoz told the President that there was unrest in Puerto Rico concerning its relationship with the United States. He proposed a study by U.S. and Puerto Rican experts on how various governmental functions such as immigration, agricultural subsidies, tax benefits, and food stamps could be enhanced to stave off the efforts of the Republican Party in Puerto Rico, which was pressing for statehood. Munoz believed the proposed improvements were desirable and even necessary. He supported an enriched commonwealth status as opposed to statehood, which he regarded as unattainable. Munoz wanted the exercise to be conducted in secret, since he believed that if word got out about the project, the pressures on both sides would be tremendous. Our first session was at the Hay-Adams Hotel, across Lafayette Square from the White House, with Munoz using an alias, and our trips to Puerto Rico were shrouded in secrecy. The Kennedy administration was in general agreement on almost all of the Puerto Rican proposed changes (many of which would require Congressional action), but my recollection is that the assassination pushed the matter onto the back burner. The question of the relationship lives on today. Munoz did not run for re-election after serving four four-year terms, but supported his Secretary of State, Roberto Sanchez, who was elected governor. Munoz, ever the thoughtful one, moved to Spain so that he would not be a drag on his hand-picked successor, who by all accounts was not nearly as successful in his administration of Commonwealth affairs as Munoz had been.

In addition to the Puerto Rico assignment, I was the White House liaison with the United States Virgin Islands, which was also under the jurisdiction of the Interior Department. President Kennedy had appointed a businessman from the island of St. Thomas, Ralph Paiewonsky, to be the Governor of the Virgin Islands. There was to be a fundraiser on St. Thomas, known as Kennedy-Paiewonsky (or K-P) Day. My wife and I were put up in a nice little guest house and had a couple of sightseeing days.

At the K-P dinner, I had the pleasant assignment of announcing that the Kennedy administration was asking Congress to enact legislation by which the Islands would elect their governor rather than have the office filled by presidential appointment. Messengers who bring good news are treated better than messengers who bring bad news, and my brief speech was very well received. The legislation was enacted, and today Virgin Islanders elect their political leaders.

Bureau of Outdoor Recreation

President Kennedy issued an executive order creating a Bureau of Outdoor Recreation within the Department of the Interior, directing the various agencies with responsibilities in recreational activities to coordinate their activities and to work with non-governmental organizations to enhance recreational opportunities. Included in the group was the National Forest Service, a part of the Department of Agriculture.

One Sunday afternoon, our family was at a little center in Rock Creek Park (one of the great amenities of the Washington, DC metropolitan area) with some kids on slides and swings and having a picnic, when Orville Freeman, the Secretary of Agriculture and former Governor of Minnesota, who lived nearby, showed up with his wife, Jane. He said he was surprised to see me at the park. I explained that a picnic lunch was OK, but my idea of outdoor recreation was to play pool on a screened porch. He occasionally reminded me of that observation. But the creation of the Bureau is another of the Kennedy administration accomplishments that has stood the test of time.

THE ARMY CORPS OF ENGINEERS

The Army Corps of Engineers brought me a bit of notoriety early on. The Corps had planned a dam site in southern New York State that would flood some tribal lands owned by the Seneca Indians, who were not happy about the proposal. A letter writing campaign to the White House supporting the Indians' position resulted in a slew of letters to the President piling up in my office, which I sent to the Corps for a suggested response. Because the proposed reply seemed reasonable, I signed the responses and out they went over my signature. Many of those who received the replies didn't like them and sent them on to Hugh Downs, a member of NBC's "Today" show cast. Mr. Downs, in his deep voice, wanted to know who this "Lee C. White, Assistant Special Counsel to the President," was answering the President's mail. I called Major General Bill Cassidy, the Deputy Chief of the Corps of Engineers and asked if he was absolutely confident that the Corps' answer was valid and would stand up under scrutiny. When he assured me it would, I told him I was going to ask the "Today Show" to have him on the program to explain the rationale for the decision. He was apoplectic—there was no way he wanted to go on any TV show, especially a network show; but I insisted. He went on the show and did a fine job of explaining the Corps' planning process and what it was doing to assist the Senecas. The furor subsided. As a World War II First Lieutenant, I had to admit to a bit of pleasure in being able to tell a General what to do.

A harrowing experience grew out of my scheduled participation in a panel discussion at the 1962 annual convention of the National Rural Electric Co-operatives Association in Atlantic City. Major General Bill Cassidy was also on the panel, and he suggested I fly to Atlantic City with him in a Corps airplane. I liked the convenience of it, but my happiness faded when it became apparent that we were flying into a major storm. The pilot told Cassidy that the Atlantic City airport was closed because of the storm. But Cassidy told the pilot that they had to open it up so we could land. Curiously enough, the airport authorities agreed. (I remember thinking that's one special privilege I could do without.)

We landed and the wind was blowing everything every which way. We made it into the terminal building only to learn that the causeway connecting the mainland where the airport was located with the barrier island where the city is located was flooded and impassable. When Cassidy asked if they had a helicopter that could fly us over to the city, we were told that the winds were way too dangerous for such a flight. We waited an hour and the storm never let up and the causeway never was open to traffic.

We went out to the Corps four-seater plane which had been tied down with ropes to prevent it from blowing away. After we struggled into the plane, a crew untied the plane and the very skilled pilot got ready to take off. I noticed a helicopter not too far away with its rotor spinning. I said to Cassidy that I thought they said it was too dangerous for those things. His answer was, "Oh, that's just there in case we crash." We didn't crash, but the Deputy Chief of the Corps of Engineers had the pilot fly up and down the coastline to view personally the ravages of one of the worst storms to hit the mid-Atlantic area, including the destruction of the Steel Pier at Atlantic City.

THE FEDERAL POWER COMMISSION

One area of activity that fell naturally in my lap was dealing with electric power matters. With my Tennessee Valley Authority background and holding an electrical engineering degree (which really was not terribly significant, but sounded good), I was the White House staff man that dealt with the Federal Power Commission and related issues. This was so even though, for the most part, Mike Feldman was the staff person for regulatory agencies, demonstrating the pragmatic manner in which assignments got parceled out. In addition, the fact that the Chairman, Joe Swidler, had been my boss at TVA, and his extremely able assistant, Dave Freeman, was one of my closest friends didn't hurt. I understood the independence of regulatory bodies and never discussed specific cases or proceedings before the commission. When one of my White House colleagues asked me to call Swidler about a contested case involving Wyoming, I explained that it was inappropriate. Besides, knowing Swidler, he would probably go the other way and publicly denounce my intervention. Joe and Dave discussed with me their plan to take a hard look at the electric utility industry, hoping to lay out where it was and where it could expect to move in the future. The various phrases proposed as a title included "investigation," "inquiry," "study," or "review" didn't quite sound right, so we settled on "survey." The National Power Survey was a highly useful document and was well received by all interested parties, including the industry.

Another tie-in was my relationship with Alex Radin, the principal staff officer of the American Public Power Association, the trade association for the nearly 4,000 municipally owned and operated electric systems. I had worked with him on legislative matters while serving on the staffs of Senator Kennedy and, especially, of Senator Cooper, who was a member of the Senate Committee on Public Works and had a Kentucky interest in TVA. Alex and I and our families were and are close. Most APPA members were comparatively small communities, but there were some very large cities, such as Los Angeles, Memphis, Seattle, Jacksonville, Cleveland and Omaha. They had their problems, mostly with the investor-owned utilities, which for the most part were the dominant suppliers of electricity in the country, serving about eighty percent of the national load. The group had not fared too well in the Eisenhower administration and was pleased to see the Kennedy crowd come into office.

Alex was a native of Chattanooga and our good friend Milt Shaw, who headed the Atomic Energy Commission's unit that approved nuclear reactor projects, was from Knoxville. Dave Freeman, later one of the most important individuals in the electric power world, was also a Chattanooga native. With my background at TVA, and later the Federal Power Commission, I fit into a small cabal which jokingly was known as the East Tennessee Jewish Power Mafia.

The rural electric cooperatives were greatly assisted by the creation of the Rural Electrification Agency as part of the Roosevelt New Deal program in the 1930s. The trade association of the approximately 1,000 cooperatives, the National Rural Electric Cooperatives Association, was headed by Clyde Ellis, a former Arkansas Congressman and an energetic Democrat. In a meeting with President Kennedy, Clyde persuaded the President that although the membership was rural and conservative, they loved the government subsidized interest rates and, thus, NRECA was a good group to court. I was assigned to attend the regional meetings NRECA held around the country each year and to deliver a message from the President. In doing so, I enjoyed the opportunity to visit some interesting smaller cities around the nation.

At about the end of the first year of the Kennedy administration, the two electric power groups asked to meet with the President and were not able to find much to complain about. The major complaint was that a year had gone by and Elmer Staats, the Deputy Director of the Bureau of the Budget, was still there. They said he was the villain of the Eisenhower group who opposed initiating any new hydroelectric projects. I explained that he was only carrying out the policy directives of that group and that now he was implementing the policies of the Kennedy administration, the very ones that they had just applauded.

A CHARGED JOB

My work with Interior, the Army Corps of Engineers, and the FPC and electric power groups was certainly not very glamorous, but it fit with my Tennessee Valley Authority experience and, the truth to be told, any assignment in the White House was automatically important and interesting. During my more than five years there, I got a charge every morning when I went to work. It is, of course, the center of governmental activity and, in a sense, it sets the tone for the nation.

Chapter Nine

Domestic Programs and Policies

The practice of deciding who the smartest guy or gal in the room may be and relying on him or her is a fairly standard approach. As a generalist, I asked the experts (or the so-called experts) for their take on the big picture issues and kept my fingers crossed.

THE HOUSING AND HOME FINANCE AGENCY

The Housing and Home Finance Agency was an independent agency that reported to the President. A principal entity within HHFA was the Federal Housing Authority, which guaranteed loans to individuals seeking to purchase homes. In addition to the decision to place the mass transit program in HHFA referred to earlier, another principal function was urban renewal, a program designed to help cities and communities revitalize some of their rundown areas.

Among my continuing assignments was the periodic fixing of the Federal Housing Authority's interest rate. Because I was the "White House Guy," I was involved in those decisions. In truth, even though I knew what the group assembled in the Office of the Council of Economic Advisers was deciding, I had no independent judgment on how the various factors that went into the decision were to be evaluated and integrated into a decision; but I did know that the late Kermit Gordon, a member of the Council of Economic Advisors and later the Director of the Bureau of the Budget, was the smartest economist in the room. When he recommended a rate, I might ask a few general questions, but I would be heavily influenced by Kermit. The interest rate committee apparently needed a White House presence, and because HHFA was in my bailiwick, I was it. In general, I believed the right decisions were made because the program functioned well and there were no complaints.

I was also impressed with Robert Weaver, the Administrator, and his top lieutenants. His general counsel was Milt Semer, whom I had known as an aide to Senator Muskie of Maine. (Later, Milt became my partner in the first law firm I joined upon leaving government in 1969.) Phil Brownstein, the Federal Housing Commissioner, was highly regarded and probably was the ablest to serve in that capacity. He was a lifelong friend and neighbor until his death, living with his lovely wife, Esther, in the complex adjoining the one that I have lived in for nearly thirty years. Bill Slayton, a fellow alumnus of Omaha North High School, was the Urban Renewal Commissioner and over-saw the first urban renewal project of the Kennedy administration in South-west Washington, DC, where the Brownsteins and I have lived.—Long after we were no longer in the government, Phil, Bill and I would get together for lunch every couple of months. Unfortunately, Bill died in 1999, and Phil died less than six months later.

Equal Housing Opportunity

During the 1960 presidential campaign, JFK chided the Eisenhower adminis-tration for its failure to move to eliminate discrimination in housing through-out the country by claiming that all it would take would be an executive or-der by the president or to put it in campaign lingo, "a stroke of the pen." Well into the second year of the administration, no executive order and no "stroke of the pen" had materialized. Concerned organizations started a campaign to get the President's attention. The preferred approach was to send the Presi-dent a letter enclosing a pen he could use to sign the executive order. The pens came in by the hundreds and wound up in boxes in my office. JFK's cam-paign commitment was so specific and well publicized that he had no alter-native but to issue an executive order. So, working with HHFA people and Burke Marshall, the Assistant Attorney General for Civil Rights, I started drafting the order.

When word got out that the President was intending to honor the commit-ment he had made, Larry O'Brien reported that a significant number of Dem-ocratic members of Congress, many from suburban districts, had quietly asked him to tell the President that if the order was issued before the No-vember 1962 election, he should not expect to see them re-elected. Included in that group were some very liberal members who did not want their views to be aired publicly because they feared a backlash. As tough as it was to at-tack discrimination in employment and education, housing was clearly the most sensitive issue.

The major issue for the President was how far should the order extend in its scope. For example, should it include banks and other lending institutions? In November, after the election, but before Thanksgiving, a meeting of the key players assembled in the Oval Office, along with the Attorney General and Douglas Dillon, the Secretary of the Treasury. (Incidentally, referring to an historian's question over thirty years later about where Bob Weaver was standing, my recollection was that he was not able to be at the meeting.) After listening attentively to the positions and arguments advanced, JFK stood up, paced the room for what seemed like fifteen minutes, and announced his decisions. Burke Marshall and I were assigned to modify the draft order accordingly. The President had decided not to include lending institutions. (When housing legislation was enacted in 1968 which, among other things, codified the Executive Order, its scope was expanded to include banks and other lending institutions.) The President told me that the press release announcing the order should be issued on the Friday after Thanksgiving, the weakest news day of the year.

The Executive Order called for a director of the Office of Equal Housing Opportunity to be located within the White House. Although presidential appointments were not my assignment, I came up with the name that proved to be the winner: former Governor of Pennsylvania David Lawrence. He had been the Mayor of Pittsburgh for a number of years before being elected governor and, most importantly, was one of the political bosses who threw his state behind John Kennedy in the 1960 selection of a presidential candidate. Although the governor was along in years, he was able to bring along with him a sharp young man who had been a key aide to him as governor. Progress was slow, as had been anticipated, and did not get a good start until the Housing Act of 1968 provided a statutory base to the difficult field of equal housing opportunity.

THE VETERANS ADMINISTRATION

The Veterans Administration (now the Department of Veterans Affairs) was headed by Jack Gleason, an affable, back-slapping Irishman from Chicago who had been the top officer of the American Legion and was in the banking business. He called everyone "comrade," which may have been a term used appropriately in the American Legion, but had a slightly uncomfortable flavor to it during the Cold War.

One very strong recollection I have of Gleason is seeing him at a budget review session at the Bureau of the Budget. These review sessions provide the opportunity for department and agency heads to meet with the BOB team that has gone over the budgets the departments submitted for the coming fiscal year. BOB serves as the President's agent in pulling all the budgets of the Executive Branch together for the President's consideration. It is a critical function, and in general, some of the brightest federal employees are in BOB, but except for the Director and maybe the Deputy Director, they are virtually anonymous. Ideally, they are non-partisan and untouchable. The sessions are quite large with the Director, Deputy Director, Assistant Director, section leaders, and the working stiffs (called analysts), as well as a host of agency people. For department and agency heads, these were, and I presume are, very important sessions. As the White House staff working with some of the involved agencies, I would frequently attend their review sessions.

At the first such session for Gleason, a relatively low level budget analyst named Pierre started at the top of the VA proposed budget and began to rip it apart. He obviously knew more about the agency than the head and most of the key staff that had accompanied him. It was clear that Gleason was most uncomfortable, and when the session ended after perhaps four or five hours, he said what many department and agency heads have said, "Let's hire that guy and get him on our side of the table." He never got Pierre to join the VA. But he did have some able people in the agency: Bill Driver, the Deputy Administrator; and Phil Brownstein, in charge of veterans' housing programs and the same fellow who became the Federal Housing Authority Commissioner, were first rate.

One memorable event occurred as a result of a decision to close a Veterans' Hospital in Lincoln, Nebraska. Periodically, surveys would be made to determine whether shifting veteran populations and numerous other factors would dictate that some VA facilities would have to be closed. After one such review, the Lincoln hospital had to go. This bad news had to be delivered to the local Congressman and Senators by the President's Congressional Liaison, Larry O'Brien. It's hard to think of a lousier task. But Larry was so well respected and so sincere in his regrets that when he had to tell Clair Callan, the one-term Democratic Congressman from the First Congressional District (an extreme rarity), that the Lincoln hospital was to be closed, Callan thanked Larry for the news and for getting it in advance—a courtesy that is now a rarity.

Because of the political sensitivity of military base and VA hospital closings, Congress was persuaded to adopt an approach by which an independent commission would make recommendations to the President and Congress. The President could eliminate some installations from the list; but the list, as sent to the Congress, had to be accepted or rejected as a package. When Ramsey Clark, who subsequently became Attorney General, was a White House staff member, he worked with the commission that recommended closing a military base in Montana, the home state of Senator Mike Mansfield. Senator Mansfield was then Majority Leader of the Senate, and I'm told that President Johnson figuratively landed all over Ramsey, explaining that you do not close a facility in the Majority Leader's state. So much for independent commissions.

THE INTERAGENCY TASK FORCE ON NARCOTICS

In the early1960s, the federal government was concerned with drug abusers and maintained some facilities for incarceration and for rehabilitation, notably a large operation in Lexington, Kentucky. Because of the considerable number of agencies with various responsibilities, including, for example, Health, Education and Welfare; Justice; Treasury; Veterans Administration; Defense; and Agriculture, an interagency task force was established. I was the White House staff handling the task force. In assignments like that, someone from one of the agencies with a significant interest in the work of the task force would prod me to schedule a meeting and would assist in developing an agenda.

During one of these meetings, someone said that President Kennedy, while campaigning in 1960, had said that if elected, he would convene a White House Conference on Drug Abuse. I had not heard that and, for reasons that I can't recall, I sent a note into the President at a meeting he was conducting, asking, "Did you promise to have a White House conference on drug abuse?" His answer: "I don't know. Did I?" It turned out that during the campaign, Mike Feldman had prepared a position paper on the subject which, indeed, promised such a White House conference if Kennedy was elected.

As the staff member heading up the task force, I prepared a draft of the President's remarks opening the conference. He glanced at the draft and said, "Geez, this is dull. Sex it up a little." So, I undertook to "sex" it up. In the President's limousine on the way to the State Department auditorium where the conference was meeting, he said, "Geez, this is dull." Of course, I was not asked to write any more speeches. As the nation's drug problems grew and exploded, clearly they would not be handled by a staff member with some major assignments on his hands.

PRESIDENTIAL PARDONS AND
EXECUTIVE CLEMENCY

One of the first problems facing President Kennedy was the scheduled execution of a soldier who had been court-martialed for assaulting and raping an eleven-year-old German girl and leaving her for dead in a stream near a small village. The Court Martial convicted him of rape and attempted murder and sentenced him to be executed. President Eisenhower approved the sentence, but before it could be carried out at Fort Leavenworth, Kansas, President Kennedy occupied the Oval Office. An appeal was made by the soldier and by local lawyers on his behalf on grounds that the victim did not die and that racial prejudice was involved because the soldier was black. (President Eisenhower had permitted the execution of some black soldiers but had commuted the death sentence of two white soldiers.) Major General Chester "Ted" Clifton, the President's Military Aide, and I worked together on the case. After thoroughly reviewing the extensive file on the case and discussing it at length, we met with the President to report to him on our findings. In a session lasting about an hour and a half, we reviewed the case in detail, and the President read significant portions of the file and peppered us with questions and asked for additional information, including the psychiatric evaluations.

After about six weeks, we met with the President with the requested materials. I remember how astonished I was that he seemed to recall every detail of the case. When he heard my recommendation that the sentence be reduced to life imprisonment, he said, "But you don't approve of the death sentence in any situation." I replied that he was right about that, but I had to concede that I believed the crime was so heinous it could warrant the death sentence in a case where the victim survived, if one had no basic problem with the death penalty. He paced the room and finally said that he was not going to change the Eisenhower decision.

So the word went out to Fort Leavenworth. The arrangements were made, and I was supplied with an open line to the scene of the execution in case of any last minute problems that might arise. None did.

THE DISTRICT OF COLUMBIA

The limited home rule enjoyed by the District of Columbia today did not exist in 1961. Back then, the President appointed the three members of the Board of Commissioners that ran the city. One member of the Board was designated as the Engineer Commissioner, and normally was a very high ranking officer of the United States Corps of Engineers. The remaining two were basically good old patronage appointees with varying degrees of ability and experience. President Kennedy had intended to appoint Frank Reeves, a Washingtonian who had been very supportive during the campaign and who would have been the first black to serve in that position. Although District citizens could not then vote for the president, the District did have some votes at the Democratic and Republican Conventions that selected their respective nominees for the presidency. But Frank had neglected to pay his income taxes and didn't make it to the Commission.

JFK had appointed another supporter, a fairly low-keyed but highly respected Washington lawyer, Walter Tobriner, to be the President of the Board of Commissioners. I was the White House liaison with the Board. The nature of the issues that came my way were basically nuts and bolts matters. One somewhat visible item was securing approval for the nursery school to be held in the White House for Caroline Kennedy and a small group of her playmates. Mrs. Kennedy wanted the school properly accredited, which meant obtaining certification from the District's Superintendent of Education. A phone call to Walter was all that it took to start the process and there was little doubt that it would be approved.

One of the prerogatives of the Board was to assign low-numbered license plates to cars registered in the District. Walter's assistant called my secretary and asked what number I would like. The response went back that I really had no preference. When I wound up with number 138, Walter called personally to see whether that was low enough. Can one believe the sort of things that occupy people with big jobs?

A significant matter involved the Kennedy administration's commitment to building a subway system in the Washington, DC metropolitan area. The principal owner of the DC Transit Company, which owned and operated the streetcar and bus systems in the area was O. Roy Chalk, a flamboyant and aggressive business tycoon who also owned a chunk of Pan American Airlines. When an item appeared in one of the local newspapers about the administration's support of a publicly owned subway system, Chalk came to see me and proclaimed that there was no way that such a new system would be built. I am not particularly confrontational, but I made it clear to him that, yes, indeed, a subway would be built. Of course, the Washington, DC metro system was built, and it is one of the nation's most highly regarded public works projects.

Probably my most memorable contribution resulted when President Kennedy called me to his office and said that Phil Graham, the publisher of *The Washington Post*, had recommended that the President appoint a Special Assistant to the President for District of Columbia Affairs. He asked me what I thought of the idea. In my very best staff manner, I said that the President had often referred to the thesis in Dick Neustadt's book about the presidency that White House staff should be generalists who clearly and obviously owe their loyalty to the president, not to some particular interest group—there were enough advocates in the departments and agencies. Neustadt was a Harvard professor who had served on the staff of President Truman, and was a highly respected expert on government, especially the presidency. I went on to say that the President had appointed Walter Tobriner to be the President of the Board of Commissioners, and, obviously, he would be greatly undercut by someone in the White House who could be seen as a force to overrule Tobriner. I was rather pleased with my answer and went on about my business. A few days later, the press office announced that JFK had appointed the late Charlie Horsky, a very distinguished lawyer and, incidentally, a resident of Montgomery County Maryland, to be Special Assistant to the President for District of Columbia Affairs. So much for perfect textbook arguments.

As it turned out, Charlie was an excellent choice. He had the right personal style and worked well with Tobriner, and we became close friends. Charlie and I would take my sons, Murray and Sheldon, to wrestling matches and other sports events. Charlie came from Montana, and spent every August horseback riding and camping in the mountains. He could never understand why I didn't take him up on his offer to go with him.

THE COMMISSION ON
PRESIDENTIAL CAMPAIGN FINANCING

Shortly after taking office, President Kennedy decided that he wanted to set up a blue ribbon group to study the problems he perceived in campaign financing, especially as they related to presidential campaigns. I was the staff person for the group. I don't recall how the seven-member group was put together, but it was politically balanced. The chairman was a neutral, Alex Heard, a distinguished political science professor from the University of North Carolina (and later the Chancellor of Vanderbilt University) who was one of the country's most respected authorities on campaign financing. There were two prominent political fundraisers—one a Democrat and one a Republican. There were two other political science professors and two former Congressmen: John Vorys, Republican from Ohio, whom JFK had worked with when he was on the House Labor Committee; and Neil Staebler, former Democratic member from Michigan, who had also served as Chairman of the Democratic National Committee. The staff director they chose was Herbert Alexander, a protégé of Professor Heard.

An interesting sidebar to forming the group had to do with obtaining the agreement of Neil Staebler to serve on the commission. I had contacted everyone but Staebler, only to learn from his Michigan office that he was in Greece and couldn't be contacted. The White House operators were not used to hearing that somebody could not be reached, so they got on the case.

Within a couple of hours, he was located in a very small village in Greece, which had only one telephone. The connection was not very good but we could communicate. The first thing he said was, "How in the hell did you find me?" Of course, he was delighted to serve.

The standard procedure for launching groups of that sort was for the members to assemble in the Oval Office for a brief visit with the President and for photographers to be ushered into the office for what are called "photo-ops." In this particular case, JFK ushered them into the Cabinet Room, had them take seats and explained that he regarded this matter to be of great importance. He wanted these experienced people to focus on the problems inherent in financing a presidential campaign and to develop some positive recommendations. He then told a story about his 1960 campaign going into the final days. The strong recommendation of his political advisers and media people was that he had to have a half hour speech on national TV. There were no readily available funds (even his father for whatever reason was not in a position to produce the necessary funds). He told the group that in desperation he (or maybe someone on his behalf—I'm not certain) asked an official of the AFL-CIO for $10,000 (boy, have times changed).—In a sense, every thing that was done right was responsible for JFK's victory in the extremely narrow race with Nixon.—Then he said, "I hope I will have the strength to consider any request they make of me without regard to their having bailed me out at that crucial moment. No president should have to face that kind of situation."

The group's principal recommendation was that public funds should be available for candidates who choose to avail themselves of those funds in return for accepting a limit on their total campaign funding. The money was to be raised by individual taxpayers indicating on their tax returns that they wished one dollar (two in the case of joint returns) of their tax payment to go into the pool. This was enacted and the basic concept is still in operation. But when the White House press office released the President's statement thanking the commission and announcing that enabling legislation was being sent to Congress, I had a call from an outraged Joe Rauh. Joe was a liberal Democrat and an outstanding civil rights advocate. He also was Washington counsel to the United Automobile Workers. He told me that we were about to kill the unions in this country. I told him I didn't know where he had been—this entire process was done with the maximum publicity we could manage and nobody from the UAW or any other union had said a word. He was not assuaged. Happily, I never had to deal with what would have happened if Joe and others had poured in on the administration before the proposal was a done deal and had been announced publicly. Maybe JFK would have had to face the problem he told the group he thought was wrong to impose on the President.

THE COUNCIL OF ECONOMIC ADVISORS

Because I had worked briefly with the Council of Economic Advisers at the very beginning of the administration, I would sometimes get pulled into their activities. For example, when the Kennedy tax cut was being considered, I raised the issue of whether regulated utilities should be eligible for credits on their investments in plants. I argued that since they had an obligation to build facilities, an incentive for them to build didn't make any sense. My position did not prevail.

The Council was truly a gifted group of economists. The Chairman, Walter Heller, from the University of Minnesota, had the ability to make economic points in language that mere lawyers could understand. He said that JFK was one of his better students. He explained to the President that the difference between monetary policy and fiscal policy was easy—just remember Martin (William McChesney) the Chairman of the Federal Reserve Board went with monetary, and Fowler (Joe) the Undersecretary of the Treasury (and later Secretary) went with fiscal. Kermit Gordon from Williams College, another council member, later became Director of the Bureau of the Budget under President Johnson and, subsequently, the President of the Brookings Institution. Professor Jim Tobin of Yale, the third member, later received the Nobel Prize in Economics.

THE CIVIL SERVICE COMMISSION

John Macy, the Chairman of the old Civil Service Commission which oversaw federal employees, came up with the idea of establishing federal regional centers in those cities which contained fairly substantial and numerous federal agency offices. Bill Carey, a senior BOB official, John and I constituted the traveling team that pulled the various offices together and launched a more efficient way of getting the word out in matters of broad governmental application, such as federal personnel issues, anti-discrimination policies, and small business contract setasides. We went to about a dozen major cities to promote the idea, to explain how it would operate, and to let it be known that the White House supported the concept. Easily, the most interesting experience occurred in our Dallas visit. Our meetings went well and we left for the airport to return to DC. The first thing that happened was that the Civil Service Commission regional director, who was also traveling to Washington, DC, took John Macy and me to the airport (Carey did not make that trip). Imagine his embarrassment when Macy, his boss, and the "White House

Guy" were traveling coach and he was in first class. After that experience, the rules were changed about who could travel first class.

We were about forty-five minutes out of Dallas, when it became clear that there was serious trouble with the plane. We could see that one engine was not working; then a second conked out. The pilot informed us that we were turning back, but that we would have to discharge much of our fuel to minimize problems when landing. The atmosphere in the cabin was mighty tense and most didn't seem to worry or care about where that fuel being discharged might land. When we approached the airport, the ambulances lined up and the foam on the runway did not present a cheerful picture. The pilot made a smooth uneventful landing and announced on the loud speaker, "Well, ladies and gentlemen, that was Dallas-to-Dallas, nonstop." I'm not known as a generous big-time spender, but I said to John Macy, "I've got forty bucks in my pocket that would have burned up if we had crashed, so I want to buy you and your regional director a few drinks."

KEEPING MY FOOTING

The White House Police were under the supervision of Kenny O'Donnell, the Appointments Secretary, but there were some issues that came to me. Thus, I was on rather good terms with them, despite my initial run-in with Sgt. Lanier my first day at the White House. The White House Police were a local of some larger law enforcement union. They held periodic meetings in a not-too-fancy building in a grubby neighborhood in nearby Maryland, owned by the Veterans of Foreign Wars. When I was asked to meet with the group, I wanted to know what I should talk about. I was told to be pretty light-hearted about it and I should tell some jokes since I had a bit of a reputation in that direction. That suited me fine and I went prepared with some of my favorites, most of which ranged from risqué to downright dirty. After about thirty or forty minutes, it was time to call it quits. I had another drink and left. Many of the fellows (there were no women present) told me that they appreciated my coming and I felt pretty good about the evening. A week or ten days later, one of the police saw me coming into the building, stopped me and told me how much his wife had enjoyed my stories. I asked him what he was talking about and he told me that, unbeknownst to me, the whole evening had been recorded and the tape was making the rounds.

I worked closely with the talented people at the Bureau of the Budget. Dave Bell, the first JFK Director, had served on President Truman's staff. He was one of JFK's first selections and worked in the transition group taking over from the Eisenhower administration. He was so good that President

Kennedy appointed him head of the Agency for International Development, asserting that if he couldn't administer it effectively, nobody could. It did shape up under his steady hand.

BOB occupied the old State-War-Navy office building (now the Eisenhower Executive Office Building). The exterior was in bad shape and the use of space was most inefficient; thus, the question became whether to tear it down and rebuild on the site or sandblast it and do some internal renovating. The decision was to clean up the outside. So, I told Dave that he used to have a dirty old ugly building—now he had a clean old ugly building.

My work with the National Security Council was quite limited. Carl Kaysen, one of McGeorge Bundy's deputies managed to get me involved with the issue of the Japanese over fishing the waters of the Bering Sea in the North Pacific. The United States fishing interests, particularly in the state of Washington, wanted the government to do something to alleviate the problem. Their major congressional advocate was the late Senator Warren Magnuson, Democrat of Washington, then Chairman of the Senate Commerce Committee. I don't recall what we did about the problem, but I distinctly recall how the meeting froze when Maggie, as the fairly rough hewn character he was, announced that the trouble was that ". . . we didn't kill all those [bleeping] Japs in the war."

Finally, long after my experience with Congressman Porter Hardy and the aid program in Peru involving the issue of executive privilege, Ted Sorensen gave me the foreign assistance Message to Congress to oversee. I asked the late Arthur Schlesinger, the famed Harvard historian who was on the White House staff, to go over the draft. I even had the temerity to change some of the material he suggested. Imagine!

Chapter Ten

JFK and Civil Rights

In the midst of the 1960 presidential campaign, Martin Luther King, Jr. was jailed in Atlanta. Harris Wofford, who worked with JFK and the staff on civil rights issues, is credited with suggesting that JFK call and speak with Coretta King while her husband was in jail. It was a most propitious stroke because news of it solidified what was then called "the Negro vote" in what became an exceedingly close election. Any event that tipped the scales was significant, and it was generally believed that the call to Mrs. King could have been the factor on which the election turned. After the election, Harris joined the White House staff as Assistant to the President for Civil Rights. In November 1961, Harris was transferred to the State Department to help develop the concept of an international peace corps, and Ted Sorensen told me the President wanted me to take over Harris's responsibilities. In light of what I was already doing, there was an off-the-wall quality about it. I was never told as much, but I believe that the President did not want a high-profile big-name assistant handling civil rights issues and attracting attention. That made me a natural to take it over. It was one of the many chance events that became a formative experience in my career.

Realistically, the assignment should have been handled by someone with much more time to devote to the subject than I had, and perhaps a prior association with the subject. There was no fanfare about my taking over the portfolio, but there also were no complaints (that I was aware of) that the Kennedy Administration was deliberately downplaying civil rights. The way the Kennedy White House typically functioned, any domestic matter that rose to a major level of presidential concern would be bumped up to Ted Sorensen, with the rest of us in the Special Counsel's office playing a subordinate role. In the case of civil rights, Attorney General Bobby Kennedy and various Justice Department people, such as Deputy Attorney General Nick Katzenbach and Assistant Attorney General for Civil Rights Burke Marshall, were the major players.

THE BLACK LEADERSHIP

The black leadership was (and is) a high-powered group. The most respected and even revered player was A. Philip Randolph, the organizer and longtime leader of the Union of Sleeping Car Porters, who had been in a position of leadership for decades. He was a distinguished soft-spoken gentleman but, as he was getting along in years, he was frequently represented by his brilliant assistant, Bayard Rustin. Roy Wilkins, the head of the National Association for the Advancement of Colored People, was the *de facto* chairman of the group and, in my view, was a statesman and the intellectual leader of the group. Whitney Young of the Urban League was an idea man. Jim Farmer, the head of the Congress of Racial Equality, was a large man with a strong baritone voice who was almost always a little more aggressive than the rest. Dr. Martin Luther King, Jr., headed the Southern Christian Leadership Conference. His voice was not an especially dominant one in the group discussions. Dorothy Height headed the United Negro Women, and although not as vociferous as the others, she often had a good point or two to make, making her truly "one of the boys." John Lewis (currently a highly effective U.S. Congressman from the Atlanta area) represented the Student Non-Violent Coordinating Committee, but rarely traveled with the group. They were an able bunch and, not surprisingly, there was some jostling and elbowing going on among them.

At the time I took over civil rights issues, the black leadership was—as it should have been—pressing for more action on civil rights. Although I frequently had the feeling that we were trying to appease the leadership and that they didn't appreciate what had been and was being done, I counted myself lucky to be at the center of one of the major administration activities.

What was clear to the black leadership and to blacks across the country was that the Kennedy Administration was far more in tune with their needs and aspirations than was the Eisenhower crowd. President Kennedy had courted the black community in the election of 1960, and owed his victory to their support. With the margin over Nixon being so narrow, Kennedy had a response ready for each group that told him that if it hadn't been for them, he wouldn't be President. He'd jokingly say, "You know, you're right. Every group tells me the same thing." But it was true.

WORKING WITH CONGRESS

Larry O'Brien, President Kennedy's Congressional Liaison, knew his business and advised the President with realistic appraisals of what could and could not be accomplished. The congressional committee chairmen were then mostly southerners. In those days, southern states tended to re-elect and re-elect their legislators. With a strict seniority system in effect, many of these chairmen were in positions to influence the progress (or lack of it) of other legislation equally critical to the administration.

The U.S. Civil Rights Commission, as it was created by Congress in 1957, had no power other than the right to hold hearings on matters it deemed relevant to finding abuses and to recommend corrective action. But its members knew how to gain press attention and were almost always proposing such drastic action as cutting off federal funding to states with lousy civil rights records and practices. The Executive Director was Berl Bernhard, an old buddy of mine with whom I could work; but under the leadership of Father Theodore Hesburgh of Notre Dame University, and later former Harvard Law School dean Erwin Griswold, the Commission served as an unwelcome prod to the administration.

Similarly, there were individual legislators pushing their favorite programs. For example, California Congressman Jimmy Roosevelt, the son of FDR, was pushing a Fair Employment Practices Act. Again, even though the administration and the people in it may have been sympathetic, such a bill would have had no chance of enactment. Essentially, these positions of reluctance rested on the belief that this was a booby-trapped field, and the administration had better ideas about what was achievable.

THE PRESIDENT'S COMMITTEE ON
EQUAL EMPLOYMENT OPPORTUNITY

Because of the basic feeling that the views of blacks were welcome and that a sympathetic administration was in office, when progress didn't come as quickly as might have been desired by the black leadership, the disappointment was sharp. I never heard President Kennedy say he wanted to go slowly in pushing civil rights; but it was clear that he preferred to press on with executive actions that he could take while legislation was too divisive and unlikely to succeed. Such efforts could await a second term. Thus, in March 1961, he created by Executive Order the President's Committee on Equal Employment Opportunity, headed by Vice President Johnson, to encourage businesses to make special efforts to eliminate discrimination in hiring and to promote minority employment affirmatively. He followed up on President Truman's order to integrate the Defense Department by establishing a committee headed by Gerhard Gesell (later a United States District Court Judge) to make specific recommendations for accomplishing a meaningful integration.

Because the committee was created by Executive Order, it did not have the statutory base (supplied by Congress in1964) for enforcing anti-discrimination in employment; thus, its efforts were hortatory. The committee had a number of businessmen in leadership roles: Bill Miller, the head of Textron (later, Secretary of the Treasury), working with the committee's able staff director Hobart Taylor (a black lawyer from Texas, and the son of a longtime supporter of LBJ), developed a program called "Plans for Progress," which called for a voluntary commitment by individual companies to increase their minority employment. Bobby Troutman, an Atlanta lawyer, also served on the committee. Partly because of Troutman's southern background, rumors circulated that these "Plans for Progress" were sweetheart deals arrived at only for public relations benefits.

As the White House liaison with the committee, Attorney General Bobby Kennedy asked me to check into the committee's activities. I inquired and concluded that, because it had to rely solely on voluntary actions, its progress was limited. Yes, there may have been a little puffing of the committee's accomplishments, but all-in-all it was operating fairly and with some success. The strain between Bobby and the Vice President was no secret, but Bobby accepted my assessment.

PRESIDENTIAL APPOINTMENTS

Although there had been an occasional black presidential appointee in past administrations, the gates opened wide in the JFK Presidency. JFK named Robert Weaver to head the Housing and Home Finance Agency. Carl Rowan was posted as Ambassador to a major European country. Leon Higginbotham was appointed a United States District Court Judge, and Thurgood Marshall was the first black appointed to the United States Court of Appeals. Subsequently, Thurgood Marshall was appointed by President Johnson as the first black to serve on the United States Supreme Court.

A KEY PLAYER

A key player in all civil rights activities was Louis Martin. Louis had taken leave from his position with the *Chicago Defender*, an African-American newspaper, to advise the Kennedy team in the 1960 campaign. He was a self-effacing guy with a wry way about him and one of the shrewdest political minds in the business. Louis was not only the Deputy Chairman of the Democratic National Committee, but also, and more importantly, was an unofficial adviser on all matters affecting the black community and all Democratic political issues. He could walk into the President's office at almost any time, and he had the delightful habit of calling everyone "Chief."

Louis was a playful fellow. One of my responsibilities was to answer the President's mail dealing with civil rights sent by important officials, such as governors, mayors, and local elected officials. If the letter warranted a presidential response, I'd prepare the letter; otherwise, I'd refer them to the Civil Rights Commission, the Justice Department, or to Louis for suggested drafts for my signature. One letter from a local councilman or officeholder had a rather bitter tone, and we sent it off to Louis. His draft letter was pretty salty, something like, You don't know what you're talking about. Why don't you crawl back in your hole. I told the secretary to type up the letter as Louis had proposed, destroy the original, and send the carbon copy (this predated Xerox copies) to Louis. The next day, Louis called. "Hey, Chief, you didn't send out that letter, did you?" "What letter, Louis?" "You know, the one to the councilman." "Oh, Louis, I don't go over the drafts that you prepare. Kathy must have typed it up, and I signed it and sent it out." "Oh no!" After letting him stew for a few minutes, I let him out of his agony.

One day in early 1963, Louis said to me, "Chief, you know, we ought to put together a legislative proposal to eliminate discrimination in public accommodations. Even if it doesn't get enacted, the 'brothers' will know that the Kennedy's have their hearts in the right place." That was the beginning of what turned out to be the most significant civil rights legislation ever enacted.

President Kennedy's Special Message on Civil Rights sent to the Congress in the spring of 1963 was fairly limited in that it was primarily about public accommodations. But it served some very useful purposes. Public accommodations discrimination was for many blacks the most visible and humiliating aspect of discrimination in the nation. As Louis Martin had predicted, it demonstrated to the black community that the administration was concerned. It also provided a base for additional legislative proposals. And it preceded the eruption in Birmingham, Alabama, which precipitated national outrage.

THE BIRMINGHAM OUTRAGE

President Kennedy's move to press civil rights activities vigorously was occasioned by the outrage of Birmingham, Alabama, in the summer of 1963.

The use of fire hoses and cattle prods by "Bull" Connor, the Birmingham Public Safety Commissioner, and Alabama state troopers against protesters in Birmingham had been caught by television cameras and broadcast all over the nation and the world. Those vivid pictures made a difference, a significant difference.

The President decided to make a speech to the nation, carried by television and radio, about the situation and scheduled it for later that afternoon. Sorensen went to work drafting it. I was not in the President's office when he made the decision, but I knew about it quickly, because Kenny O'Donnell called and told me I ought to get down to Sorensen's office because Ted had just been given an almost impossible job to do. O'Donnell and Sorensen were not the closest of buddies, but Kenny felt that Sorensen was in a tight spot and needed help. Of course, two people can't write a speech, especially when Ted was dictating to his secretary, Gloria Liftman, and she was typing the copy as he dictated. As pages came out of the typewriter, they were shuttled over to the President, who had already begun delivering the address. It was a close race, but the President ran out of text and continued extemporaneously for a short time.—Later, when I told Ted that no one would know where his words stopped and President Kennedy's took over, he said, "That's not right." Of course, Ted was right: both he and the President knew.—A few months later, in a meeting with civil rights leaders in the Cabinet Room, President Kennedy made his much-quoted observation that they should erect a statue of Bull Connor because of his great "contribution" to the cause for which they had fought so hard.

A TOTAL ADMINISTRATION EFFORT

A short time later, Bobby Kennedy asked Ralph Dungan, a Special Assistant to President Kennedy, and me to meet him in his office. I don't recall why Ralph was there, but it may have been because he worked on presidential appointments and Bobby wanted to fill him in. In any event, Bobby told us of a meeting he had had with owners and operators of national retail chains that operated in southern states. Ten-cent stores and drug chains with lunch counters, hotel chains, movie theater chains, bowling alleys, for example, were represented. The Attorney General asked those assembled to use their influence to eliminate discrimination in the way the companies operated various business enterprises in the South. He told us that one fellow from New York, after listening to the Attorney General, said that he was afraid the AG didn't understand. He continued, stating that his company and the others were businesses operating in areas where it was not up to them to change the mores and customs of the region. They were there to conduct business, hopefully to make a profit and be good neighbors, not to impose their ideas of proper conduct on the local communities. But, he told the AG, if you have legislation enacted, telling us what we must do, you can be sure that we will comply with the law.

In the discussion that followed, we came up with the idea that the President should hold a series of meetings with various leadership groups to let them know that they had a role to play in building a national consensus in support of federal legislation. Those meetings were held during the summer of 1963. Included in the groups that were invited to the East Room of the White House were religious leaders, educators, labor leaders, local governmental officials, business executives, and lawyers.

President Kennedy told me that he wanted the Attorney General and the Assistant Attorney General for Civil Rights Burke Marshall to be present, and he especially wanted the Vice President to be there. He said that he wanted it to be crystal clear that this was a total administration effort. Vice President Johnson was to be there because of his Texas background. The President didn't say so, but I had the impression that he also wanted Johnson to be involved in case the whole exercise failed.

As the White House staff person responsible for setting up the meetings, I would pull together the list of the individuals from each group that should be invited. I also prepared a short memorandum for the President telling him who would be present, where I had obtained the names, and some points that he could make in his presentation. I would dictate the memorandum for the President fifteen or thirty minutes before each meeting was scheduled to begin. With only carbon copies available, the Vice President and I would be in the Oval Office with the President going over the original; I would be reading the carbon copy. On occasion, I would forget to bring a copy for the Vice President, so the two of us would be standing there with Vice President Johnson looking over my shoulder (he was 6 feet 4 inches, and I was 5 feet 7 inches), asking if he could share my copy.

Each meeting was aimed at what the members of the group could do to work within their area of activity to promote awareness of the national problem, to take actions to eliminate discrimination, and to urge Congress to act. For example, the lawyers' group, headed by Harrison Tweed of New York, and Bernie Siegel of Philadelphia, created the Lawyers Committee for Civil Rights, an aggressive organization supplying legal assistance and support for victims of civil rights abuses. The Lawyers Committee for Civil Rights continues to this day.

The President hit the religious leaders especially hard, expressing dismay that with the great moral issue facing the nation, they for the most part were silent. To labor leaders, most of whom had supported him in 1960, he pointed out what they already knew, namely, that there was widespread discrimination in their unions. The one group that astounded me was the business leaders. When the President and Vice President walked into the East Room to start the session, they remained seated. No other group had done that. When I mentioned it to the President, he said he hadn't noticed.

Not all the meetings were this cold. I recall an earlier meeting of civil rights leaders that was full of smiles and laughs. It included some local Washington, DC activists and was held in the Cabinet Room on March 17th. The late Aaron Goldman, the head of the Macke Vending Company in Washington, DC, and an active foe of discrimination, told the President, "Mr. President, for over sixty years my name has been spelled a-a-r-o-n, but I want you to know that on this special day, my name on your White House list of attendees at the gate was spelled er-i-n."

The meetings were deemed a great success in raising the level of attention and concern across the country and in increasing public pressure on the Congress. Although the meetings were not open to the press, the press had access to the participants following each meeting, and the coverage was wide and generally favorable. On one occasion, an AP photographer got into one meeting, and the next day, a news story, accompanied by Photo 10.1, appeared in the Washington, DC *Evening Star*.

The Subcommittee on Civil Rights

On the side of the federal government, I had established a group of fairly high ranking individuals from key agencies to monitor activities within their agencies. Called the Subcommittee on Civil Rights, it was extremely casual and met whenever it seemed appropriate. An example of what we would discuss was a minor but sticky situation that would occur when an administration official accepted a speaking engagement only to find on arrival or just prior to arrival that the audience was segregated. This resulted in my sending a memorandum to department and agency heads advising them to establish procedures to avoid such situations.

THE 1963 MARCH ON WASHINGTON

In the summer of 1963, the black leadership let us know that they were planning to stage a march in Washington, DC to demonstrate the concern of the black community for a change in national attitude and to put pressure on Congress to enact civil rights legislation. The leading figure was A. Philip

Photo 10.1. President Kennedy conducted a series of meetings with various leadership groups to build a consensus on civil rights issues. The President addressed a group of lawyers on their role in civil rights at a meeting in the East Room of the White House on June 21, 1963. A Lawyers Committee for Civil Rights that was formed at the meeting continues to exist today. L-R: President John F. Kennedy at the podium; Assistant to the President Ralph Dungan; Assistant Attorney General for Civil Rights Burke Marshall; Assistant Special Counsel Lee C. White is shown standing to the left of the mantle. Photo Credit: AP Wirephoto. Published with permission of Associated Press.

Randolph, who had attempted a march in the early 1940s, but had been dissuaded from doing so by Eleanor Roosevelt, among others. The administration clearly had no enthusiasm for such an undertaking. We envisioned a tremendous crowd that could get out of control, despite the leaders' efforts. The District of Columbia Police Department was inexperienced in handling such crowds, and many of its policemen were not sympathetic to the goals of the would-be marchers. We saw enormous logistical problems in handling a crowd of hundreds of thousands. Most importantly, we were concerned that the march could have the opposite effect its planners intended in that it could alienate the Congress. But what could we do?

The First Amendment to the Constitution guarantees the right of peaceable assembly, and there was no law we could point to that limited the number of participants. We might have been able to have the National Park Service, which has jurisdiction over the grounds on the great mall, impose limits on the number who could participate for safety reasons, but that approach was simply unacceptable.

The march was not government-sponsored, but it was obvious that the administration had to do everything possible to make it work. The lead for the administration was the Justice Department. Bobby Kennedy generally used his top staff however he thought they could be useful. For example, Louis Oberdorfer, the Assistant Attorney General for Tax Matters (and later a distinguished U.S. District Court Judge), was from a prominent Birmingham, Alabama, family. Bobby had dispatched him to Birmingham to play a mediating role in the situation there. When it came to the March on Washington, Bobby designated John Douglas, the Assistant Attorney General for Civil Matters (and the son of the great United States Senator from Illinois, Paul Douglas) to oversee the logistics of the massive undertaking. John's counterpart from the leadership was Bayard Rustin, the brilliant aide to Mr. Randolph. Secretary of the Army Cyrus Vance (later Secretary of State in the Carter Administration) worked with Bobby to station seasoned troops as inconspicuously as possible around the Washington, DC metropolitan area in case a riot developed. I was kept advised of what was going on from the government's point of view and kept in contact with Mr. Rustin.

On the day of the march and earlier, in many cases, people poured in from all over the country. The crowd at the program in front of the Lincoln Memorial was estimated at roughly 250,000. All speakers were effective. It was reported that some of the older members of the leadership had to lean on John Lewis, the head of SNCC, to tone down his criticism of the administration. Clearly, the speech that captured the imagination of the crowd and, indeed, of the nation was Martin Luther King, Jr.'s "I Have a Dream" speech. I was in the President's office watching the activities on television, and, as I recall, the

President was greatly impressed by King's speech. Its content, its cadence, and the powerful voice made it clear that you had just heard a powerful and electrifying speech.

Ted Sorensen was at the Naval Hospital in Bethesda, Maryland, that day, so I prepared a draft of a statement for the President to issue on the occasion of the march. The President looked at it and said, "Who wrote this?" Recalling his decidedly negative reaction to the draft opening remarks I had prepared for the White House Conference on Drug Abuse, I answered with some trepidation that I had. He replied, "Not bad."

Of course, it was a great relief that the march had gone off without a major hitch. The President's meeting with participants, including Walter Reuther, the head of the United Automobile Workers, was one happy gathering. And the nation had a new hero in Dr. King, whose stirring speech had moved the country.

Chapter Eleven

The Assassination

Few events are so overwhelming that, years later, one recalls the exact circumstances when he or she learned of it. When word of the attack on Pearl Harbor was announced to the world, I was at the ΣAM fraternity house in Lincoln, Nebraska. I was at a gas station in Fort Monmouth, New Jersey, when the service station attendant told us that President Roosevelt had died. And I was having lunch in the White House mess when I learned that President Kennedy had been shot.

It was a sunny Friday afternoon, and I was at the table where staff ate when they did not have guests, a round table accommodating seven or eight. Jack McNally, who worked in Kenny O'Donnell's operation, came into the mess and announced that the President had been shot. My initial reaction was that McNally was a dolt for making such a terrible joke; but when I looked at his face, the realization sunk in that he was not joking. At that time, the only television set in the West Wing was in Pierre Salinger's office. Leaving the table, I went up the stairs to the main floor, walked down the inside corridor to the inside entrance to the press office. As I went down the corridor, I passed the Oval Office, where the door was open, and noticed workmen replacing the pale green oval rug with a brilliant red one. The furniture had been moved to the sides and the office was in shambles.

When I walked into the press office, I saw Helen Gant, a long time White House staff person, and a young lady whom I did not recognize. They were standing in front of the television set with tears running down their faces. Joining them, I stared at the set as reports were coming out: initially with a bit of hope; then with the increasing realization that there was no hope; and, finally, the somber report by Walter Cronkite that the President was dead.

By this time, reporters had started to drift into the office. The reporters who normally covered the White House were in Texas with the presidential party or taking the weekend off. Press Secretary Pierre Salinger was en route to Japan with a group of cabinet officers for a scheduled conference with their Japanese counterparts. Andy Hatcher, the Assistant Press Secretary, was at a horserace track in nearby Maryland; and Malcolm "Mac" Kilduff, the other Assistant Press Secretary, was in Texas with the President. Helen and the young lady were in no condition to handle the press, so I became the self-designated Acting Press Secretary.

SECURING THE OVAL OFFICE

Chaos reigned. Mac Bundy, the President's National Security Adviser, called me to ask what I knew. I told him I only knew what television was reporting. It simply did not enter my mind that the assassination might be a part of a grander plan and that special security measures were warranted.

As the press office filled up, someone asked whether they could see the President's office. Without much thought, I agreed and started to lead the bunch through the door to the inside corridor and down the hall to the Oval Office, when, all of a sudden, I recalled what the room looked like and decided it would be stupid to let a crowd of reporters into that office under any circumstance. I stopped the parade and steered all of them back into the press office without anyone objecting.

A couple of hours later, Charlie Horsky, the President's Assistant for District of Columbia Affairs, came by and relieved me. I then passed by the Oval Office and realized that there were some materials there that should be preserved and set aside. Because the President was away, the usual Secret Service agents were not on duty at the entrance to the Oval Office. I found Gwen King, one of Kenny O'Donnell's secretaries, and asked her to bring some large envelopes so we could empty each drawer of the President's desk, placing the contents of each in a separate envelope. She was not enthusiastic about the assignment, but I assured her it had to be done. I also felt strange in that period of shock, but realized that we couldn't simply leave that office unprotected. She locked the envelopes in her desk and later turned them over to the Secret Service. After emptying the desk, I asked the Secret Service to secure the Oval Office.

A SHATTERING EXPERIENCE

Mac Bundy was organizing a group for the helicopter ride to Andrews Air Force Base, just outside of Washington, DC, to meet the plane returning from Dallas. By chance, I sat next to Walter Jenkins, who was the longest-serving and undoubtedly the most loyal of all of Lyndon Johnson's staff people. He wasn't in shock, but he was stunned and worried out loud about what would they do and how could such a thing happen.

It was dark by the time the plane landed and there was a chill in the November air. A small crowd, including a group from Congress, was present. Bobby Kennedy went up the portable steps, entered the plane, and then emerged with Mrs. Kennedy. Next came the coffin, and as it appeared at the door of the plane, the full force of what had happened hit me: it was a shattering experience. It was not an easy job negotiating that coffin down the narrow steps; but before long, it had been put into the back of the waiting hearse that then sped off. I vaguely remember President and Mrs. Johnson emerging from the plane. Within a short time, we were back in the helicopter headed back to the White House.

THE SOLEMN EVENT

At the White House, an informal command center was set up in Ralph Dungan's office. Someone had arranged for the White House mess to be in operation and people drifted in and out until late at night. There were about a half a dozen of us, with R. Sargent Shriver, the dead President's brother-in-law and the Director of the Peace Corps, in charge. He was in contact with Bobby, who was with Mrs. Kennedy at the Naval Hospital in Bethesda, Maryland. The major decisions were being made by Mrs. Kennedy or Bobby, or both, and passed on to "Sarge," as questions about the mechanics and logistics of the funeral preparations and execution were being worked on. Almost magically, a solemn fellow from the State Department showed up with a large loose-leaf folder that contained a wealth of historical materials about how presidential funerals had been conducted and what decisions had to be made to have events occur on a timely basis.

In the case of the death of a family member, preoccupation with the funeral decisions and details serves to divert, if even only partially, the impact of the death. And so it was in this instance. I don't recall much of the details of the discussions that went on, but I remember one of my contributions. I knew that when Pennsylvania Avenue had been resurfaced, the traffic lights were installed so they could be removed for parades. It was an easy call to see that they were removed. I had seen how television camera trucks following an inaugural parade may have given pretty good coverage to some detail of marching bands, for example, but they were very intrusive. I suggested that there were very good spots along the Avenue where fixed cameras could be located and that we should prohibit the camera trucks, thereby adding to the dignity of the funeral procession from the Capitol to the White House.

The day of the funeral was cool but filled with bright sunshine. Those asked to march from the White House in a procession escorting the casket to Saint Matthew's Church for the funeral service, a little over a mile, formed in a loose formation at the White House. The group included many foreign dignitaries, including the French President Charles de Gaulle, and I felt privileged to be marching in that group. At the church, there were seats for my wife and me. One had to marvel at how smoothly the solemn event was handled.

THE UNTHINKABLE

Working in the White House is a heady experience at any time, but these were special times. The Kennedy White House exuded a pervasive sense of vitality and excitement. Things were moving. It was the place to be. In all my days there, I never stopped thinking how lucky I was to have the opportunity to work in that place. My relationship with JFK was easy and comfortable. I was not in the closest tight ring around him, but I may have been in the second or third ring. As was well known, JFK had a quick mind. He was a demanding boss but a cool one.

The tragic and untimely death of John F. Kennedy demonstrated the axiom that no one — not even the President — is indispensable. We will never know what might have been. But life goes on even after such a terrible loss.

One jarring incident occurred the afternoon and evening of the assassination. Bud Wilkinson, the University of Oklahoma football coach called a number of White House staff (not including me) to get someone to say that President Kennedy would have wanted the final game of the season between arch rivals Oklahoma and Nebraska to go on the next day. Of course, nobody would have or did say any such thing, but the game was played. It was one of the very few athletic or entertainment events throughout the country that was not cancelled that weekend. When I later asked Nebraska Governor Frank Morrison about it, he practically blew me over by saying that Wilkinson had told his Nebraska counterparts that the game would be considered forfeited if Nebraska didn't show up. And, Morrison added proudly, Nebraska won the game. Unbelievable!

Having focused on the areas of activity and events in the Kennedy Administration, one is reminded that the sharp cleavage between the Kennedy and Johnson Administrations was, of course, the unthinkable: the assassination of President Kennedy. What a cataclysmic horrendous act!

Part Three

THE JOHNSON WHITE HOUSE

Chapter Twelve

The Johnson Years

As the work week began following the funeral, the first order of business was to submit a letter of resignation to the new President. All cabinet officers, heads of agencies and White House staff did so. Initially, I believe President Johnson intended to keep the letters, but changed his mind and had them returned. He told me, as I believe he told each person individually, that he wanted me to stay. In his words, "If President Kennedy needed you, I need you even more." For me, it was not a difficult decision to stay. When the President of the United States looks me in the eye and asks me to remain, especially under such circumstances, there was no way I was going to refuse.

There were those who, for whatever reasons, were not able to continue. I believe that some had always had disdain for LBJ. Others were simply so shattered by the assassination that they couldn't remain.

All cabinet officers agreed to stay on. In the case of Larry O'Brien and Kenny O'Donnell, two of the earliest, most loyal and talented political advisers and staff to Kennedy, Kenny had to leave; Larry agreed to stay. Whether Larry agreed to stay because he wanted to help LBJ enact the Kennedy legislative program and intended to leave as early as he could or because he, too, found the new President's plea irresistible has been debated. On the basis of what he told me, it was the latter.

There was considerable scurrying around as the new folks were blended into the JFK holdovers. Walter Jenkins, George Reedy who had worked for the Equal Employment Opportunity Committee, and Bill Moyers, who had been an official in the Peace Corps in the Kennedy administration, were well known to me and the transition was fairly smooth. For the most part, the LBJ people were a competent group and I found it easy to work with them.

Ted Sorensen left and Bill Moyers took over his duties as the domestic policy chief honcho. I prepared a memo for the new President setting forth all

111

the various activities I was engaged in, indicating what was contemplated and asking how he wanted to proceed. One illustration was a meeting scheduled for JFK with a Congressional delegation representing the northern Great Lakes states of Michigan, Minnesota, and Wisconsin, seeking support for the creation of an economic development program for that area comparable to the Appalachian Regional Development Agency. He could refuse to reschedule the meeting or set it for a later time. After a few days he told me to go ahead and reschedule it. JFK had approved having a White House conference on campaign financing the next spring, and he had decided to have an exhibit in the federal government pavilion at the 1964 World's Fair in New York, by which visitors could donate to the political party of their choice. President Johnson told me to go ahead with the plans.

THE JOHNSON STYLE

President Johnson was totally different in style and in how he operated from President Kennedy. LBJ was a swarmer who would pop up all over the White House. His energy level was always on full-speed-ahead in my dealings with him. Reports of his periods of self-doubt that others witnessed were not evident to me. He would take a nap, wake up refreshed and raring to go again. I thought he should have two staffs—one for before his nap and one for after. His mind was sharp and his memory remarkable, but with all that, he had to struggle with the ghost of the martyred President. He was proud and vain, but to this amateur psychiatrist, he suffered from some unusual form of self doubt. I believe it had something to do with his having attended San Marcos State Teachers College in rural Texas and being surrounded by a number of Ivy League graduates. To me, he was as smart as anybody in the room.

One of his favorite devices was to convene a good-sized meeting of administration people to discuss an issue that had bubbled up to him. If it weren't controversial with some people for and some against, it wouldn't have gotten there. He would listen to the various arguments presented and pretty soon you could tell by his questions and observations which way he was going. Everyone in the Cabinet Room where this type of session would be held knew where he had come out on the matter being discussed. As depicted in the photo 12.1, he would then go around the table asking each person what he (or she) thought. He wanted each person to tell him what he or she had decided, so if it came a cropper, he could say that every one of his aides had advised him to take that action. When I agreed with his decision, I would say so when he got to me; but if I didn't agree, on occasion when I felt

Photo 12.1. On controversial issues, President Johnson typically convened a meeting of administration people to discuss the issue. He would listen to the various arguments presented and then go around the table asking each person what he or she thought. This meeting in the Cabinet Room on August 31, 1965 was one such occasion. Clockwise from 9 o'clock: Assistant to the President Harry McPherson; Assistant Walter Jenkins; Special Counsel Lee C. White; Assistant to the President Bill Moyers; President Lyndon Johnson; Assistant to the President for Education Douglas Cater; National Security Advisor McGeorge Bundy; Assistant to the President Jack Valenti; Assistant to Lee C. White Clifford Alexander; Assistant to the President Joseph A. Califano, Jr. (Also in attendance but not pictured: Hayes Redman, Hal Pachios, Jake Jacobsen, Marvin Watson, Joe Laitin, Horace Busby, Paul Glynn, Nicholas Katzenbach) Photo Credit: Yoichi R. Okamoto. (Personal Collection of Lee C. White)

strongly about the issue, I would say I didn't agree with the others. I thought of his informal survey as a challenge to my manhood and I was reluctant to play that game. He'd scowl a bit and pass on to the next person. Undoubtedly everyone present understood the game but didn't deem it worth struggling over.

I don't know whether it was a positive characteristic, but LBJ seemed never to take time from the burdens of the office. When JFK left the office in the evening, for the most part, he left the problems there. LBJ's idea of a pleasant night was to have a committee chairman over for drinks and dinner so he could find out what was going on in Congress and, incidentally, catch up on the gossip. When Vietnam mushroomed, obviously he was, to coin a phrase, "Sleepless in Washington." For a man who had suffered a major heart attack when he was Majority Leader of the Senate, his energy level was almost always on full throttle.

If a member of the staff submitted a memorandum for LBJ to Juanita Roberts, his personal secretary, before 7:00 p.m., by the time the staff person got to the office the next day, LBJ would have read it and replied. He developed a pattern by which each memo would have at the bottom three separate items: Approved; Disapproved; or, See Me. I used to joke that one time when I received a string of "Disapproveds," I tried to fool him by casting the memo with my actual recommendation set up to call for "disapprove," and, of course, that time it came back with "Approve" checked off.

Francis Bator, of the National Security Council, once came to my office late one Friday afternoon to ask for my help. There was a document requiring presidential signature that had to be signed that day. So, what was I supposed to do about that? He wanted me to go to President Johnson's office with him to ask the president to sign the document. "Why don't you ask Mac Bundy to go with you?" I asked. "Because he's not here" was the answer. Francis wasn't exactly on a first-name basis with the President, so we headed for the President's office and by chance encountered him in the corridor. Francis and I were about eight or nine inches shorter than LBJ. I told the President that Francis has a document that must be signed today. He looked down at Francis and said, "How long have you had this?" "Two weeks" was the reply. It seemed to me that the President was in a pretty good mood. He said, "How come you get two weeks and I get two hours?" No intelligible answer. The President signed it, but he had posed a good question, and I assume it didn't happen very often.

President Johnson felt his job was important and that he should have the best people available working for him. For example, he swiped two speechwriters, Will Sparks and Bob Hardesty, from Secretary of Defense McNamara, because he read and liked something each had written. But the classic case involved a very bright young University of Texas law graduate, Perry Barber, who had led his class and who jumped at the chance to work as an assistant to Jack Valenti, handling scheduling matters for the President. Joe Califano, who had been General Counsel of the Army, and Jack Valenti thought that after a year of performing fairly menial tasks, Perry should move to a more substantive and significant assignment and made arrangements for him to be assigned to the office of the General Counsel of the Defense Department. When LBJ learned about it, he vetoed the move, asserting that he should have the "best Goddam scheduling assistant" there was. To Perry's credit, he resigned on the spot and returned to Texas, where he became a prominent lawyer.

News Tickers and Red Phones

LBJ followed the news assiduously. A bank of three television sets was installed in the Oval Office so he could watch all of the news programs and switch as he saw something that interested him. Miniature radios were distributed to staff, set to an all-news station. He had news tickers (Associated Press, United Press and Reuters) placed in a number of spots in the West Wing. Pretty clearly, he wanted everyone to keep up with the news. One time, Joe Califano asked me why he never saw me reading the news tickers. I told him I really had better things to do and, besides, I didn't have to worry. If there was a report I should know about, I'd get a call from the President saying, "Did you see AP #48? You better get on it." As I told Joe, there was no reason for both of us to be glued to the tickers.

Speaking of phones, LBJ loved gadgetry and had a phone console with more lines than any I had ever seen. One afternoon, I was talking to Mike Feldman near my secretary's desk when she answered the phone and asked if I wanted to take a call from "Leonard Nelson." I didn't know any Leonard Nelson and told her, "No, tell him to call back." Within a couple of minutes, a White House operator called and told Lorene that it was President Johnson who had called using his telephone console. Not long after, LBJ had special red phones installed on the desks of the top staff. This might have been regarded as a prestigious status symbol except for the fact that they had the loudest ear shattering ring. When that phone rang, I jumped six inches. It did get my attention.

The Many Forms of Protest

One incident showed a bit of the Johnson style. The Vietnam War was not going well and there were many forms of protest. One of the most unusual took place during the normal visitors' tour of the White House. One morning about eleven o'clock, word reached the President that a group of about fifteen or so young people who had entered with the usual line of visitors, had gotten as far as the space between the East Wing and the residence and sat down on the marble floor. They asked to see the President. This obviously was a sticky situation. LBJ called Bill Moyers, Cliff Alexander, an assistant of mine, and me into the Cabinet Room to discuss what should be done. We mulled it over with him and concluded that, if he saw the group, the visitors' tour would probably have to be cancelled since it would be regarded as a sure-fire way to gain an audience with the President. Besides, it was rude and an infringement on the rights of others. The tour was shut down as soon as the sit-in was discovered. The President said he had to meet with someone in his office but would return fairly soon.

About fifteen minutes later, he returned and said, "It may be a good way for me to show I'm comfortable in my position and big enough to respond to their unorthodox approach." Obviously, whoever met with him had turned him around. We gently reiterated our objections. Pointing to me and Cliff, he said, "You two go out and talk to them and if they ask to see me, bring them in here." We went out and they were sprawled on the floor and somewhat restless. One big fellow got up on his elbow and started to say that they wanted to see the President. He had not gotten the words out, before a number of them shushed him. The request was not made and we never knew why it wasn't. After talking with them for a while and waiting in vain for their request to see the President, we returned to him and reported what had happened. He muttered something about a couple of his brightest couldn't even get that ragtag gang to ask to see the President.

When the visitors' tour was cancelled, the word got out and every White House gate was covered by reporters and cameramen. Mrs. Johnson, out of the goodness of her heart, had coffee served to them. In fact, one of the group rushed out of the East Wing entrance and told a reporter who asked what was going on, "Man, I didn't come out here to talk to you people, I've got to take a leak." We let them remain until it was dark and had DC unmarked police cars come to the diplomatic entrance, which is fairly far from the gates and not very visible in the dark of the night. They were loaded into the cars, taken to jail and booked on trespass charges. We dropped the charges the next day and so ended the tale of the sit-in. Happily, there were no other similar attempts and the White House tours were resumed.

A major event occurred in the summer of 1965. Without any specific warning, a riot broke out in the community of Watts in the Los Angeles area. A number of lives were lost and the police had trouble bringing the situation under control. It was a Saturday morning and Joe Califano had just joined the staff from his Defense Department position as General Counsel of the Army. We were on the phone to President Johnson, who was at his ranch in Texas. He was following events by watching television and getting whatever information we were able to learn from intelligence reports. Things were not settling down. When LBJ learned that California Governor Edmund "Pat" Brown was in Europe and was en route back home because of the rioting, he told me to fly to JFK airport in New York where the governor would land and change planes. I was to brief the governor on what was transpiring. Whatever I had to tell Governor Brown could easily have been told by telephone. But LBJ, as I've noted before, was shrewd about using symbols. All radio and television stations were covering the Watts story and now there was a new piece, albeit a small one, that the President's counsel was flying to New York to brief Governor Brown on what was going on in that major crisis.

For me, this was a piece of excitement. I asked the Air Force aide's office for transportation. In practically no time, a military helicopter was on the White House lawn and I was whisked to Andrews Air Force Base, where an eight passenger military jet got me to JFK airport in less than an hour. I was immediately led into a small conference room where Governor Brown was waiting. The conversation with him was easy and there wasn't really much to tell him that he had not already learned. Instead, I told him about the time in 1958, when he was California's Attorney General and I was in Los Angeles being sounded out about joining the group of lawyers being assembled by the Assistant Attorney General to work on the United States Supreme Court law suit over the waters of the Colorado River. Obviously, I hadn't taken the job. LBJ's dispatching me to brief Governor Brown on the Watts situation may have seemed a little gimmicky to me at the time, but it had the desired effect of demonstrating the Administration's continuing involvement in the critical events taking place in Watts.

UNCOMFORTABLE ASSIGNMENTS

It was not easy to tell the President that you didn't want to do something that he asked you to do. One of the most uncomfortable assignments given me arose out of Walter Jenkins' personal tragedy. Walter had gone to a reception celebrating the opening of a new office by *Newsweek* magazine in October 1964. Later, he was arrested at the YMCA building near the reception and charged with soliciting sex from an undercover policeman in the men's room. Following his arrest, Walter called Abe Fortas, who together with Clark Clifford asked *The Washington Star* editor to sit on the story. The editor agreed to hold off unless and until the story broke, but a story as big as that one always manages to get out. Inaccurately, it was widely assumed that LBJ had called Fortas and Clifford asking them to contact the newspapers to try to squelch the story.

When Walter was arrested, Bill Moyers called me in Lincoln, Nebraska, where I had given a talk to the regional meeting of the National Rural Electric Cooperatives Association and said I'd better get back to Washington pronto. By the time I arrived, there wasn't much to do except feel great sorrow for Walter.

The real heroine was Mrs. Johnson. Without checking with anybody, she issued her own statement saying that Walter Jenkins was the most dedicated, loyal staff member; that he was the best family man she knew; and that regardless of what trouble he may be in, she stood by him as a stalwart friend. Of course, timing is everything. Within a few days, Soviet Prime Minister

Nikita Khrushchev was deposed and his story wiped everything off the front pages, including Walter's story.

Shortly after the November 1964 election, Moyers called and said that the President wanted me to review the FBI files of the entire White House staff. Presumably, every White House employee's file was available, but because Walter had been arrested a number of years previously and nobody knew about it, LBJ wanted the files reviewed. I said to tell him I really didn't want to do that job. He called back and said the President thought I was exactly the right person for the assignment: I was judicious, conscientious, and discreet. (In my mind, I added, and a Kennedy man).

It was a lousy task, but I had little choice. Besides, I'm a sucker for anyone who tells me I'm far and away the best person for a particular assignment. Sure enough with very tight security, a pile of boxes descended on me with everyone's FBI file (except mine). As is generally well known, those files are mostly unevaluated miscellaneous items such as newspaper clippings, results of FBI investigative reports on the top staff who required security clearances, rumors including any about drinking or philandering, police records and any litigation references. The procedure has been likened to a vacuum cleaner. For the most part, there were no problems and to me most of the derogatory material was not serious. In the very few instances where I thought the President should know about the material in a particular file, we discussed it, and I am happy to report that no one was eased out or even questioned about their background. It was an uncomfortable and tedious task. Fortunately, I have a well-developed capacity for misremembering.

Another not-so-pleasant task arose out of some information LBJ received about a sub-cabinet official. He asked me to look into the matter. I did and concluded that although the particular deed was not criminal, it was highly inappropriate action and would be an embarrassment to the administration if revealed. LBJ asked if he should be eased out. Despite the fact that I'm an old softy, I said, "Yes," and Johnson had me make the call and tell the fellow to resign, which I did and he did.

THE 25TH AMENDMENT

In 1964, LBJ was hospitalized at the Naval Hospital in Bethesda, Maryland, for an operation. Although it was not deemed serious, a newspaper article questioned whether LBJ had any kind of agreement with Speaker of the House John McCormack governing procedures to be used in the event of LBJ's disability. At that time, there was no Vice President and no procedure for filling the post, but we had developed such a document for LBJ, as Vice

President, in the event of a similar situation in the case of President Kennedy. We simply had not gotten around to issuing it.

The situation was handled by my drafting the agreement and sneaking into the hospital through a back entrance, where it was signed by LBJ and delivered to Speaker McCormack for his signature. I don't believe the question arose again, but I remember thinking I had just played a role in a Grade C movie.

This experience led directly to the effort to provide procedures for selecting a Vice President in the event the position was unoccupied and for handling the tricky questions of presidential disability. The lead was taken by Senator Birch Bayh, Democrat of Indiana, who was the Chairman of the Senate Judiciary subcommittee dealing with Constitutional issues. I worked closely with him and with Justice Department lawyers to develop the procedures. In early 1965, the Congress approved the 25th Amendment to the Constitution, and sent it to the states for ratification. It was well received by state legislatures and became effective in 1967, in time to be applied when Nixon's Vice President, Spiro Agnew, the former governor of Maryland, resigned under pressure from the Justice Department for accepting money from Maryland contractors in his vice presidential office. Congressman Gerald Ford of Michigan was nominated by President Nixon and confirmed by a majority vote of both the Senate and the House of Representatives to be the new Vice President. He then succeeded to the Presidency when President Nixon resigned in 1974. Former New York Governor Nelson Rockefeller became the Vice President with the same procedure being employed.

AN UNORTHODOX APPROACH

One of the stickiest and most contentious issues that came my way was the planned construction of an electric transmission line connecting the high voltage line of the Pacific Gas & Electric Company with a major experimental nuclear reactor to be built at Stanford University. The new line was to pass near the upscale San Francisco suburb of Woodside. On one side of the controversy were the landowners and residents who insisted that the line should be located underground in order to protect the beautiful vistas. They were represented by a local attorney, Pete McCloskey, who later was elected to Congress from the District. On the other side was Glenn Seaborg, the Chairman of the Atomic Energy Commission and California Congressman Chet Hollifield, the Chairman of the Congressional Joint Committee on Atomic Energy.

They argued that the cost of under grounding the line was grossly excessive and that the town of Woodside had ugly local distribution lines that were not underground. They charged that the wealthy landowners selfishly wanted to protect their views at great cost to the federal taxpayers and they didn't believe the executive branch should yield to them. A number of alternatives to putting the line underground were considered. The one that made the most sense was to construct the line above ground but instead of a straight line, it would be located close to a wooded area and the normal supporting poles would not be used but camouflaged poles designed to blend with the forest background would be put in place. Because the initial power requirement for the reactor would have to be increased in a few years, this option could be tried and if it didn't work, the parties could re-start the battle. In the meantime, we could see whether the town of Woodside had done anything about its ugly distribution lines.

The contending parties were not enthusiastic about the proposed alternative, but we had one more wrinkle to offer. Mr. Laurence Rockefeller had agreed to go out to Woodside to survey the situation and advise all concerned of how he regarded the compromise proposal. He enjoyed a solid reputation as a concerned environmentalist and a developer of facilities that harmonized with their natural surroundings. As pictured in Photo 12.2, I recall telling President Johnson about the proposal in the little office used as a makeshift barber shop in the West Wing. His question to me was: "Is this going to get me in trouble?" What could I say but, "I don't think so." And it didn't. Mr. Rockefeller reported that he thought the compromise plan could succeed and should be tried. This unorthodox approach worked to everyone's satisfaction.

There are two points to this story worth noting. First, there were those who thought I didn't have to let this get to the White House, and they were correct. But when it was discussed with me, I thought the AEC position was too flat-footed and, clearly, concerns about the environment were gaining in national consciousness. If we had not been able to come up with a plausible option, it could have caused some White House grief. The second point was the use of a non-governmental agent. On occasion, a little irregular approach can be helpful. I must add that if Laurence Rockefeller had recommended against the alternate plan, I wouldn't be using it as an illustration of ingenuity.

BOBBY KENNEDY

One of the first things the new President said to me after the assassination was that he wanted me to continue to work with Bobby Kennedy, and to keep him fully advised of what I was up to. Now, it was not a closely held secret that

Photo 12.2.   President Johnson discusses a controversial transmission line connecting the high voltage line of the Pacific Gas & Electric Company with a major experimental nuclear reactor to be built at Stanford University in the White House Barber Shop, August 24, 1965. L-R: President Lyndon Johnson; Assistant to the President Bill Moyers (seated); White House Barber Steve Martini; Special Counsel Lee C. White. Photo Credit: Yoichi R. Okamoto. (Personal Collection of Lee C. White)

there was no love lost between these two men. I took President Johnson's admonition seriously and did as I had been instructed to do.

As fate would have it, I happened to be in the Oval Office one day when LBJ was giving Press Secretary George Reedy unshirted hell. LBJ was standing behind his desk and he had some object in his hand which he was banging on his desk and shouting repeatedly, "Staff work, staff work—Goddammit, every body's got good staff work but me." I thought to myself, if he ever yelled at me like that, I'd curl up and die on the spot. But good old George who had a big head and an awful lot of hair stood there like a big old sheep dog nodding and taking it calmly. When Johnson noticed me, he said "What do you want?" I said, "It's nothing that won't wait," and got the hell out of there. What Reedy knew and I didn't know was that in an hour and a half, Reedy was going to tell his press briefing that the President had decided that no member of his cabinet would be his vice-presidential running mate in 1964. It was the day he was dumping Bobby, and he was a little uptight about it. Bobby's response was, "I sure took a lot of good guys over the side of the boat with me."

THE 1964 DEMOCRATIC NATIONAL CONVENTION

The Democratic National Convention took place in August 1964 in Atlantic City, New Jersey. With an incumbent President, and especially one who had been given highest marks for his conduct of the office following JFK's assassination, there was no doubt that LBJ would be nominated. His idea was to pump a little suspense into the convention by playing games with possible running mates. (This was one of the manifestations of his meaner side.) He publicly dangled the nomination in front of Senator Tom Dodd of Connecticut (father of the current Connecticut Senator Christopher Dodd) and the two senators from Minnesota, Hubert Humphrey and Eugene McCarthy. In the end, it was Humphrey, but not without humiliating McCarthy by letting the press speculate about his choice and waiting until the last moment. The speculation about Senator Dodd being the running mate had subsided.

LBJ had done something similar in letting Nick Katzenbach stew before nominating him to be Attorney General. When Bobby Kennedy resigned to run for the Senate in 1964, LBJ made Nick Acting AG. There is (or at least was) an obscure provision of law requiring the post of AG to be vacant no more than thirty days. I wrote a memorandum to LBJ pointing this out, but the President waited for a few months before acting on the nomination. I believe he was testing Nick's loyalty.

An incumbent really controls what goes on at a party convention, except for challenges to state delegations. Although there was no doubt about the outcome of the convention, the challenge to the all-white Mississippi delegation by an impressive competing group of black Mississippians caught the press's attention. Of course, LBJ was not happy about that. My recollection is that Bill Moyers handled negotiations with the group, which was ably represented by civil rights advocate Joe Rauh. I met with Senator Clinton Andersen of New Mexico, the Chairman of the Senate Committee on Interior and Insular Affairs, and together we wrote the natural resources plank of the party platform in a session lasting about an hour and a half.

LBJ wanted the big day when he would be nominated by the party to fall on his birthday, August 27th, but he knew that he couldn't do much about the fact that Bobby Kennedy would make a speech at the convention and that the convention would go absolutely wild; and it did. The convention was a treat for me, because I was able to bring my family to enjoy the beach and the excitement. After the convention, we drove to the World's Fair on Long Island, which was great fun. On the way home, I ran out of gas on the Delaware River Memorial Bridge. When I stalled, a Delaware state trooper magically drove up behind me weaving his way through dozens of cars on that bridge. I didn't want to baldly admit I had run out of gas, especially with all of those kids in the station wagon, so I pretended I didn't know what the trouble was. He looked at me and got in his car and pushed my car across the bridge into a gas station on the Delaware side. I expected a good sized fine since I'd screwed up traffic pretty badly, but he must have thought that I'd suffered enough with the embarrassment in front of my family and there was no ticket.

I did not play a major role in the election of 1964. However, I did work with Mitchell Cieplinski of the State Department whose assignment was to be liaison to the various ethnic groups throughout the country. In mid-1964, we scheduled a major meeting in the East Room of the White House for the leaders of organizations such as the Polish-American Congress and the media that covered such groups. Mitch knew the players and we assembled approximately three hundred people. President Johnson, whose home town of Johnson City was in an area settled by German immigrants, was right at home with the group talking about his experiences and about the administration's accomplishments and prospective programs of interest to those present. Generally, LBJ was not a polished speaker and tended to appear mechanical in speeches on television and before very large crowds. But when he was unscripted and letting his thoughts pour out, he could be most effective. That particular day, he was at his best, and he owned the audience. The prominently displayed highly favorable articles in the ethnic press constituted a real vote-getting proposition for the President.

LBJ appeared unbeatable and when the Republicans nominated Senator Barry Goldwater of Arizona, a right wing conservative, it was pretty clear that LBJ would win the election. He won it in a landslide.

"DIRTY WATER"

One of the most bizarre environmental moves resulted from an old friend of President Johnson calling him from Texas and complaining about the federal government bugging him about some polluted water. LBJ said he'd look into it and told his secretary, Juanita Roberts, to get Secretary of Interior Udall on the phone. When LBJ started to tell Udall about the call he had received, Udall told him that the program was administered by the Public Health Corps within the Department of Health Education and Welfare. LBJ said, "Stew, when I think of dirty water, I think of you." And so help me, he instructed Joe Califano and me to prepare a reorganization plan transferring the program from HEW to Interior. We had to go to Capitol Hill and explain why the transfer was being proposed. Senator Muskie, chairman of the Environmental Subcommittee, said to us, "Are you guys nuts?" Biting our tongues, we explained that a new agency with a new charge would be more energetic and more efficient.

Muskie went along with the change and everything worked out alright because, five years later when the Environmental Protection Agency was established, the program became part of EPA.

But the saga continues. The National Park Service, a part of the Interior Department, had jurisdiction over the George Washington Memorial Parkway, which served many Virginians as their route to downtown Washington, DC. It so happened that the Park Service had set the speed limit at 45 miles per hour. One morning, as Bobby Kennedy's limousine was doing about 60 mph on the Parkway, he was given a speeding ticket by a very bold Park Service policeman. When Bobby got to his office, he called Stewart Udall and said, "Why don't you raise the speed limit to 55?" What do you know—that's what it became and is now.

My favorite episode is about how the DC Memorial Stadium came to be named the Robert Francis Kennedy Memorial Stadium, or "RFK" Stadium for short. The stadium had been built on grounds under the jurisdiction of the Park Service. Udall was a good friend of Bobby Kennedy and President Johnson was not (to put it mildly). So at 11:45 a.m. on January 20, 1969, when President Johnson and President-elect Richard Nixon were at the Capitol for the inaugural ceremony, Secretary Udall issued an order re-designating the stadium. Fifteen minutes later, President Johnson was out of office.

Chapter Thirteen

LBJ and Civil Rights

Following President Kennedy's assassination, President Johnson kept me in the civil rights slot and, if anything, enhanced my role. One of the earliest issues was a Saturday night call to my home. As it happened, we had dinner guests and I was not accustomed to receiving calls from President Kennedy at home. The question was should LBJ invite some or all of the civil rights leadership group to his ranch in Texas for a get-together session over dinner. My quick response was that he had been Vice President for three years and had never met with them in a social or family setting and that it would look too gimmicky to do so now. He said, "OK" and that was that. With the passage of time, I now think that I would have given a different reply. LBJ was very good with symbolism. Such a high profile arrangement as he proposed would most probably have been helpful. However, it is safe to say that, ultimately, it made no difference because his presidency, despite Viet Nam, will be credited with doing more for civil rights than any other administration except that of President Lincoln.

The President also asked me whether he should have his daughter Lynda move out of the segregated dormitory she lived in at the University of Texas in Austin. My response was that if she was there when he was Vice President and no one had raised the issue, why draw attention to the fact, especially since she was going to move into the White House when the semester ended? I was pretty good at saying, "No."

I found myself in a bit of a bind in my own family situation. We were living in the District of Columbia in a racially mixed neighborhood, and I had worked with the District's Superintendent of Education and the principal of Paul Junior High School, which my son attended, to create an environment for harmony among the student body by adopting special courses and bringing prominent persons to address the student body. Two years later, our daughter who attended Paul told us that the atmosphere was very rough and even threatening and class work was unsatisfactory. Because we lived close to Montgomery County, Maryland, we were able to have her transfer to a junior high school in Silver Spring, Maryland, paying an out-of-state annual fee of $750, which was slated to increase sharply and did. Her mother and I were content and quite happy to live in an integrated neighborhood. I served on the board of an organization called Neighbors, Inc., which worked with great success in persuading white home owners to remain as black families moved into the very attractive area. But we did not believe that our views should adversely affect our daughter's well being and education. With a number of younger children who would have to face the inconvenience of going to school in Maryland and the great expense, we chose to move to Montgomery County. In light of my civil rights assignment, I was prepared for criticism for leaving the District. Happily, only one local newspaper made a fuss about the matter.

THE SUMMER OF 1964

By the summer of 1964, things were heating up in Mississippi. I was kept apprised of what was going on there by the FBI. The White House FBI liaison was Cartha "Deke" DeLoach, and he or some other agent would, for example, call in the middle of the night to report that a house or church was ringed by Ku Klux Klan hoodlums. Mostly, it was for information but, on occasion, I had to answer the question of what should the FBI do. The FBI had infiltrated the Klan and had remarkable information. Additionally, I was among those on their limited distribution list to receive the agency's written reports, including the infamous reports of Dr. King's peccadilloes. But the high or low point occurred when Deke told me that the director would like to meet me. So, we tootled off to Mr. Hoover's office. I waited in an anteroom wondering what my FBI file contained when Deke told me to enter. I've never been presented to a king or queen, but my imagination told me that was what I was experiencing. It was all small talk and lasted no more than nine or ten minutes.

The Mississippi Civil Rights Workers

A major event occurred in June 1964. Three young men who were in Mississippi trying to register blacks to vote were reported missing: Andrew Goodman, a white boy from, New York City; Michael Schwerner, another white boy from Westchester County, New York; and James Chaney, a black boy from rural Mississippi. Democratic Congressman William Fitts Ryan, who represented the district in which the Goodman family lived, called me and said that the parents of the missing civil rights workers would like to meet with the President. When I asked why, he said that it was to let the parents and the country know that the federal government was doing everything in its power to find the boys. He said he was also calling on behalf of Republican Congressman Ogden Reid, who represented Westchester County. They had talked to Mrs. Chaney, the mother of the Mississippi boy, who joined in the request to see the President. I told him I'd get back to him.

I walked down the stairs to the first floor and caught the President standing between the Oval Office and the large office occupied by the appointments secretary. I looked up at LBJ and told him about the Ryan call. He looked down at me and said, "It's just the beginning of summer and if I meet these folks, I'll have to meet with everyone else whose kids are in trouble." He said, "No." I replied saying something like, "It's not like we're deciding whether to invite them. I've got to go back and tell Ryan "No." "That's right. You've got to tell him 'No.'" Now, he had said "No" a second time. Still looking up at him, I said, "And I'll be saying "No" to Brownie Reid as well. *The Herald Tribune* [owned by the Reid family] will headline a story saying, 'President refuses to meet with parents of missing civil rights workers.'" Now the President was damned mad—mad at me because I kept after him after he'd told me "No" a couple of times, and really mad at the thought of *The Herald Tribune* publishing such a headline.

When LBJ was angry, there was no doubt about it. He looked down at me and saw an invisible tag saying, "Inherited from Kennedy—won't understand." Then he spied Jack Valenti in the far corner of the room looking out the French window, talking on the phone and completely oblivious of our conversation. Like a thunderbolt crossing the room, he shouted "Goddamit, Valenti, every time I see you, you're on that (bleeping) telephone!!" Of course, Valenti hadn't the foggiest idea of what that was about, but he dropped the phone like it was radioactive.

The President met with the parents, and it was a warm, emotional session. He was absolutely superb with them and they were most appreciative. During the meeting, Mr. Hoover called to report that the station wagon the boys were using had been found. Their hopes were raised only to learn later that the boys had been killed. I represented the President at the memorial service held in New York for the Goodman young man.

I use this story to demonstrate that it's possible sometime to argue with your boss and not get fired.

Camp David

One FBI report turned out to have a far-reaching impact. LBJ had decided to close Camp David as an illustration of his frugality but, happily, no announcement had been made. On the last weekend it was available in the late summer of 1964, my family was lucky enough to be there along with Secretary of State Rusk and his wife. On Saturday, Reserve Army Officer Lieutenant Colonel Lemuel Penn and three other black reserve officers were driving back home to Washington, DC, from Fort Benning, Georgia, after completing their active duty training tour. When they were at a stop light, a local car approached them and fired into their car, killing Colonel Penn. The FBI called the White House to inform me, and the White House operator, who knew where I was, put the call through to me while I was at the side of the swimming pool. I did whatever I would have done if I had been in my office.

The next Monday, I told Bill Moyers that it would be a mistake to close Camp David, and that he ought to tell the President. He said, "You do it." I replied that the President would pay more attention to him.—Moyers was a key aide to LBJ whom I had known in the Kennedy administration when he was the deputy to Sarge Shriver, the first director of the Peace Corps. He was calm and unflappable in an environment where there were many heated and excitable events taking place, and it was evident that LBJ had great confidence I him.—Moyers said, "Write him a memorandum." So I did, pointing out how a presidential aide could be readily located there (this was long before pagers and cell phones) but, more importantly, how Secretary Rusk could spend a pleasant weekend with his wife without being bothered by reporters, gawkers, or admiring autograph seekers. Moreover, it was a great place for meetings. Fortunately, the President reconsidered, and Camp David has earned a place in the history of peacemaking. Indeed, the Camp David Accords negotiated by Prime Minister Menachem Begin of Israel and President Anwar Sadat of Egypt under the watchful eye of President Carter have a special place in my recollections.

LEGISLATIVE ACCOMPLISHMENTS

How LBJ's legislative accomplishments were achieved was demonstrated during a meeting with the black leadership group who had asked to meet with the President to complain about the administration's failure to act on a particular problem (which escapes me at this time). Similar to the scene depicted in Photo 13.1, we were seated in the Oval Office, and the President leaned forward, which was his habit, and said, "I don't know what y'all want to talk to me about, but let me tell you that whatever it is, it isn't as important to yore people as the Education Bill that's up for a vote tomorrow. The count looks mighty close and we need all the help we can get. Lee, tell Larry O'Brien to

Photo 13.1.   Upon taking office, President Johnson urged the passage of pending civil rights legislation. President Johnson and Assistant Special Counsel Lee C. White are shown meeting with civil rights leaders in the Oval Office on January 18, 1964. Clockwise from center: President Lyndon Johnson (from the back); Whitney Young, Head of the Urban League; James Farmer, Head of the Congress of Racial Equality (partially obscured); Assistant Special Counsel Lee C. White; Roy Wilkins, Head of the National Association for the Advancement of Colored People (obscured); Dr. Martin Luther King, Jr., Head of the Southern Christian Leadership Conference. Photo Credit: Yoichi R. Okamoto. (Personal Collection of Lee C. White)

come down and bring his tally sheet with him so we can find out who we have to get working on."

Larry O'Brien showed up with his list and LBJ asked him who had to be "worked on." As O'Brien mentioned a particular senator's name, the President would say, "Now which one of you has some way of getting to that one?" Wouldn't you know it? The gang, putting off whatever was bothering them, walked out of the Oval Office with specific assignments and went up to the hill to do their lobbying. The bill passed and it was, indeed, important to the group's constituency.

What the incident demonstrated was President Johnson's single-minded approach to legislative objectives. He seemed to view a bill like a target on the wall, and every device and pressure he could bring to bear on that target was focused on it until the legislative goal was achieved. Then there would be a new target in place.

The Civil Rights Act of 1964

The Kennedy civil rights bill that was pending at the time of the assassination, which was greatly enhanced from the earlier version submitted in the spring, had been moving but wasn't breaking any speed records. Upon its introduction in June 1963, Bobby Kennedy had testified on it for nine days. There was some encouragement in early November, but blockbusting legislation, especially when complex and controversial, is rarely on a fast track. President Johnson, the shrewd legislative operative that he was, understood how to appeal to Congress and the nation and, in the wake of the assassination, urged passage of the pending civil rights bill, without modification, as a tribute to the martyred President who had proposed it. With Larry O'Brien and his team and the Justice Department working together, the push was on.

A key player was Senator Everett Dirksen, Republican of Illinois and the Senate Minority Leader. LBJ was at his best in courting Dirksen. In addition, an Ohio Republican Congressman, William McCulloch, who was the ranking minority member of the House Judiciary Committee was crucial to securing the passage of the legislation. Senator Cooper of Kentucky, my former boss, was among the Republicans and one of the few southern senators supporting the bill.

After Bobby Kennedy left the Justice Department to run for the Senate from New York, the Justice team, with Acting Attorney General Nick Katzenbach in the lead role, did the serious lobbying and negotiating over the language of the bill. The passage of the Civil Rights Act in July 1964, after overcoming a lengthy filibuster in the Senate, was a monumental achievement that has been eloquently described by Nick Katzenbach in *Lyndon Johnson Remembered: An Intimate Portrait of a Presidency*.

President Kennedy had often remarked that success has a thousand fathers and failure was an orphan. In the case of the enactment of this monumental piece of legislation, many factors played a part. From the Freedom Riders touring the South; sit-ins at lunch counters; the uprising in Birmingham, with Bull Connor's police dogs, fire hoses, and cattle prods; the 1963 March on Washington, DC; the killing of four little girls attending Sunday School by a bomb outside the Sixteenth Street Baptist Church in Birmingham, Alabama, in September 1963; the uprising in St. Augustine, Florida, with its beatings, acid, and an alligator in the city swimming pool; and a heightened level of concern by various national leadership groups; to the assassination of President Kennedy—the nation was ready for action. Clearly, the impact of television bringing these events into homes across the country was also a very significant factor.

The Voting Rights Act of 1965

President Johnson recognized the realities of political life and knew that blacks would gain considerable leverage if they could manage to obtain the vote and to have politicians court them for their votes. The poll tax device which had been used by many southern states to limit black voting had been eliminated, but that was not enough. So LBJ proposed federal legislation to ensure fair voting opportunities for minorities by prohibiting unfair and discriminatory qualifications, by providing monitors at voting booths, and by eliminating gerrymandering of Congressional Districts. He knew that pushing such legislation would be detrimental to the Democratic Party in many southern states, but he acted according to what he believed was the right thing to do.

A legislative draft had been prepared and we were developing a message to Congress to be forwarded with the draft bill when a group of civil rights demonstrators in Selma, Alabama, was brutally attacked by Alabama state police on "Bloody Sunday," March 7, 1965, with TV cameras focused on the event. One of the leaders was John Lewis, head of the Student Non-Violence Coordinating Committee, who was severely beaten by state troopers, as were a large number of others. The national revulsion at those scenes of brutality was the moral launching pad for the voting rights legislation.

As we were preparing to submit the legislation, I came up with a bright idea one Sunday afternoon as I was cutting the grass and trimming shrubs at home (it was easier to do it myself than to get my two teenage boys to help — besides, it was a good time for cogitating). The next day I went to see Bill Moyers and told him my suggestion and asked that he present it to LBJ. Moyers said, "You do it." I argued in vain that LBJ would be more likely to approve it if Moyers was involved.

As I explained to the President, there was no prohibition against the President addressing a Joint Session of Congress on a subject other than the annual State of the Union speech, and I suggested we arrange to have the presidential message on voting rights legislation delivered in person, rather than sending it to Congress as a mimeographed message. The only similar previous joint sessions we could think of that hadn't been for a State of the Union message were President Franklin Roosevelt's "Day That Will Live in Infamy" speech following the attack on Pearl Harbor, and President Johnson's resounding appeal to Congress and the nation on November 27, 1963, less than one week after the assassination, to support civil rights legislation as a tribute to President Kennedy.

It was a home run. LBJ called Speaker of the House John McCormack, of Massachusetts, asking him to invite the President to address a joint session. And the show was on.

The Joint Session assembled at 9:00 p.m. Eastern time on March 15, 1965, and LBJ swept into the House of Representatives chamber filled with the usual cheering crowd. The speech was carried on all national TV networks. President Johnson, who was no great orator, was at the top of his form, and the speech was one of his best, drafted by Dick Goodwin with contributions from me and others. I picked up the civil rights leadership group in a White House limousine and escorted them to a section of the gallery set aside for them. The place really rocked with LBJ's charge that ". . . it is all of us, who must overcome the crippling legacy of bigotry and injustice," followed by the refrain, "And we shall overcome." It was a smash hit.

Afterwards, we drove to the White House for a little victory reception. Everybody was in a good mood with a drink or two, engaging in a bit of self-congratulation, when at about 11:00 o'clock, LBJ said to Larry O'Brien, "Have you called Manny Celler (the Chairman of the House Judiciary Committee) to schedule hearings on the bill?" Then he turned to me and said, "Have you called Ben Bradlee (the managing editor of *The Washington Post*) to get a favorable editorial for the bill?" Again, that highly focused approach to legislation was in action. The Voting Rights Act was signed into law by LBJ less than five months later on August 6, 1965.

The Voting Rights Act has had the revolutionary effect on national politics that all predicted it would have. That includes the shellacking the Democratic Party suffered in southern and border states. At the time, LBJ predicted that the Voting Rights Act would spawn at least a generation of bad news for Democrats in those states and his forecast proved to be right on the nose.

THE DEPARTMENT OF
HOUSING AND URBAN DEVELOPMENT

Following up on a Kennedy proposal which never got off the ground because of strong political opposition to the possibility of a black cabinet officer, President Johnson decided to ask Congress to create a new cabinet department, the Department of Housing and Urban Development. It was not an easy legislative undertaking. There was criticism that the proposal was simply an elevation of HHFA to cabinet status. President Johnson tried to get as many functions from other programs to add to the basic HHFA activities without much success. After the bill was enacted September 9, 1965, speculation arose over who would be the first Secretary of the new department. Robert Weaver, a native of Washington, DC, with a doctorate from Harvard and a reputation as an excellent administrator, was the obvious choice, especially because he would be the first black to serve in a cabinet post, a factor that would appeal strongly to LBJ. But LBJ let him hang in the wind. He was concerned that appointing Weaver would lend credence to the claim that this wasn't really a new department but merely the old HHFA, a charge that could be answered by "so what?"

In addition, another possible choice was Whitney Young, head of the Urban League and a respected member of the civil rights leadership group. I was a staunch advocate for Weaver, because I knew his administrative talents and deemed him to be a natural, one who would hit the road running. Dr. Weaver was not an assertive individual and LBJ really didn't know him well, so I weighed in with some memos to the President on Weaver's behalf. Weaver felt embarrassed and even humiliated as time dragged on, and I appointed myself to be his hand-holder and adviser. I would go by his office about twice a week and listen to him tell me that LBJ could take the job and stick it in his ear. I would say, "Hang in there, Bob, I think the decision is imminent." He was finally named, confirmed, and served admirably. It was a stressful period for him, but in the year 2000, well after his death, he received proper recognition when President Clinton issued an Executive Order designating the HUD office building the Robert A. Weaver Building.

POLITICAL THIEVERY

This chapter on civil rights would not be complete without noting the masterful role of Louis Martin. Martin was as trusted and used by LBJ as he had been by JFK. At the time of the LBJ's 1965 inauguration, Louis demonstrated his finesse. The President called me and said that the FBI had advised that a group of blacks were planning to have protesters at the various facilities around the city where inaugural balls were to be held. When I relayed this information to Louis, he told me he'd get back to me shortly. He did, asking if I could get him five tickets to some of the balls. I told him I could get him ten tickets and, like magic, the demonstrations dissolved.

One day, Louis said to me, "Hey, Chief, what do you think about stealing Lincoln's birthday from the Republicans?" The next February the 12th, President Johnson had a White House reception for a few hundred of the nation's most active civil rights leaders and workers. Interestingly, when Louis pulled together the list of people to be invited, the list was submitted to Marvin Watson, who was President Johnson's "gatekeeper," or Appointments Secretary. As was the usual custom, the list was sent to the FBI for a check of police records of the people to be invited. Of course, virtually every one of them had arrest records, so Marvin told Louis they couldn't be invited.

When Louis brought this information to me, we went to Marvin to explain. Marvin had had no government experience: he had been assistant to

the President of the Lone Star Steel Company in Daingerfield, Texas. LBJ
had asked him to help straighten out the Democratic National Convention in
Atlantic City in 1964, and then to stay on and replace Kenny O'Donnell,
who was leaving the White House. Louis and I had to explain to Marvin that
we knew who these people were and there would be no problem in inviting
them. After all, President Johnson had enthusiastically approved the idea of
the reception.

The Lincoln's Birthday reception went off without a hitch. In fact, it was a
smash and garnered more favorable publicity than the usual Republican Lincoln Day Dinners, with *Newsweek* running an article with a photograph of
LBJ with the top leadership group.—It was a masterful piece of political
thievery.

GIVING AND TAKING CREDIT

One incident demonstrating Johnson's famous personal quirks was his decision that his Vice-President, Hubert Humphrey, was getting too much credit
and publicity for his civil rights activity and that he should have his wings
clipped. He called Attorney General Nick Katzenbach, Assistant to the President Joe Califano, and me to his office and told us that he wanted Humphrey
to bow out of civil rights activity. When LBJ left, we agonized over how we
could tell the Vice President who owned the oldest and greatest reputation for
leadership in civil rights advocacy that he was muzzled. Nick and I met with
the Vice President in his office and told him that the President believed a single administration voice on civil rights was desirable. Without hesitation,
Vice President Humphrey said, "Of course, tell the President that's no problem," and he stuck to the new script. As depicted in Photo 13.2, our relationships remained cordial.

What a trouper Humphrey was. He didn't say it, but I believe he thought
that if the fellow who had chosen him as Vice President wanted something
done a different way, that was alright with him. As we know, his loyalty to
LBJ's Vietnam policy to nearly the end of the 1968 campaign, in all likelihood, cost him the presidency.

We are far from having resolved our racial problems and eliminated discrimination in this country, but we have come a long way. President Kennedy
might have initially intended to hold off pressing for civil rights legislation until a second term, but he responded vigorously and effectively to the obvious
need to act on the nation's most difficult and intractable domestic problem
when the Birmingham situation threatened to get out of control. His successor,
LBJ, achieved considerable progress. Years later, some harsh critics of the

Photo 13.2.   Following the passage of landmark civil rights legislation, a cordial and relaxed mood prevailed at this meeting with the President and Vice President in the Oval
Office on September 22, 1965. L-R: Assistant to the President Joseph A. Califano, Jr.; Attorney General Nicholas de B. Katzenbach; Special Counsel Lee C. White; Vice President
Hubert Humphrey; President Lyndon Johnson. (In attendance but not pictured: Bill Moyers) Photo Credit: Yoichi R. Okamoto. (Personal Collection of Lee C. White)

Johnson Administration's Vietnam policies, such as the late, noted economist
John Kenneth Galbraith, and former Senator George McGovern, remarked that
upon hearing the tapes of LBJ's conversations about Vietnam, especially with
Georgia Senator Richard Russell, Johnson's mentor and longtime friend and
the chairman of the Senate Armed Services Committee, they realized how hard
LBJ tried to disengage in Vietnam. They observed that his great accomplishments on the domestic affairs front and, especially, in the area of civil rights
should not be held hostage to the Vietnam misfortunes. History will surely accord Presidents Kennedy and Johnson considerable credit for progress in this
vital area, and I can take some satisfaction in the knowledge that I had the opportunity to play even a small part in that progress.

Chapter Fourteen

Leaving the White House Staff

Toward the end of 1965, I began to think about leaving the White House. As great as the job was, I'd been there nearly five years. My biological clock seemed to be set somewhere between three and three and a half years: I was in the Army for three and a half years; law school for three years; TVA for three and a half years; Senator Kennedy's office for three years (with an eight month gap with the Hoover Commission); and Senator Cooper's office for three years. The oldest of our five children was then seventeen years old and the specter of college tuitions presented itself. I didn't believe I was burned out, but it just seemed to be the right time. My wife and I discussed the situation and the decision to move on was made.

I had observed that people who left LBJ were regarded by him as disloyal ingrates, maybe traitors, but certainly deserters. The one major exception was Horace "Buzz" Busby, who seemed to flit in and out of LBJ's orbit rather smoothly. So I got in touch with Buzz and asked him what the key was. He said, "You've got to give him a reason he can't really object to because he can't do anything about it." When I told him about the genuine need for money for college for a gang of kids, he said that was a winner. And so the letter was written in January 1966 and hand delivered to LBJ's secretary, Juanita Roberts. Interestingly, LBJ's reaction was to call Bill Moyers and raise hell with him because he hadn't told LBJ I was thinking of leaving. He expected Moyers to know what was going on among the staff and to keep him advised. But, of course, Moyers didn't know.

THE MASTER PERSUADER

In the summer of 1965, a little dance was going on between Joe Swidler, the FPC chairman and LBJ. Joe's term was expiring and the question of his reappointment was being considered. Joe had done an excellent job in turning around the agency that former Harvard Law School Dean, Jim Landis, had called the worst of all. Because Joe, who was my boss at TVA, and I were old friends, I was the middleman. I believed Joe wanted another term but he was pretty stiff necked and wanted LBJ to ask him to stay. LBJ could be a little rigid himself and wanted Joe to ask to be reappointed. While this was going on, Joe's term ended; but under the governing statute, he was authorized to remain until his successor was confirmed.

In October, Joe said he was leaving. He and my very good friend Dave Freeman, who was Joe's principal assistant at the FPC, decided to start their own law firm and leased space in a building near the White House. Before they could leave and move into the newly rented space, the massive power failure hit New York and the Northeast. Joe and Dave agreed to stay on at the FPC to conduct the investigation into the blackout.

I had not been deluged with offers to take jobs in the private sector. There was one exception. I had worked closely with Nick Katzenbach of the Justice Department in developing legislation creating Comsat (the Communications Satellite Corporation), a hybrid organization supported with federal governmental funding in its formative period with the expectation of its ultimate transformation into a privately financed and operated company. LBJ had named Leonard Marks to the Comsat Board. Leonard was a communications lawyer who had helped the Johnson's in their radio and television licensing and other matters. I knew Leonard from my very close friendship with one of his law partners, Stanley Cohen. Leonard told me he would like to propose me as the general counsel of the new outfit. It promised to be an interesting and lucrative job, but it was easy for me to decline the offer. I doubted that President Johnson would have let me go, but more importantly, I did not want to be Leonard's man in the job. Quite a bit later during the 1972 presidential campaign, he became the Treasurer of Democrats for Nixon, aligning himself with Nixon's Treasury Secretary John Connelly, who resigned and headed Democrats for Nixon.

I wanted to move into the private sector and had held discussions with Berl Bernhard, my old buddy from the Civil Rights Commission, and a small congenial group of lawyers. Jim Verner had held a high post at the Civil Aeronautics Board, and Gene Liipfert represented a major trucking firm. We seemed to get on well, although nothing had been signed and sealed when the FPC matter heated up.

The blackout report was wrapped up in January 1966, just as my letter hit LBJ. I had been involved in the FPC succession matter from the outset and considered it quite possible that LBJ might offer the spot to me.

The first emissary from LBJ was my old friend and colleague John Macy, Chairman of the Civil Service Commission, and LBJ's major appointment headhunter. I told John I had given the FPC spot serious consideration and had decided against it if it were offered, and I went through the song-and-dance about money. Next came Bill Moyers with the same pitch that LBJ thought I was the right fellow, and he got the same response.

Then the master persuader himself asked me to come down to see him. We went into the very small office adjoining the Oval Office and started to talk, although I was doing more listening than talking. He explained that this was a difficult slot for him to fill because of his Texas background: "They all think I'm a Texas President, but I'm a United States President." He told me that my background was ideal for the job, that he knew me to be conscientious and fair-minded (of course, I agreed with all that)—and that I had something else: identification with President Kennedy. He said that he knew that I was concerned about money and he would ask me to commit only to two years. As far as money goes, he said, "You know that Tommy the Cork [Thomas Corcoran, one of FDR's well known aides] has made a fortune representing utilities before the FPC. I tell you that after two years there, those utility guys will be lined up outside yore door and they'll have to take tickets like they do at meat markets. You won't have to ever worry about money."

Then he got to the clincher: He pulled out of his jacket pocket a copy of a letter he had written to Abe Fortas about going to the Supreme Court. Basically, it said that LBJ had just signed an order sending an additional 75,000 troops to Vietnam, and they didn't have the option of saying "No." Abe had told him "No" three times, and, by God, LBJ wasn't taking that answer again. I thought to myself that I'd be willing to go on to the Supreme Court if he wanted me to.

I hadn't said much but I told him that when the President of the United States asks me to do something, I certainly have to consider it seriously. I would discuss it with my wife and get back to him soon. He didn't look overjoyed and as soon as I left, he called Marvin Watson, his gatekeeper, sitting immediately outside of the office. According to what Marvin told me, the President said, "Marvin, tell Macy to send me some names, that sumbitch ain't going to take it." Through the grapevine, I learned that after I left his office, he had asked Manny Cohen, the very effective Chairman of the Securities and Exchange Commission, to move over to the FPC, and Manny had turned him down.

Well, that "sumbitch" thought it over, discussed it at home and decided to accept. I liked the notion of being in charge. I agreed that it was a tough spot for

LBJ to fill and I liked the idea of being of help to the President of the United States. I especially liked the fact that, unlike most appointees, I didn't seek the job, it sought me. So, I would not, in the slightest, be beholden to any groups, including those I was sympathetic to for their support. That's about as independent as one can get. And LBJ was probably right. I would be able to make a living after being at the FPC, although I didn't quite see that long line of utility executives outside my law office holding numbered cards. I did not want to cut off my relationship with the Kennedy's so I visited Bobby in his senate office and told him what I was contemplating. He said, "By all means, do it."

I told the President I had decided to take the post and he was pleased. I knew how LBJ worked and was not surprised that I was asked to sit on the information until the White House could make the announcement. What LBJ did was attempt to offset the departure of a deputy press secretary named Fleming (I don't know whether he jumped or was pushed) by announcing my appointment and that of Elmer Staats to be the Comptroller General at the same press briefing. Our jobs, especially Elmer's, were fairly big and the Fleming story was lost in the shuffle.—LBJ at his best.

NOT A HOUSEHOLD NAME

The press reaction was almost totally positive. My name was not a household word, but I had worked with many reporters and enjoyed a reputation for fairness and it was a good feeling to read good things about my appointment. Elmer's reception, if anything, was more positive. *The Washington Post* ran a good-sized, front page article in the "Style" section with pictures of my wife and all the kids. It was a happy time.

My nomination was referred to the Senate Commerce Committee, where I was in happy hands. The chairman was Warren Magnuson of Washington, and the ranking Republican was Norris Cotton of New Hampshire (my former secretary in Senator Kennedy's office, Elva Benting, was now Cotton's secretary, so I knew him fairly well). I had worked closely with the key staff members, so it looked like and was a cakewalk. The presidential certificates of office at the White House had listed me as a resident of Nebraska, so the nominating papers had the same designation. I asked the two Nebraska senators, Roman Hruska and Carl Curtis (both mighty conservative Republicans) if they would accompany me to the nomination hearing and say a word on my behalf. Both agreed to, as did my old boss Senator Cooper; so I was in pretty good shape on the Republican side.

My son Bruce was a Senate page, and he told me that one day he got on the little trolley-like car heading to the Capitol and Senator Curtis got on. He asked where Bruce was from. He was very interested to get the answer "Nebraska." When Bruce answered the next question as to who his father was, the conversation stopped cold.

There really were no tough questions, but I had a stray thought as I sat in the witness chair: "I wish I'd paid more attention to the law school course on Government Regulation of Business." The nomination moved without any difficulty.

The swearing-in was to take place in the East Room of the White House; thus, there was no serious limit on who could be invited. Lots of relatives and friends, the FPC Commissioners and principal staff, White House staff, and other government associates were there on March 2, 1966. My mother, who hated to fly in airplanes only partly because they cost so much, flew to Washington, DC for the event. I asked Judge Barrett Prettyman, of the U.S. Court of Appeals for the District of Columbia, to swear me in, because I had done some work with him and I thought highly of him. The President's remarks were not exactly world-shaking, but you're forced to be complimentary when talking about someone you have appointed. He didn't say I'm losing the ablest fellow to ever work here. He said, "He always told me what he thought, not what he thought I thought."

And so my days at the White House came to an end. When I left the best staff job there is and went to a relatively obscure agency as a member and Chairman of the Federal Power Commission, I remembered Martin Luther King's refrain from the Negro spiritual with which he concluded his "I Have A Dream" speech during the 1963 March on Washington: "Free at last! Free at last! Thank God Almighty, we are free at last!" I had been treading softly with someone else's reputation, and now I was on my own. Assistants would figuratively tug at my sleeve, telling me to vote this way or that way, dissent, blast the other side. But it would be my decision and I could be as bold or timid as I wanted to be.

Part Four

MY LATER CAREER

Chapter Fifteen

The Federal Power Commission

I was sworn in as Chairman of the Federal Power Commission on March 2, 1966. The FPC, which was succeeded by the Federal Energy Regulatory Commission in 1977, was an independent regulatory agency created by Congress in 1935 with responsibility for implementing the Federal Power Act and the Natural Gas Act. The Commission consisted of five members appointed by the President and confirmed by the Senate. No more than three of the five could be from the same political party.

The four commissioners I was to serve with initially were Charles Ross, a liberal Republican from Vermont; Lawrence O'Connor, a fairly conservative Democrat from Texas; David Black, a liberal Democrat from the state of Washington; and Carl Bagge, a conservative Republican from Illinois. In 1966, there were roughly a thousand employees, and regional offices in New York, Chicago, Houston, and San Francisco.

Prior to the Kennedy administration, the FPC was regarded as one of the least efficient and least effective of all federal regulatory bodies. A review of regulatory agencies undertaken by James Landis, the former Dean of Harvard Law School and former Chairman of the Securities and Exchange Commission, at the request of President Kennedy, deemed the FPC the worst of all. Under the leadership of Joe Swidler, my old boss from TVA days, it had been turned around and enjoyed a good reputation. Swidler was a very intelligent and determined fellow who wanted to get a lot accomplished, but he tended to be autocratic and didn't believe he had to do a lot of handholding. This had been most apparent in the follow-up of the Commission's response to the massive power failure in the Northeast in November 1965. As the new fellow, I didn't have the personality or intensity to accomplish what Swidler did, but that was not what the Commission required. My softer approach was well received by my new colleagues.

143

THE FREEST BIRD IN THE SKY

I came to the Commission as the freest bird in the sky. Almost always, candidates for regulatory agencies seek support from interest groups, whether industry, consumer or other quarters. Frequently, they are sponsored by members of Congress. A key factor in my decision to go to the FPC was that the President knew me personally and had made the pitch to get me to accept the position. I didn't totally accept the fact that I was doing him a favor by accepting the appointment, but I believed there was a kernel of truth there. That's about as good as it gets. LBJ never once called to ask me to tilt one way or the other. Only one White House staff person called about a case, and I promptly turned him off.

I got a relatively free ride with the general press; the trade press was another story. The Commission and I got generally lousy reviews from trade publications, especially the *Oil & Gas Journal*. The only time I complained to the Washington editor was when an editorial criticizing me used the wrong middle initial for me. He said he knew darn well I'd complain about that.

For the most part, the independence of the regulatory bodies is respected by all: the members, the staff, the Executive branch, the Congress, the practitioners, and the press. Occasionally there are lapses, some of which rise to the level of scandal. One notable exception was the Congressional outcry at the Federal Energy Regulatory Commission's handling of the electric power crisis in California in the late 1990s.

Shortly after I got to the Commission, Dick McGuire, the Chairman of the Democratic National Committee, called and asked if I would be willing to meet with Walker Cisler, the CEO of Detroit Edison Company. Because there was no case involving the company before the Commission, I said I'd see him. I did and it was a cordial session. When I learned that McGuire had received $5,000 for arranging the visit, I joked that I'd have set it up for $1,500. Of course, I saw many utility executives, and I couldn't imagine why anyone would have thought you had to have an intermediary set up a meeting. There was a fraternity of lobbyists retained by many companies to keep tabs on what the FPC was up to, to try to get to staff and members, as well as to learn what was happening and even to sway a decision. I was spared that, and I believe most commissioners were not susceptible to that kind of pressure. But there was an interesting story involving one such individual.

Back in my White House days, my wife told me she had received a call from a woman who wanted to invite us to dinner. The caller said she and her husband had met us at Tom and Mary Clark's house. Tom Clark was an associate justice of the Supreme Court. I said there was something screwy about this because we had never been to the Clarks' house. Because I didn't know who he was, I said, "Let's just say 'No.'" One night after I had moved to the FPC, my wife told me about some woman who had called to invite us to dinner and said she and her husband had met us at Tom and Mary Clark's house—the identical spiel. Because her husband was an FPC lobbyist, this time I could say, "Because I know who he is, let's just say 'No.'"

THE CHAIRMAN'S RESPONSIBILITIES

The chairman had certain responsibilities in the administration of the agency, as distinguished from his vote on matters before the Commission where each member's vote was his (it was a long time before a woman was named to the FPC). For example, I could replace the heads of the various units within the agency. One of my first decisions was to replace the executive director who was a very decent fellow but wasn't really up to what I thought the office should do. I brought over an old and much admired friend from the Air Force General Counsel's Office, Murray Comarow. Another major move was to ask Jack O'Leary, an economist from the Department of the Interior, to head the Bureau of Natural Gas. O'Leary had impressed me while I was in the White House, and although the Department could ill afford to lose someone with his talent, I was thinking about the FPC. From Swidler, I inherited a brilliant, if offbeat, General Counsel, Dick Solomon, and a first-rate group of lawyers. Stewart Brown, the Chief Engineer, was a highly competent understated leader who did an excellent job. In general, the Commission ran rather well and by the time I arrived, it had recovered from its reputation as one of the worst regulatory bodies.

One rather strange action involving the Department of the Interior was a three-way switch engineered by the late Senator Henry "Scoop" Jackson, Democrat of Washington. When I got to the Federal Power Commission, Dave Black, a protégé of Scoop was on the Commission. Thus, we could claim that the FPC with Commissioners Black and White was the only "integrated" commission in Washington. But Scoop persuaded LBJ to transfer Chuck Luce, who was the Administrator of the Bonneville Power Authority, the governmental agency which controlled the power generated by the numerous dams on the Columbia River and its tributaries, to become the Undersecretary of the Interior. The current undersecretary, John Carver, was to be appointed to the FPC, and Dave Black was to be named the Administrator of the Bonneville Power Administration. I was not happy with the switches, but there wasn't much I could do about it since Scoop was the Chairman of the Senate Committee on Interior and Insular Affairs.

Supreme Court Justice Abe Fortas, who had himself been the Undersecretary of the Interior in the FDR New Deal days, presided at the swearing in of

Dave Black as Bonneville Administrator, which I attended. I had grown a Van Dyke beard while my family and I had been at the beach, so Fortas jokingly said, "You sometimes sound like a Bolshevik, you don't have to look like one, too." The next time I was scheduled to testify before Congress, I took his advice and shaved the beard.

During my tenure, Ralph Nader had a crew of young bright followers called "Nader's Raiders" who undertook to examine federal agencies, rate them, and issue public statements generally sharply critical of them. After reading about the shellacking the Raiders gave the Federal Trade Commission, I had someone contact the Nader people and tell them that we welcomed the Raiders because it would help us determine where we were deficient. Of course, they never came.

COMMISSION UNDERTAKINGS

Pending before the Commission when I arrived was a blockbuster case pitting some of the major natural gas companies in the country against each other in a comparative proceeding to determine which group would be certificated to supply the vast markets of Southern California. Oral arguments had already been scheduled. I was asked if I wanted to delay consideration of the case because of its significance and complicated issues. I chose not to delay it. Each commissioner had assistants and the chairman three, so I was able to obtain input that sharpened the issues for me. Because the chairman has the prerogative of assigning which commissioner is to author an opinion, I assigned this big one to myself. The procedure then (and I believe now) starts with a discussion of the case among the members of the commission after which each member states his view of how the case should be resolved; the authoring member, working with staff, prepares a draft opinion which is circulated to the other members for review and comments. If there is unanimity, the draft is polished into final form and issued. If there is a dissent, the draft is circulated and is issued together with the majority opinion. In the Southern California case, Commissioner O'Connor dissented.

Among the major undertakings during my time at the Commission was the effort to achieve improved reliability of electric power service and to set the prices to be paid to natural gas producers in a major producing area, southern Louisiana, which covered the vast offshore producing area of the Gulf of Mexico. There was a steady diet of applications for certificates for new and enhanced natural gas pipelines, including pipeline gathering systems to bring gas from the deep wells in the Gulf of Mexico; applications for new hydro-electric projects; rate cases for electric utilities; issues dealing with importation of gas from Canada; and proposed mergers and acquisitions of natural gas pipeline companies.

The massive power failure in the Northeastern portion of the country in November 1965 shook confidence in the reliability of the nation's power supply. The review of the failure pointed to inadequate transmission line capacity, coordination among utilities, and monitoring of the interconnected systems. Working with staff, the Commission developed a program which would grant the FPC considerable authority over the utilities within each region of the country to monitor and to require overall coordination. A unanimous Commission with some diverse ideological members proposed the program to Congress for its consideration.

An alarmed industry which certainly would be averse to governmental involvement in "their" business found a Paul Revere-type in the person of Phil Sporn, the head of one of the nation's major utilities, the American Electric Power Company, operating in a number of mid-western states. Mr. Sporn, an engineer and a very effective executive, went around the country telling his fellow utility executives that they had to establish regional reliability councils capable of making the required improvements in electric reliability in those regions. He had not been elected president or chairman; he simply seized the initiative. And he had a great selling point: if the industry didn't do it, five pointy-headed bureaucrats at the FPC in Washington would. Nine regional councils under the guidance and leadership of a national electric reliability council (which was expanded to include Canadian operations) were created and funded by the industry. I confess that in the commission's consideration of the legislative proposal we offered Congress, the thought that we might just spur the industry to do what they had not previously done did cross my mind.

The partial deregulation of the industry, and the greatly increased concern about sabotage that has occurred since September 11, 2001, has prompted attention to be focused again on electric reliability. The massive power failure in August 2003, stretching from Detroit to Long Island, brought the issue forcefully to the nation's and the government's awareness. A legislative solution vesting ultimate enforcement responsibility and control in the hands of the Federal Energy Regulatory Commission is essential.

Another major legislative effort involved the rules and principles that would govern the renewal of licenses for hydroelectric dams. Most original licenses were granted for a fifty-year period. As the terms of many projects would be coming to an end in a few years, the Commission went about recommending to Congress legislation to govern the re-licensing procedures. Important issues included the conditions that must be applied to new licenses, reflecting the heightened interest in environmental and fish protection concerns. Also, there was the need to consider what weight to accord to licensees who had operated the projects in the event of competing applications for the right to take over the license and the amount, if any, that the original licensee should receive in compensation in the event another applicant was successful. Like the right to use the air waves regulated by the Federal Communications Commission, the power in the flowing rivers is owned by the public and must be regulated by the government.

THE STAFF-COMMISSION INTERACTION

Hydroelectric licensing happened to provide an interesting illustration of the interaction between the staff and Commissioners. At stake in the particular license proceeding before the Commission was the reach of the Commission's jurisdiction over the transmission lines leading from the hydro project. Charlie Ross and I argued for the maximum distance, while the three other members tended to support a narrower determination. As the debate wore on, Carl Bagge changed his position and went with Ross and me. I then realized that Stewart Brown, the Commission's Chief Engineer, had sat through the entire discussion without saying a word. Everyone in the meeting room knew that the debate was over and that it had gone my way and, also, that I had the authority to replace the staff personnel. Thoughtlessly, I asked Stew what he thought about the issue. He said quietly that he believed the shorter distance was the correct ruling, so Bagge jumped back. The lesson from that experience is that the staff really did think they were to call the issues as they saw them. That, of course, is the way it should be.

In the very controversial Phillips Petroleum decision, the United States Supreme Court in 1954 held that the FPC was required by the Natural Gas Act to fix the price at which gas was sold by producers at the wellhead to the national transmission companies that delivered the gas to local distribution companies, which sold to the ultimate consumer. Despite efforts to reverse that decision by legislation, Congress had not done so. (I earlier referred to the Senator Francis Case scandal that erupted over the legislation.) The FPC under Joe Swidler had struggled to come up with a price for gas from the area known as the Permian Basin. The case had been appealed to the Supreme Court, but our Commission believed we had to go forward to fix the rate for the much larger Southern Louisiana area. The Supreme Court affirmed the Permian Basin procedure and we were deep at it. The record consisted of thousands of pages of testimony before the Commission and hearing examiners, with hundreds of exhibits. The staff plowed through the record and provided analyses, and, finally, it was up to five fellows to see if they could agree on an appropriate price. Each of us wanted the decision to be unanimous, if at all possible. The five of us gathered in my office and simply went back and forth until we reached a decision very close to that which the Chief Hearing Examiner had recommended. It was unanimous.

A RELUCTANT MINORITY

As chairman, I was reluctant to be in the minority. But somewhere in my third year, I couldn't persuade my colleagues, and I couldn't possibly agree with their judgment. I did try to lobby my fellow commissioners (we are pictured in Photo 15.1) sometimes successfully and sometimes not. Carl Bagge, a big extroverted Chicago lawyer who had represented the Santa Fe Railroad, was my favorite target. When I would go to his office, he'd say, "Now what do you want me to do?" I'd tell him I just wanted a ride home because we did not live too far apart. But once in his office, I'd do my best to convince him that he really should vote with Charlie Ross and me. Charlie and I were almost always

Photo 15.1. Lee C. White served as Chairman of the Federal Power Commission from March 1966 to July 1969. Members of the Commission are pictured in the Commission Meeting Room at FPC Headquarters, Spring 1969 (L-R): John A. Carver (Idaho); Lawrence O'Connor (Texas); Chairman Lee C. White (Nebraska); Carl E. Bagge (Illinois); Albert Brooke (Kentucky). Photo Credit: Unidentified FPC photographer. (Personal Collection of Lee C. White)

on the same side of an issue, but we often needed a third vote. Frequently, I got Bagge to go along.

Charlie was a Vermont Republican who had served on the Vermont Public Service Commission and was a true liberal who had distinguished himself by a vigorous dissent in one of the earliest major environmental battles. Before I got to the Commission, it had approved an application of New York City's Consolidated Edison Company to build a pumped storage hydroelectric project, including a major dam, on the Hudson River. A pumped storage project operates by using electricity to pump water from a lower reservoir during low peak usage times to an upper reservoir and releasing it at high peak periods when the electricity generated is more valuable. Charlie's dissent was adopted by the U.S. Court of Appeals for the Second Circuit in reversing the Commission. The Scenic Hudson Preservation Conference decision was a major milestone in environmental law.

John Carver, who had been the Undersecretary of the Interior, brought his keen analytical mind and a somewhat feisty attitude to match that of Charlie Ross. The two were almost always on opposite sides of issues. Each worked hard and was an effective advocate. I deemed that arrangement to be highly useful because the three of us in the middle of the argument would benefit from a sharp debate and, hopefully, would reach a sound decision.

One incident involving Carl Bagge was extraordinary. An assistant to U.S. Senator Dirksen called Bagge and told him he had better vote right on the controversial Southern California gas supply proceeding (mentioned above) or he would regret it. When the story got to me, it was decided that we couldn't ignore such a crude threat; so Charlie Ross, Dave Black, and I (O'Connor was out of town) went to see Nick Katzenbach, the Attorney General. He shooed his staff out of the room and told us he would handle it personally because it was such a sensitive and potentially explosive matter. He told us to forget about it unless he got back to us. That was the end of the story. That was a happy result, because the FPC had had its share of previous scandals and conflicts.

There is an interesting story about Bagge's reappointment. Quite a few months before his term was ending, I wrote John Macy, LBJ's top headhunter, and told him that Bagge quite often voted right (meaning he went along with me), and because by law the slot had to be filled with a Republican or an independent, we probably couldn't do much better. But there was a juicier part to the story. Senator Everett Dirksen, Republican of Illinois, had been Bagge's initial sponsor. Bagge had been a lawyer for the Atchison, Topeka & Santa Fe Railroad, and was expected to be a strong industry supporter. For the most part, he voted an industry line, but occasionally he crossed over. I was certain some industry folks would tell Dirksen that Bagge had been a disappointment and that he ought to be dumped. If LBJ announced Bagge's reappointment fairly early, when Dirksen complained, LBJ could tell him, "Ev, I did it because I knew he was yore man." And that's exactly what happened, much to LBJ's delight. He and Dirksen were experienced horse traders, and LBJ savored having outfoxed him on this one. Bagge subsequently left the Commission to head the National Coal Association.

HEROES AND VILLAINS

One case that took a peculiar bounce involved a proposal by El Paso Natural Gas Company, a natural gas transmission company which served the California market, to acquire the Northwest Natural Gas Company, which served the Northwestern states. The Commission had rejected the acquisition and the issue was on appeal to the courts. Drew Pearson, the muckraking columnist, ran an item saying that President Johnson was ill-served by two of his staunchest allies: Clark Clifford and Lee White. Clifford, who had been an assistant to President Truman and a practicing lawyer, was widely regarded and respected as an adviser to presidents, including LBJ, who subsequently named him Secretary of Defense. The Pearson piece said the two of us had supported the merger and that would surely be counter to what LBJ would believe to be in the public interest. I had had some dealings with Pearson while on the White House staff and they were all positive. But I had thought to myself that it would be just fine if I did not appear in a Pearson column while at the FPC, either as a hero or a villain. I'm sure it wasn't always the case, but there was a presumption that the heroes in his columns had given him the story.

In any event, my first call of the day was to Marvin Watson, who was then the President's Appointments Secretary and sat right outside of the presidential office. I explained that the story was incorrect insofar as I was concerned because I had voted the other way. Clark was a lawyer for El Paso, but I wanted LBJ to know my position. Happily, I did not hear a word about the matter from Watson or anybody else. I called Drew Pearson and told him he had screwed up and that I knew who had given him the false story: a member of the California Public Utilities Commission. I asked why he didn't check with me. He said, "You know, I thought about it but I didn't get around to it." He said, "Don't worry; I'll make it up to you." Before that happened, Pearson died.

TESTIFYING

One of the responsibilities of the chairman is to testify before Congressional committees on behalf of the Commission. Occasionally, in major matters, for example, in presenting our reliability proposed legislation, the entire Commission would be present, but for the most part, it was the Chairman. In preparation, the standard approach of a dry run (or war games) was used to get me briefed and ready. Principal staff would array themselves as though they were committee members and I would sit in front of them in the witness chair. They would pepper me with questions and then follow-up questions and some of them would get pretty aggressive and even a little nasty. I knew they were helping me but I couldn't help but believe they got too much pleasure out of pushing me around. As it happened, I never had a question from a member of Congress that I hadn't heard in the dry run in a sharper and more vigorous fashion.

One question I really wasn't sure how to handle came from Congressman Eddie Boland, of Springfield, Massachusetts, who was the chairman of the House Appropriations Subcommittee that handled the FPC appropriations. I had known Eddie from my days in Senator Kennedy's office and the White House. When the hearing was concluded and the stenographer recording the proceeding had stopped, Eddie said, "Are you getting all the money you need?"

LIFE IN THE BUREAUCRACY

A beautiful illustration of the happenstance of life in the bureaucracy started at a cocktail party that Jack O'Leary, the head of the Bureau of Natural Gas, attended. He met Dr. David Rosenbaum, a mathematician with a heavy scientific bent. David headed a small group of about half a dozen brilliant mathematicians from Princeton, Stanford, and some other universities that were expert at network analysis. The group had been retained by the Office of Emergency Preparedness (OEP), headed by Price Daniel, the former Governor of Texas, and an LBJ appointee. The group's assignment was to analyze the nation's electric power grid and to demonstrate the effects of natural disasters and sabotage on the delivery system.—That was in 1968; today, undoubtedly, the Homeland Security Department is busily working on this potential disaster.—For reasons I never understood, OEP decided not to pursue the project even though OEP had paid for it. O'Leary told Rosenbaum that he ought to talk to me about a matter the FPC could offer the group as a challenge.

Large numbers of wells were drilled in the vast area of the Gulf of Mexico that produced both oil and natural gas. The oil could be removed from the deep ocean platforms by tankers, but the gas had to be fed into gathering systems in regions of the Gulf, with each system consisting of an intricate series of pipes that fed into the onshore transmission pipelines that routed the gas throughout the nation. Any gathering system had to be certificated by the FPC as necessary, thereby enabling the approved expenditures for the construction of the system to be included in the company's rate base for the purpose of determining how much companies using the system could be charged for the gathering service. There were many variables that had to be considered: the location of the wells, their anticipated output, the size of each pipe in the system (larger pipes obviously cost more to install), the depth of the wells, and the energy required to propel the gas through the system. Traditionally, these systems were designed by experienced engineers—it essentially was a highly specialized art form.

Rosenbaum said the group would be happy to undertake the project and OEP had given its blessings to the gang coming to the FPC. No member of the group had any experience with natural gas, but approached the assignment as a mathematical problem with a host of variables. They spent about a month or so talking to the Commission's engineers, reviewing systems that had been previously approved, determining the pressures that were required, and the safety factors that had to be built into the system. They then reduced the system to a computerized software program where the pertinent data could be fed into the program and at the touch of a button, the optimum system—meaning the most efficient and thus the most economical one—would be produced. O'Leary and his engineers examined the software program and declared it to be workable.

After reviewing what the group had done and seeing it demonstrated, I announced this remarkable development at a press conference with pride and a bit of trepidation. Present were representatives of the companies that operated in the Gulf. They snickered at me, saying they were delighted that we at the FPC had discovered computer technology—they always used computers to test their designs. I was pretty sure I was on firm ground when I responded that our program did not test a design but rather created the optimal design. I explained that the federal government had paid for the development of the software and that it would be available to the industry at no cost. The kicker was that the industry didn't have to use our system, but whatever was proposed to the Commission would be tested against our optimal system. I was pretty proud of what had flowed from a cocktail party. The end of the story is the sad part—within a year after I left the Commission, the program was nowhere to be found.

"FRIENDLY" CONSUMER ADVOCATES

A significant benefit of my chairmanship was the opportunity to represent the Commission in numerous conferences and seminars. One special meeting was arranged by American and British legal groups to provide a forum to compare the administrative law practice in the two countries. The meeting at Ditchley House about sixty miles from London was held in an impressive palatial house in beautiful rolling hills. Our group of about ten included jurists, two regulators (Nick Johnson of the Federal Communications Commission and myself), and two or three private practitioners who practiced before regulatory agencies. The original designated head of our delegation was Abe Fortas, an associate justice of the United States Supreme Court, who had been nominated by President Johnson to become the new Chief Justice.—Later a serious flap developed over his nomination and he was forced to withdraw from the delegation. In his place, Judge Warren Burger, of the United States Court of Appeals for the District of Columbia Circuit, assumed the leadership of the delegation. Fortas was forced off of the Supreme Court and President Nixon nominated Judge Burger to be the Chief Justice—quite an ironic twist.

Another Court of Appeals judge, Henry Friendly, of the Second Circuit, was also in our group. It was very clear from the first session that there was a disconnect between the two groups. Our administrative law practice involved regulation of business, while the British administrative practice was primarily zoning and local governmental practice. But we marched on. My set piece was to explain a relatively new movement in the United States pressing for the establishment of consumer advocates to participate in regulatory proceedings on behalf of the public. When I finished my presentation, Judge Friendly, who possessed a strong national reputation for handling major complex regulatory cases on appeal, rose and in a scathing tone said that he could not believe that he would ever hear a regulator argue that he needed an outside advocate to tell him where the public interest rested.—All I wanted to know was who in the hell had named him "friendly."—Today, there is hardly a state or federal regulatory body that does not have an Office of Consumer Advocate. I'm very proud of my role in achieving this result.

Another piece of the "consumer advocate" story took place in Columbus, Ohio. A member of the Ohio House of Representatives invited me to testify before the committee considering legislation to create an Office of Consumer Advocate. I welcomed the opportunity because I liked the topic and it was my first time before a state legislative committee—also my last. After I made my pitch, a member of the committee who was obviously an opponent of the proposal, asked me, "How did you get here?" I told him by plane. He said he wanted to know who asked me to attend and who paid for my trip. I said that the committee chairman had invited me and that the Federal Power Commission was paying my expenses. "Do you mean to say that we federal taxpayers are paying for you to come out here and tell us yokels what to do?" he thundered. The chairman stepped in and rescued me. Happily, the bill was approved by the committee.

INTERNATIONAL CONFERENCES

I attended a hemispheric conference in Lima, Peru, in 1968, where the Peruvian President, Terry Belaunde, held a reception for the conference participants. I attended the World Power Conference in Tokyo in 1967, and in Moscow in 1968. The gathering in Moscow had a first night reception for probably 500 attendees in a beautiful modern building within the Kremlin. Some members of our U.S. delegation, as luck would have it, were next to a group of Czech representatives. Despite the language barrier, we were enjoying the lively antics of the Czechs who had done some vodka-imbibing, as had we. The next morning we learned that there had been an uprising in Prague the night before and the Russians had sent troops and tanks to quell the rioters. The Czechs who had been at the conference were gone. The first person to tell me of the Czech situation was Sir Henry Jones, the Chairman of the British Gas Council and a rough counterpart to my FPC position. He was a dapper gentleman with a distinguished appearance. However, I could not get out of my head a ditty I had heard many years before: "Save the bones for Henry Jones 'cause he don't eat no meat."

In our delegation was Senator Hugh Scott, Republican of Pennsylvania, and Senator Frank Moss, Democrat of Utah. The two senators and I went to the U.S. Embassy to check on what was going on in Prague. The U.S. ambassador was in Washington, DC, but the chargé d'affaires told us what little information the embassy had received indicated that this was a very serious matter. Two days later, the chargé d'affaires escorted our group to the Moscow airport. He told us where to walk to board the bus that would take us out to the plane we were to take to Paris. A young Russian soldier with a big rifle, but no English, pointed us to the bus. As he did so, the chargé d'affaires came running to the terminal door yelling that we were headed to the wrong plane—that one was going to Prague. We were very happy to have missed what would have been a fascinating sensation when two United States senators got off the plane in Prague.

Upon my return, a CIA contact asked me to come to the headquarters in Langley, Virginia, for a debriefing of the Soviet experience. There was very little to report, but I sort of felt like a secret agent while at the headquarters.

POWER FAILURES

A totally different experience, not normally in a day's life at the FPC, arose out of a power failure in the Philadelphia area in 1967. It was nowhere as massive as the 1965 blackout in New York and much of New England, but it got the attention of Eastern Pennsylvania. I was asked to appear on the Mike Douglas program, which originated in Philadelphia and was widely syndicated. It was a mid-morning talk show and I was on with Smokey Robinson and his musical group and with Carol Lawrence, a beautiful and talented singer. Incidentally, the creative producer of the show was a scrawny blond young man named Roger Ailes (now the head of Fox News and no longer scrawny). As I was about to finish a little spiel about the cause of the local power failure and its likelihood of recurring, the studio went completely black for twenty or twenty-five seconds. When the lights came back on, everybody had a good laugh, and Mike Douglas asked me what I thought of our own little blackout. I said, "It would have been better if I had been sitting next to Carol Lawrence."

Later that year, I was addressing the National Association of Regulatory Utility Commissioners (the association of state regulators) in Las Vegas when a power failure hit the city. Although it was fairly short-lived, there was quite a mess with hospitals and many other vital functions without power for a while. However, the newspapers reported that all of the casinos had emergency generating equipment that kept the juice flowing during the blackout. I believe every major Las Vegas facility now has back-up power.

A fascinating seminar was held in the West Texas town of Midland, the focal point of a large oil and natural gas producing area known as the Permian Basin. I was asked to participate and because I had not previously been to that area and liked the idea, I accepted, even when I found out who the others would be on the panel: Allen Shivers, then the President of the Texas Chamber of Commerce, who as the Democratic Governor of Texas had refused to support the presidential candidacy of Adlai Stevenson; Congressman George Mahon, in whose Congressional District Midland was located and who was then the Chairman of the House Appropriations Committee (he participated by telephone); Stanley Learned, the Chief Executive Officer of Phillips Petroleum Company; Paul Harvey, the conservative radio commentator; and Air Force General Curtis LeMay. We were quite a gang of liberals. As President Lincoln said, "People little noted nor long remembered" what was said there. I can report that I did not win any arguments.—It was at this seminar that I had to return a gold watch with my name engraved on it because of the Executive Order governing what federal employees could accept, which I had helped draft.

When I arrived at the Midland/Odessa airport for the meeting, I was met by the publisher of an oil and gas magazine called *Drill Bit*. He was to escort me and asked if his wife could go along with us to the opening barbeque and sit in on the lectures. Of course, I had no objection. When the program was over and he was returning me to the airport, he said he had a little confession to make. The reason his wife wanted to go along was that she had never met a "liberal" before.

A few years later while attending a get-together of LBJ alums at the University of Texas in Austin, I saw Governor John Connally. Because it had been quite some time since I had seen him, I started to introduce myself, and he said something like 'every body in Texas knows who you are.' It didn't sound like a particularly positive recognition.

A symposium at Phillips University in Enid, Oklahoma, focused on energy issues; the main event was a debate between me and an economist from Texas A & M University. It was a little hard to understand everything he said because of his heavy drawl, but he was forceful and argued effectively. I thought I did a pretty good job on the issue of whether natural gas prices should be de-controlled. He ultimately won the argument when he later became a Republican senator and helped change the law. His name is Phil Gramm, and he switched parties after being elected as a Democratic congressman from Texas.

TRADE ASSOCIATIONS

I tried to get to as many industry trade associations as I could. TIPRO (Texas Independent Petroleum and Royalty Owners) invited me to talk to them in Austin. This was a pretty rough and rugged group who introduced me to jalapeno peppers at the pre-meeting reception. I knew they expected me to gasp for water and run to the men's room, but I have a high tolerance for that sort of stuff and pretended that I really enjoyed it. At the first meeting I attended of the American Gas Association (the organization of local distributors of natural gas) in late October in New Jersey, I told a few of the people attending the meeting how great the mild weather had been. They looked at me as if I were crazy. Then I remembered who I was talking to.

A BELATED APOLOGY

Every year when the Washington area conducts its United Way drive, one administration official is designated by the President to head the federal government's participation in the drive. And so President Johnson, in consultation with John Macy, the Chairman of the Civil Service Commission, named me to that "honor." A professional staff does all the work and the federal representative gets his picture taken presenting a multi-million dollar check to the campaign. There was a "Victory Luncheon" at the Mayflower Hotel with a cast of hundreds. A few people at the head table were to report their successes and that's where I went haywire. Just before my turn to say a few words, a very well meaning matronly lady from Silver Spring, Maryland, a nearby suburb, spoke. She wanted to recognize the fine folks who had served as her captains and workers who had done such a great job. She must have been listing names for eight or nine minutes and it seemed like hours. When she concluded, I got up and said that by far the largest amount of the whole campaign was contributed by federal workers and I was going to read each of their names. This, of course, resulted in a lot of snickering. Immediately after the words left my mouth, I regretted what I had done to the poor lady. I tried to apologize, but I would guess that even after nearly forty years, she's still mad at me.

THE ADMINISTRATIVE CONFERENCE

During my time at the FPC, the Administrative Conference of the United States began operation and each government agency could designate a representative to the Conference. I named myself. The group consisted of government and private practicing lawyers and was to consider and make recommendations for improving administrative procedures and practices. There was to be a steering committee of ten members who would set agendas and run the conference as a Board of Directors. John Macy put my name on the list submitted to LBJ. When he came to my name, he told Macy, "He's had enough, take him off the list." That was sort of a characteristic Johnson operational technique. I really liked working on the conference and had an extra benefit. One of the private practitioners was Carolyn Agger, a prominent tax attorney and the wife of then Justice Abe Fortas. Ms. Agger was a small woman who smoked cigars and was widely noted for that somewhat unusual habit of hers. Many friends would present her with cigars, but she would only smoke slender ones. So we had a mutually beneficial arrangement: She would give me her fat cigars and I would give her my skinny ones.

In 1968, the Congress enacted a new housing act. One provision established a program whereby nongovernmental organizations, including not-for-profit and for-profit entities, could engage in building housing projects for low- and moderate-income families. The federal government would provide financial subsidies to qualified participants in the program. It was a natural for utilities because they were accustomed to acting comfortably with regulations. Moreover, many cities had undergone heavy damage to central portions of their cities from the wave of riots that had flared in the 1960s, and this program offered a way to rebuild some of those blighted areas. My old friend

Secretary of Housing and Urban Development Robert Weaver asked me if the FPC would convene a meeting of utility executives to urge them to participate in this new program. I was enthusiastic about the program and we had a very successful session with a few hundred utilities represented. Only a handful actually built projects, but those that did made a real contribution to their communities and were honored for doing so.

NO KIDDING

When President Johnson was putting the arm on me to go to the FPC, he told me that I would only have to stay two years. In mid-March of 1968, I went to see him. It was a very amiable conversation, as it should have been. I told him that the two years was up, but that if he would prefer that I stay at the Commission, I was very willing to do so. I told him I would be glad to stay through the November election. He was in his rocking chair and I was on a couch right next to him. He leaned over, gently grabbed my knee and said, "I'm not so sure I'm going to run." I thought to myself, "Who does that old goat think he's kidding." On March 31st, he announced that he would not run for reelection.

THE BEST STORM WINDOWS

Obviously, I could not be involved in the campaign of 1968 between the two former vice-presidents: Richard Nixon and Hubert Humphrey. My sympathies were, of course, with Humphrey. During my time at the FPC, my wife and I had bought the Humphrey home in Chevy Chase, Maryland, so we had that extra bond.—Whenever he saw me, he reminded me that that house had the best storm window-screen combination that cost $6,000. There is absolutely no way they could have cost that much, but why would I argue with the Vice-President.—As I recall, my contribution to the campaign was the suggestion that his anti-crime platform should stress the benefits of greatly improved street lighting. In any event, with the election of Nixon, I still had the remainder of my term which ran to May 1970.

MY SUCCESSOR

When President Kennedy announced Swidler's appointment as Chairman of the FPC, Jerry Kuykendall, who was then Chairman, pointed out that there already was a chairman. President Eisenhower had designated him and, as

Kuykendall read the Federal Power Act, he was chairman until his term on
the Commission ended. We in the White House scurried around and, working
with the Department of Justice, concluded that, even though it was somewhat
ambiguous and we might persuade a court that the President could designate
someone else to serve as chairman, it could be pretty messy and we were not
about to change the locks on the chairman's office in the dark of the night. A
deal was struck with Senator Everett Dirksen, the Senate Republican leader,
to allow Kuykendall to continue to serve for a few months, after which he
would resign from the Commission and Swidler could move from being a
member to being chairman. And that's what happened.

The issue of whether President Nixon could designate a different chairman
had not been raised, so I continued on until I attended a major policy meeting
conducted by the new Secretary of Labor, George Schulz, who later became
Secretary of the Treasury and subsequently Secretary of State. The session
dealt with the question of whether to impose quotas and tariffs on residual oil
from abroad. It was an issue I'd dealt with in Senator Kennedy's office years
ago, so I had a bit of a feel for it, but any way you examine it, there's a healthy
political component to it. I was the only non-Nixon appointee in the room,
but, as FPC Chairman, I should have been there. I was uncomfortable for two
reasons: I should not be inhibiting a frank political discussion; but more importantly, if anything leaked about the meeting, I'd be the prime suspect.

I could have chosen to ask the President to designate one of the other members of the Commission as chairman and stay on as a member until the end of
my term. In fact, that is exactly what my friend Mike Pertschuk did at the
Federal Trade Commission after Nixon took office. However, I did not want
to stay on as a member. I let it be known to Peter Flanagan, President Nixon's
staff person handling regulatory appointments, that I was willing to leave,
which was very well received. I chose July 31, 1969, as my last day. To my
surprise, Flanagan asked if I would like to meet briefly with the President as
I was leaving. The administration was quite happy with my decision, although some groups were not pleased that I was leaving ten months early. In
any event, I met with President Nixon for what I thought would be a ten
minute handshake affair. But he was relaxed and started asking about regulatory policies and philosophy and the conversation went on for over half an
hour. I was thinking to myself that surely he must have more important things
to do with his time. Later, Flanagan told me that Nixon had said to him, "Why
can't we (the Administration) find some Republicans like me?"

A strange thing happened upon my departure. *The Congressional Record*
carried a brief statement by Senator Warren Magnuson, Chairman of the Senate Commerce Committee, commending my service at the FPC. Two days
later, a similar but somewhat lengthier statement appeared in the *Record*. I

learned that one of my friends on the committee staff had prepared and had inserted into the *Record* the longer item, unaware that Senator Magnuson had on his own expressed a similar thought earlier. It took me back to the days when I used to do things like that, namely inserting items in *The Congressional Record* for my boss.

Chapter Sixteen

My Law Practice

Once I had announced that I was leaving the Federal Power Commission, I began receiving calls from law firms interested in the possibility of my joining them. Whatever enthusiasm they may have had evaporated rather quickly when I informed them that I had made a personal decision not to practice before the FPC. I had not made this a public statement, but before long reporters were calling to learn more about my decision. I knew they wanted to portray me as the "good guy" and, by doing so, criticize the "revolving door" practices of many who leave government. I didn't mind being the good guy—I do find many revolving door activities unsavory—but, more importantly, I wanted to explain why I preferred not to practice before an agency I had led.

There were two reasons that I chose to forgo FPC practice. First, I thought I would find it demeaning to appear on behalf of commercial clients before people who had been under my supervision. Second, I felt that the rate hearings and other aspects of FPC practice were mighty dull, and I'd rather make a living another way if I could. That killed the "good guy" stories.

Quite a few years later, I did accept a matter before the FPC, when my friend Bill Hyland, of New Jersey, asked me to represent a colleague of his who had been ordered by the FPC to leave either his position on the board of a savings & loan association or the board of Public Service Gas and Electric Company. Because of how the two organizations operated, there was no conflict or the appearance of a conflict; but the Commission's narrow view of its authority had resulted in a rather ridiculous decision. The clincher, in my very short memo to the Commission, was: "It's decisions like this that give regulation a bad name." The FPC changed its decision.

A reception noting my departure from the FPC was held on my last day at the Commission, July 31, 1969. My old friend from the White House, Mike

Feldman, played a key role in putting on the party. The biggest surprise was that my secretary, Lorene Baier, had arranged for my dearest friends, Ann and Don Farber of New York, to attend. I had heard a clever remark by an honoree at a recent dinner and intended to use it: "I accept your nomination to sainthood." Because all of the speakers thought they should roast me rather than praise me, no gushing comments were made, and I didn't get to use the line.

After nineteen years as an employee of the federal government, at age 46, I was entering the private sector. I had briefly considered teaching and a political career. The only serious teaching feeler had come from the University of Nebraska Law School, and that had been a number of years before and would involve relocating to Nebraska. A political career would also entail moving to Omaha, the only jurisdiction where I thought there might be a prospect for success. I knew I would have to try to get the support of labor for funding, and I was most reluctant to start down the path of being beholden to some group or groups, even those with whom I normally agreed. I had not lived in Nebraska since 1950, so it would take time to re-establish myself; and I didn't believe I should aspire to a congressional race without some apprenticeship in local politics. I also considered that if somehow I were successful and secured a congressional seat, I would be at the bottom of the seniority list and, like most Nebraska House Democrats, would have a hard time staying in office. Clearly, I did not have the necessary burning desire to give it a whirl. Plus, there were those kids in college and those headed there.

So, I did what seemed like the natural thing: I entered into the practice of law in Washington, DC. I didn't have the experience, flair, or desire to be a trial lawyer. Appellate practice also didn't seem to be my cup of tea. But I was familiar with the legislative process and, although I had intended to forego FPC practice, I knew the federal regulatory world quite well and was comfortable in it.

SEMER, WHITE & JACOBSEN

I wanted to be in a small firm where I thought I would have a big voice in its management, and Semer, White and Jacobsen was a small firm. Milt Semer and I were the two Washington partners, and Jake Jacobsen, who had his own law firm in Austin, Texas, spent most of his time there. We had one associate, Gavin O'Brien, a bright young lawyer who was a graduate of Catholic University Law School. I had worked with Milt when he was the General Counsel of the Housing and Home Finance Agency, and I was on the White House staff, and I had found him knowledgeable and easy to get along with. I had

Chapter Sixteen

known him from my Capitol Hill days when he had been on the staff of Senator Edmund Muskie of Maine. Milt, too, was a Maine native. Jake had been one of the Texans that President Johnson brought to the White House, and although I had not worked closely with him, I liked his understated style. He was gracious, natty, and a pretty shrewd operator. Thus, Semer, White & Jacobsen opened for business on August 1, 1969, with offices at 15th and M Streets, NW, across from the Madison Hotel.

As is customary, announcements were sent far and wide to let the world know that I was ready to start my private law practice. The problem was that nobody seemed to want my services as a lawyer, I believe, in part, because of my decision not to practice before the FPC. I also discovered to my dismay that I didn't seem to have the golden touch to bring in clients. It didn't help that I was a card-carrying Democrat during a Republican administration. At least four months went by without my nailing down one client. The financial arrangement with Semer and Jacobsen called for me to receive a minimum of $40,000 annually, which had been my departing salary at the FPC. Thus, although we were still eating at home, I was growing a bit anxious. Occasionally, I recalled President Johnson telling me about those clients who would be lined up outside my office with numbers to get to see me.

Although hustling business did not come easily or naturally to me, I began to ponder what I could do to drum up some business. I explored with Milt an idea I had by which we could establish an entity to stimulate and assist utilities to participate in the Housing Act of 1968 program that subsidized the construction of housing for low and moderate income families. At the FPC, I had enthusiastically supported the program and had convened a meeting of a few hundred utility executives in the Old Executive Office Building, where Secretary of Housing and Urban Development Robert Weaver had made the pitch for utilities to become interested in the program. This was a logical blending of my expertise with utilities and Milt's deep knowledge of federal housing programs.

The Utilities Housing Council

I contacted a handful of utility executives I deemed to be more socially concerned than was customary and received a favorable response. Thus, the Utilities Housing Council was born. We attempted to encourage the utilities to take advantage of the federal subsidies available for builders of housing for low- and moderate-income families in their service areas. The utilities contributed whatever amounts they felt appropriate, and the meetings held three or four times a year at my call would also provide a governmental official to discuss energy, housing, and general Washington hot topics. It afforded executives the opportunity to discuss issues of interest and to exchange ideas with people who were making policy at the federal level.

Very few projects were actually built, but one outstanding example was built in downtown Detroit by the Michigan Consolidated Natural Gas Company. Much of the area had been laid waste by riots in the 1960s, and the company's distribution lines were unused. The new construction could help restore the usefulness of that infrastructure, and the local politicians loved to see sections of downtown come to life. Unfortunately, the Securities and Exchange Commission held by a 3 to 2 vote that the company, as a holding company, could not engage in that activity because it was outside of the scope of the utility's business.

With this blow, the group re-invented itself into the Utilities Council on Community Development and continued its programs. When Congress enacted a program to provide grants to assist low-income families to meet home heating and electric bills during winter, our group could provide the know-how to make the program as efficient and effective as possible. After more than twenty years, the council died of old age.

Who Would I Be Fooling?

Somewhere in our third year, trouble hit Semer, White & Jacobsen. One of Jake's Texas clients was a milk producers' cooperative with headquarters in Oklahoma. It was active politically and made substantial political contributions. Prosecutors of the United States District Court for the District of Columbia brought a criminal action against John Connally, the Secretary of the Treasury in the Nixon Administration, alleging that he had accepted $10,000 in cash in his Treasury office from the milk producers cooperative which was delivered by Jake Jacobsen. This was pretty big in the "he said - she said" category of legal actions, with Connally denying he took any money, and Jacobsen saying he did. No one else was present at the alleged meeting. The jury held for Connally, and that proved to be a heavy blow to Jake's reputation and to his Austin, Texas, practice. He resigned from our firm and wound up in a business enterprise elsewhere in Texas.

Next, Semer and I got into a disagreement over money, and we concluded that divorce was the best solution. He left the offices, and I remained with the furniture and equipment and the lease to handle. By this time, my former White House and FPC secretary, Lorene Baier, was also at the firm.

The few months of solo operation proved to be the most successful period in terms of income for me up to that time; but I had never contemplated a solo practice. I had always wanted the opportunity to discuss matters with a colleague; and although I was pretty healthy, I thought that there should always be backup available. Thus, I was interested when a large New York City firm was looking for someone to head its Washington office, which had been dormant for a couple of years. I went to a meeting in New York with about a dozen of the firm's partners and it went very well.—If I do poorly in a meeting, I know it; by the same token, I know when it goes well.—My well-meaning contact at the firm called to say that everyone agreed that things had gone nicely, but there was one question some of them had after I left: I had not sounded as if I thought the most important goal in my life was to make the Washington office a major profit center. The firm would send two partners to feel me out on the question.

Sure enough, they came and I knew what it was they wanted to hear from me. After reflecting upon what had been my motivation up to then and where I would like to go, I could not, in good conscience, say to them that my primary motivation was to make the Washington, DC office a lucrative legal powerhouse. I had concluded that it would be unfair to them and to me to tell them what they wanted to hear if it wasn't what I truly believed and could be comfortable with: who would I be fooling? So they left without hearing what they had come to hear. Thus, that story ended and a new one began.

WHITE, FINE & VERVILLE

Phil David Fine, an old friend from the Kennedy Administration, who headed a Boston law firm, heard I was on my own and discussed my situation with his younger brother Ralph, who had served as an intern in our White House Counsel's Office. Ralph said that a Columbia Law School classmate and close friend of his was leaving the Department of Health, Education and Welfare and had no particular plans. With Phil's active imagination and slightly aggressive style, he invited me and Ralph's friend, Dick Verville, to breakfast at the Madison Hotel. The two-hour breakfast ended with the creation of White Fine & Verville in August 1973. Initially, the name was White Fine & Ambrogne to dovetail with the Boston firm's name; but I got a kick out of calling the firm White Wine & Vermouth.

The new firm expanded slowly and successfully. We had very competent lawyers and worked congenially in a generally relaxed environment. In the firm's nearly twenty-five years, Verville and I never had an argument. He brought into the firm a young lawyer, Bob Saner, who had worked for the Price Control agency set up by the Nixon administration. Bob stayed throughout the firm's existence and was clearly the ablest lawyer in our midst. Next came Jim Murphy, who had worked as an Assistant Attorney General of Missouri under Tom Eagleton, and had worked on his senate staff.

We were one of the first DC firms to have a black woman partner: Goler Butcher had been the staff director of the African Subcommittee of the House Foreign Affairs Committee. Peter Leyton came to us from the Government Accounting Office, and Stan Freeman, the son of very old friends Dave and Marianne came directly from Georgetown University Law School, as did Becky Burke. Ron Schwartz came from Health, Education and Welfare. Dick Fulton came from a medium-sized Washington, DC firm and represented a number of vocational schools and brought considerable business with him. John Atkisson joined us from the staff of the House Committee on Commerce and was easily the best mentor for young associates and developed some very good litigators. One partner, with the felicitous name of Grace Monaco, left to manage a National Institutes of Health cancer funded program. Arnie Havens who joined us from a Pittsburgh law firm was the managing partner until he left to be a member of the congressional liaison staff of the first President Bush. Peter Thomas, an amputee, played a key role in the enactment of the Americans with Disabilities Act.

Two of our best office managers were Kit Holden, followed by Kim Stephens. For a long time, we probably had the city's best receptionist: Trisha Naffin was superb on the phone and made every one who came into the office happier with her constantly cheerful disposition. Lorene Baier, my loyal secretary, was most efficient, as was Melva Poky. Catherine Dorsey, Dick Fulton's secretary, was also a professional belly dancer, but not in the office.

Almost every firm has some stories to tell, but one that created a bit of a furor in our firm occurred during a Christmas party held at Dick Verville's home in Georgetown. I was divorced and dated an attractive redhead, Bernice Shurman (later my wife), who worked at the Internal Revenue Service. She had met the firm's lawyers and spouses, but none of them knew or had met her daughter, who was a student at the University of Tennessee. Lori, a very lovely young lady, was coming home for Christmas vacation, and I arranged to pick her up at the airport and planned to meet Bernice at the party, who would come directly from work. While driving to Verville's, Lori and I cooked up a little scheme. I introduced her as Summer Olson, and treated her as if she were my date. There were some hard stares directed my way and then came the big moment: Bernice arrived. It seemed that some of the women were on the verge of apoplexy, and some of the men were wondering how I was going to handle the situation. Things settled down when Bernice hugged Lori and introduced her as her daughter.

Subtenants

We had a fascinating variety of subtenants. Alan Baron, a brilliant political observer and commentator had been press secretary to Senator George Mc-Govern. A nice Jewish boy from Sioux City, Iowa, Alan asked if he could rent a desk in our suite. Of course, he livened up the place, and his newsletter became so successful that he was given an office and assistance at the *National Journal*, a prestigious publication on governmental affairs. Unfortunately, his health was poor and he died at an early age.

Milton Shaw, a nuclear engineer, had worked closely with Admiral Hyman Rickover, the head of the Navy's nuclear submarine program, and transferred to the Atomic Energy Commission where he headed its nuclear reactor program. Known as "Gold Plate" Shaw, he insisted that every required step be executed properly even if the cost were significantly greater. He didn't want any naval nuclear submarines to blow up or any utility's nuclear power plants to melt down. He tangled constantly with Dixie Lee Ray, the Chairman of the Commission, and resigned in frustration. Rather than join a large consulting firm, he established his solo consulting practice in our office. He had a knack for fixing our office equipment, permitting us to boast that we were the only law firm in town who had a nuclear engineer changing its fluorescent light bulbs.

Capital Associates, a two-person lobbying firm consisting of Terry Lierman and Debbie Hardy, worked primarily in the health care field, often in conjunction with Dick Verville and Bob Saner. Their very successful operation outgrew our limited space and moved to a townhouse on Capitol Hill. Deb married Arnie Havens, our firm's managing partner, who was appointed General Counsel of the Department of the Treasury at the end of 2003 and served until early 2007.

Princeton University's Washington office was tucked away in our space and, we claimed, brought a bit of class to the place. The mix seemed to work. Somewhere I have orange underwear with the picture of a tiger on it.

When Congressman Wayne Owens of Salt Lake City was defeated in his run for the Senate, he asked if he could join our firm on an "Of Counsel" basis. He had joined a Salt Lake City firm, but thought he could do quite a bit of business in Washington, DC. Within 45 days, the Mormon Church hierarchy made Wayne an offer he could not refuse: he was to head the Church's proselytizing program in Canada. Four years later, he returned to Utah and ran for his old Congressional seat. We agreed to provide him an office to house his fundraising effort, which resulted in a young Salt Lake City fellow, Tod Cohen, working the telephones and generally filling the place with his own brand of noisy exuberance. Wayne was elected, and Tod went to law school and went on to become a senior eBay executive.

Another temporary occupant of one of our offices was Warren Rudman, who had been nominated by President Ford to be the chairman of the Interstate Commerce Commission. Rudman was the Attorney General of New Hampshire with a distinguished record in office. Our Boston partner Phil Fine had had some dealings with him and suggested that he contact me. We were delighted to provide him an office where he could manage his campaign for confirmation. In part, because President Ford nominated him very close to the New Hampshire primary in 1980, and in part, because the Democratic senator from New Hampshire, John Durkin, feared that the position would give Rudman a platform from which to challenge Durkin, the nomination was held up in the Senate Commerce Committee. Rudman stuck it out for a while and then concluded he didn't like what was going on and asked that the nomination be withdrawn. It was, and he returned to the state, went into private practice, and trounced Durkin when he was up for re-election. Nobody had ever heard of a chairman of the Interstate Commerce Commission (or any other regulatory body) being elected to the Senate, but Senator Rudman served two very distinguished terms in the U. S. Senate.

A Defining Moment

By 1994, the firm had gone through a name change, reflecting the importance of Dick Fulton's practice (representing a wide range of vocational schools) to the firm's finances, Bob Saner's seniority and steadying influence, and the demise of our Boston affiliated firm of Fine & Ambrogne. In a partnership, every partner is responsible for all debts of the partnership. Thus, facing a multi-year extension of an office lease can constitute a defining moment as each partner contemplates the future and what he or she hopes to achieve. I had passed seventy years of age, and Dick Fulton was only a year or two behind; so it made sense to consider alternatives. A number of our lawyers were involved in health care practice and had found a firm that dealt exclusively in that practice area and made a comfortable jump to that firm. Others went to different firms, and one started his own. I accepted the invitation to join my old friend and client, Ron Linton and his consulting firm, where I worked on some cases I brought with me and handled the firm's legal matters.

SPIEGEL & MCDIARMID

When Ron sold his consulting firm to the Carmen Group in late 1995, I joined the law firm of Spiegel & McDiarmid on an Of Counsel basis on the first of

January, 1996. The arrangement has proved to be one of the best moves I ever made. My relationship with the firm rests on an understanding that if I bring business to the firm, I will receive a portion of the revenues realized from that business; and if I work on the firm's cases, I will receive some compensation for that contribution.

This arrangement provides great flexibility for me at this stage in my life. But far and away, the most significant feature is the group of lawyers. Spiegel & McDiarmid's cadre of thirty or so highly capable lawyers takes on investor-owned utilities, advocating the public interest and consumer interests on behalf of municipally- and cooperatively-owned electric utilities as well as communications systems and airport authorities. This type of practice makes for stimulating work, and the combination of their advocacy, persistence against overwhelming odds, and the firm's commitment to representing public and consumer interests has been instrumental in changing the structure of the utility industry.

A number of the senior lawyers had been my contemporaries at the Federal Power Commission, so we go back over thirty-five years. The late George Spiegel, a co-founder of the firm, had earned a reputation at the FPC not only for his deceptive "aw shucks" demeanor but also for developing the sophisticated use of anti-trust laws to protect relatively small and impecunious publicly-owned utilities from over-reaching on the part of utility power suppliers. That spirit of creative lawyering at Spiegel & McDiarmid, which has been described by Mark J. Green in *The Monopoly Makers*, and John T. Landry and Jeffrey L. Cruikshank in *From the Rivers*, continues to the present.

Within the utility industry, Spiegel & McDiarmid has earned a reputation as the "gold standard" of law firms in its category. One of the factors contributing to this reputation has been the firm's longstanding emphasis on hiring exceptionally talented attorneys. The analytical and lawyering skills of the firm's co-founder and name partner Robert C. "Bob" McDiarmid set a standard among its attorneys; and as the firm celebrates its fortieth anniversary in 2007, Bob's leadership and management skills continue to guide the firm's longevity and success.

Spiegel & McDiarmid has been a natural fit for my career interests. The firm has been a happy home to me for over a decade, and the flexible Of Counsel arrangement suits my lifestyle.

THE MANY FORMS OF PRACTICE

The practice of law takes many forms. Some lawyers spend most of their time litigating in court; others are corporate lawyers drafting contracts, merger agreements and personnel guidelines; some are lobbyists attempting to assist legislators and administrators to do their jobs; some work in government; and some leave government to capitalize on their experience. My work on the Utilities Council on Community Development that I began at Semer, White and Jacobsen was the kind of activity I felt good about doing. We were making a difference, although minimally, but to find utility executives to think outside their fairly narrow boxes was an accomplishment. As my private practice took shape, I had the opportunity to serve on a variety of associations, task forces, and agencies with a public policy focus. I also stayed politically involved with the Democratic Party.

The Association of Metropolitan Sewerage Agencies

In the early 1970s, Senator Edmund Muskie, Democrat of Maine, the chairman of the Environmental Subcommittee of the Senate Committee on Public Works, began his remarkable string of legislative enactments that got the nation started on cleaning up the country's rivers, lakes and streams and our polluted air. It quickly became evident that the first major effort was going to be aimed at cleaning up the waters of the country.

The Water Pollution Control Federation, a trade association that focused on water quality matters, had been in existence for many years. It was a large organization of at least a thousand members including academics, consulting engineering firms, manufacturers of equipment for pollution control, and state and local governmental agencies charged with responsibilities for protecting the waters within their jurisdictions. The executive director of the Seattle municipal sanitation agency, Charles "Tom" Gibbs, a very thoughtful fellow, explained to the agency's local attorney the problem he saw in the WPCF's structure. The issues facing the large metropolitan sewer agencies could get lost in the Federation's processes and there were bound to be conflicts of interest because of the diverse interests in the group as Congress progressed through the legislative process. Of special concern to Gibbs was the fact that Seattle and many other local agencies had substantial claims for funds from the federal government that had not been paid under then existing programs. Together, he and the attorney, Jim Ellis, developed a rough framework for an organization limited to big city agencies. Gibbs then got in touch with some of his counterparts in other large local agencies to see about establishing such an organization.

Seattle's attorney was Jim Ellis of Preston, Gates & Ellis, and one of his partners was Gerald Grinstein, whom I had known and worked with when he was administrative assistant to Senator Warren Magnuson of Washington. Gerry called me and asked if I would meet with the convening group and give them a hand in getting started. That was in the summer of 1970; twenty five years later I retired as counsel to the group known as AMSA. It was an ideal assignment for me. These were local governmental people, and they were truly doing the basic job of cleaning up the rivers and lakes in their jurisdictions. Their primary impetus resulted from the obligations of local governments to protect the health of their citizens.

As the Muskie Subcommittee went about drafting a new comprehensive Clean Water Act, AMSA testified and generally supported the effort, although where it believed the subcommittee was off base, it was not bashful about saying so. Senator Muskie's key staff was Leon Billings, whom I had known through his earlier employment with the American Public Power Association. He respected AMSA's members and would, on occasion, call me, the group's counsel and lobbyist, while the bill was being drafted by the subcommittee and ask what would be the effect of a particular provision being considered. I would respond by saying, for example, I'll have Ben Sosewitz of the Chicago Sanitary District call you right away," and Ben's explanation would be accepted at face value. We clearly did not win all of our battles, and I recall telling Leon that our group was split down the middle about him: half wanted to strangle him and half wanted to shoot him.

My old boss Senator Cooper was the ranking Republican on the subcommittee and his key staff person, Tom Jorling, worked very closely with the Democratic staff. That particular Committee had a tradition of close working relations between the majority and the minority. When the bill was signed into law, Tom, in a highly unusual gesture, wrote me a letter thanking me and the organization for our assistance.

The AMSA's first meeting in 1970 of about a dozen men from big cities across the country was held in a hotel room in a Holiday Inn two blocks from my office. Today, it is a stable organization with a couple of hundred member agencies and a staff of ten and is known as the National Association of Clean Water Agencies. It works closely with the Environmental Protection Agency and with various congressional committees and other organizations with similar interests. It is an important association, and I was fortunate to be there during its formative years. There remains much to do in cleaning the nation's waters, but enormous strides have been made throughout the country since the 1970s.

The AMSA was the kind of client I appreciated. Its earlier membership was made up of a fairly wild fun-loving bunch compared with the more button-down groups that came along in later years. One incident from the early days that probably has grown in the retelling was the night in Duluth, Minnesota, when a bunch of us commandeered a city bus the Duluth waste water agency had chartered and made a rollicking tour of some of the few night spots in Duluth. The Association got into a pattern of four meetings a year held in the home cities of the membership. Thus, we traveled all over the country, and in each host city, the member agency went all out in providing educational and entertaining activities for the convening groups. For me, that was a most welcome side benefit.

The ultimate was a European tour put on by Ron Linton, an old friend from my senate days, who became the group's initial Executive Director. We checked on sanitation facilities in London, Paris, Warsaw, the Netherlands, and Germany. I liked to kid the gang by saying that they didn't pay much but they gave me all the crap I wanted. Sure enough, a fifty-pound bag of processed sludge to be used on golf courses and other green areas arrived in my office one day.

Consumer Federation of America Energy Task Force

My good friend Alex Radin, the Executive Director of the American Public Power Association (a trade group of about 4,000 municipal electric systems), had been instrumental, together with a few other non-profit organization leaders, in creating the Consumer Federation of America. The CFA was funded by labor organizations, APPA, the National Rural Electric Cooperatives Association (NRECA), Consumers Union, and other groups to provide a voice for the consumer in public policy issues. It commented on proposed legislation, offered recommendations, participated in regulatory proceedings, and sought to inform the public on issues of concern to consumer groups and to individual consumers. Compared to the U.S. Chamber of Commerce and the National Association of Manufacturers, it was a pretty puny and underfinanced organization, but it had verve and developed techniques for gaining attention for those issues it pursued.

In 1973, Alex asked me if I would be willing to head up a CFA task force to focus on energy issues that were being discussed and debated widely because, in large part, of the gasoline shortages that were creating havoc across the country, as well as the great interest and controversy over what course the nation should follow. My Federal Power Commission experience gave me a fair grounding in electricity and natural gas industries. Oil issues were another story. My old friend and buddy Dave Freeman from TVA days had played a major role at the FPC during the Swidler era, had been an energy maven in the office of President Nixon's Science Advisor, and had chaired a major and well-received energy study under auspices of the Ford Foundation. I asked him for advice. He told me I could pick up the oil industry issues fairly easily, but there were a raft of other issues and I could be kept awfully busy, especially in light of the modest retainer CFA could afford. The idea of

being a consumer's energy spokesman appealed to me, and the CFA Energy
Policy Task Force was hatched.

The first assignment was to find a staff person to assist me. Word filtered
through the labor-consumer universe of the new task force and my comrade
in arms, Mike Pertschuck, who had been the chairman of the Federal Trade
Commission when I was at the FPC, sent me Ellen Berman, a very bright
young woman who had worked with Mike. Though she had little experience
in the energy field, she learned quickly and we worked well together. Alex
Radin and his counterpart from the NRECA, Bob Partridge, and representatives from the Steelworkers Union, the United Automobile Workers, and the
International Machinists Union were among our board members.

The CFA was rather impecunious and we had to raise our own money.
Most of it came from unions, including a significant contribution approved by
Lane Kirkland, then head of the AFL-CIO. One notable fundraising luncheon
held at a downtown hotel was attended by Senator Phil Hart of Michigan. Although I knew he had been invited, I was bowled over when he walked in the
door and urged those attending the fundraiser to support our efforts. Senator
Hart was almost everybody's favorite senator, and the high regard his colleagues had for him is reflected in the name of the newest Senate Office
Building.

We issued policy papers and I testified before congressional committees so
frequently that during one session before the House Subcommittee on Energy
of the Commerce Committee, Congressman Clarence "Bud" Brown of Ohio,
a very conservative member who disapproved of almost everything I said,
commented when I had concluded my testimony, "Mr. White, I believe you
left out a point you usually make." And he was right.

One of the major issues we supported was maintaining regulation of the
price of natural gas at the well head. Originally, President Carter had opposed
abolishing the regulation of natural gas producers, but he changed his position, which, of course, he had every right to do; but he soured many of us with
that switch. I was at a meeting in the White House on the natural gas issue
where there were fifteen or twenty of us at a table in the Roosevelt Room. Jim
Schlesinger, then an assistant to President Carter, was presiding. The President entered the room and sat down at an empty chair on the side of the table.
He was one of the "boys" and Schlesinger kept on running the meeting. I
couldn't believe it. That would never have happened with the two presidents
I worked for.

I believed the rates the FPC set for wellhead natural gas were generous
enough for producers to operate profitably. I suggested a few approaches, but
one was especially interesting. As a TVA alumnus, I thought perhaps a federal agency operating as a natural gas producer would provide the govern-

ment and the public with experience and information that would permit a fair evaluation of how the industry really functioned. In shorthand terms, a "yardstick" by which the industry could be measured. Unfortunately, the title I proposed was the Federal Oil and Gas Corporation. It did not receive broad support, and the acronym FOGCO didn't help.

I served as spokesman for consumer positions and gave talks to various groups all over the country, and, for the most part, I enjoyed it. I debated an independent oil producer from Texas on the "Today" show, appeared on the McNeil-Lehrer Newshour, and was pretty good about finding TV cameras wherever I went. *Time* magazine ran an article on our group and my activities. One group I especially enjoyed was the Women's National Democratic Club, because my old friend and neighbor, the late Eleanor McGovern, the wife of Senator McGovern, introduced me. On another memorable occasion, the late Millie Jeffrey, the Democratic National Committeewoman from Michigan, and United Auto Workers official, picked me up at the airport in Detroit, where I later addressed a UAW gathering. Driving into town in her Plymouth, we watched her odometer turn over to 000,000.

While participating in an energy seminar in New Jersey, a gentleman I did not know came up to me and struck up a conversation about the consumer slant on energy issues. We hit it off very quickly, and he was in sympathy with our stance on issues. Leopold Wyler was an industrial businessman from the Los Angeles area who ran with a liberal Democratic clique and had sold them on the idea of funding a major effort to support consumer views on national energy policy issues. Included in the group was Miles Rubin, whom I had known from the McGovern-Shriver campaign. The shocker was that the group also included Paul Newman, Robert Redford, and Stanley Sheinbaum, a wealthy Californian contributor to many liberal causes. In short order, Wyler contacted me with a go-ahead message.

My good friend Dave Freeman from TVA, one of the nation's outstanding authorities on energy policy issues, had just finished a project, so I urged that he be included as the full-time director of the undertaking because I did not want to leave my law firm. Wyler agreed and asked the two of us to come to Los Angeles to talk specifics. So off we went and were ensconced in a snazzy Beverly Hills hotel. Wyler picked us up in the morning and told us we were going to see Paul Newman and, sure enough, we drove up to a fancy home with a large wall and gate and were waved in. Newman was getting ready to go to the airport to take a plane to Canada, where he was making a film and told us to ride with him. Before leaving, he introduced us to his wife and I told Mrs. Newman I was pleased to meet her.—I had no idea that she was Joanne Woodward, the much honored movie actress, thereby demonstrating my limited knowledge of the Hollywood scene.—During the half hour drive, we discussed what we could do and what he and Redford could do if they were willing. It went well and then there was another little surprise in store after we had a meeting with Stanley Sheinbaum. We were going to a reception at Norman Lear's house in Malibu Beach. I had been around presidents and other politicians and had met a host of celebrities, but this was a concentrated dose of the glitterati.

On our return to Washington, DC, Dave scouted around and found office space near the Capitol, and we prepared for a meeting with Wyler and Miles Rubin. We had worked up a potential full-page ad in *The Washington Post* announcing "Energy Action." It was being reviewed and amended by the group, when Rubin excused himself to meet with an old friend from the McGovern campaign, Frank Mankiewicz, who persuaded him that Jim Flug, a former staffer for Senator Ted Kennedy, was the guy they should hire. Rubin outranked Wyler, and Rubin was adamant: he wanted to retain me to advise Flug at a fairly high retainer. I flatly rejected the idea. I knew Flug was an able fellow and did a good job for the group, but no one was as qualified and able as Dave Freeman. I was so angry I could hardly contain myself.

There is a footnote to the story. Before the fateful meeting, Robert Redford was in Washington filming "All the President's Men" about the Watergate scandal. He called me but I was out of the office. The ladies in our office were all a-twitter, but he never called back. Our law office was in a building that adjoined The Washington Post's offices, and from our windows we could watch the filming that took place on the top of the Post garage, which proved to be quite a distraction.

When it appeared that I might hook up with Energy Action, there was some annoyance and resentment on the part of Consumer Federation leaders. Thus, we decided to sever the relationship and create a freestanding organization called the Consumer Energy Council of America, which continued in substantially the same operation as the Task Force had pursued. When it was time for me to move on to other pursuits, CECA was left in the capable hands of Ellen Berman, who led the organization into an even broader range of activities for many years before it disbanded in 2007.

We were not successful in opposing the natural gas industry's drive to get Congress to deregulate gas prices. Many years have passed, and I now admit that deregulation proved to be far more successful than I had predicted and argued it would be.

The Election of 1972

My friend and former colleague Larry O'Brien became Chairman of the Democratic National Committee, and when he was getting ready for the Democratic Convention in 1972 in Miami, I volunteered to help. He asked me to be his liaison with the Rules and Credentials Committees. Rules dealt with the mechanics and procedures of the convention, while Credentials handled the seating of the various state delegations. The DNC headquarters office was in a relatively new office building that was part of the complex in Northwest Washington known as The Watergate.

I went to headquarters on afternoons and on Saturdays, and had a small office adjoining O'Brien's. We worked on modifying the rules of the convention, attempting to prepare for any anticipated credential battles, and generally structuring the program for the convention. One Saturday morning, I wandered over to the Watergate Office Building, only to find a cluster of maybe twenty people standing in front of the steps to the building. No one seemed to know what had happened until Stan Gregg, O'Brien's deputy chairman and a former Democratic Congressman from Sioux City, Iowa, came out of the building and told us that there had been a robbery during the night. The police were looking things over, but at the moment there was nothing to report, except that there was some suspicion that the party platform being put together may have been the reason for the break-in. He said the office where the work was going on was in a shambles. Not long after, John Stewart who headed that program showed up, went into the building, and came out to advise that that was exactly how they had left it the night before.

The convention headquarters in Miami was at the Fountainbleau Hotel, then the newest and fanciest in the area, where O'Brien had a penthouse suite which served as his command center. We met there to do the final program planning and to report on how the various committees were getting along. As the Chairman's men, we had identification cards that we wore around our neck, which entitled us to go anywhere in the Convention Center. Early one afternoon, I was walking around the Convention Center smoking a cigar when I came upon a bit of a problem. Driving a big rental Continental, Bob Strauss was trying to enter the chain link fence gate to a parking lot. The posted guard told Strauss he needed credentials to go into the complex. In the car with Strauss were his wife and South Carolina Governor Bob McNair and his wife. Strauss was not the least bit happy with that guard. With my go-anywhere card, I told the guard that Mr. Strauss was "the DNC Treasurer, and he paid for the whole damned convention and you better let him in." And he did.

As the convention opened, the two most likely candidates were Senators George McGovern of South Dakota and Edmund Muskie of Maine. In 1966, my wife and I had bought the house that Vice President Hubert Humphrey had owned in Chevy Chase, Maryland, and our next door neighbors were the McGoverns, so we knew the McGoverns well.

McGovern had nailed down the convention votes, and O'Brien and all the folks around him played the game absolutely straight. All possible nominees were treated fairly. I liked McGovern's policies but there was absolutely nothing wrong with Muskie. He had gotten a bum rap in the New Hampshire primary when the very conservative *Union Leader* newspaper of Manchester had published a nasty front page editorial critical of Mrs. Muskie and the senator was perceived to have cried about it. The follow up raised questions as to whether the bitter cold temperature had made him appear to have tears in his eyes. But what if he had cried, what was the big deal? Today he would have been praised for his sensitivity.

McGovern's selection of Missouri Senator Tom Eagleton to be his running mate was regarded as an excellent choice until it was revealed that Tom had been treated for some mental illness—I believe depression—whereupon the selection backfired, and McGovern's expression of one thousand per cent support for Eagleton came back to haunt him when Eagleton was pushed off the ticket. McGovern's efforts to secure a running mate were widely publicized and the numerous rejections didn't help the situation. The seventh choice was Sargent Shriver, the brother-in-law of President Kennedy, who accepted the invitation to run with McGovern. He had been the first director of the Peace Corps, the head of the Office of Economic Opportunity, and Ambassador to France.

The second major disaster occurred when we, the convention managers, permitted speeches by a large number of candidates for presidential and vice-presidential office to go on and on. Although we had made a commitment for that speechmaking, we should have—and undoubtedly could have—stopped it so that McGovern's very important acceptance speech could be delivered at a reasonable hour rather than at nearly 2:00 a.m. east coast time. We were derided, properly, for putting it on in prime time in Guam. All in all, it was not a very successful convention, to put it mildly.

Although I had known Sarge Shriver, I had not worked with him in the Kennedy-Johnson administrations. So, I was mighty surprised when he called and asked me to meet with him to discuss my becoming his campaign manager. As he was McGovern's seventh choice, so I believe I was his seventh choice. My responsibilities at the law firm were such that I could undertake the assignment, and I liked everything he told me at the first meeting. I agreed with enthusiasm and never regretted the decision.

Gary Hart was McGovern's campaign chairman. Hart had come to my office in early 1972 to inquire about what sort of fellow this George McGovern was who had asked Hart to join his campaign. He became the campaign manager and later a United States Senator from Colorado.

A number of Shriver's associates who had been with him at the Peace Corps had dropped what they were doing and joined the fray. We had a fairly lively and talented crew. Included were Bill Josephson, a law partner of Shriver and Peace Corps general counsel; Mickey Kantor who went on to be President Clinton's Trade Representative and Secretary of Commerce; Michael Novak, a friend of Shriver and a fairly conservative commentator on religious matters, especially Catholicism; Bill Barnicle, noted columnist for *The Boston Globe*; George Frampton, who later headed the National Park Service in the Clinton Administration; and Mark Shields, syndicated columnist and TV commentator. Shields had worked in the Muskie effort to obtain the presidential nomination and, when that ended had told his wife Ann that he was through with campaigning for a while. Shields was correctly perceived to be a skilled political operative, who we needed, and we made a pitch to get him to join our effort. He told me I would have to persuade his wife, so I went with him and sweet talked her into giving her assent. To no one's surprise, he turned out to be terrific.

There were a few quirks in the campaign. There was an athletic cheer that went something like "Da ta da ta da; da ta da ta da (pause) Charge!!" Somebody on the campaign trail had gotten the audience to go through the chant and end with "Sarge!" He thoroughly enjoyed it and we tried to do it as often as possible.

Within a campaign headquarters there is usually some optimism and despite the discouraging polls, we kept thinking that there would be a dramatic turnaround at the end of the campaign, as had happened in the Humphrey-Nixon campaign four years earlier when Humphrey nearly overtook Nixon. But it was not to be, and we took a shellacking. But what a great experience it was to have been involved in a presidential campaign, even a losing one.

The National Regulatory Research Institute

In 1977, the National Association of Regulatory Utility Commissioners (NARUC), the state agencies that regulate electric gas, telephone, bus and trucking within their states established a regulatory institute (a think tank) to provide research assistance to those bodies as they faced new and more complicated issues. Known as the National Regulatory Research Institute (NRRI), it was located at Ohio State University in Columbus. NRRI was initially proposed by Joe Swidler, while he was Chairman of the New York Public Service Commission, and the Board was comprised of state regulators, NARUC's Executive Director, academicians who taught regulatory policy, and a few "public members" of which I was one and Joe Swidler was another.

NRRI was just getting started and the growing pains were evident. The main problem was financing: getting fifty different agencies to pony up the money required for such an undertaking was a formidable task.

The underlying rationale for the Institute was that regulators should be able to look to their own people for analysis and guidance on issues of concern to them. A good analogy resulted from the congressional debates on whether the United States should follow Great Britain and France in building supersonic airplanes. The committees were flummoxed when some of the nation's best scientists and engineers testified in favor of going forward and an equally impressive group testified against; both groups were handsomely compensated by those business interests who would lose or gain depending on how the issue was resolved. Following that experience, Congress concluded that it would be well advised to set up its own Office of Science and Technology to assess issues of that character. They hired bright people to staff the office, but the most important consideration was that they owed their loyalty to Congress and could be expected to be objective in the advice they provided Congress. The office worked as it was intended to and its reports and recommendations were relied on heavily by congressional committees. Unfortunately, the Republican revolution of 1994 resulted in the office being abolished.

My ten years on the NRRI board provided an opportunity to keep up with many of the fundamental changes taking place in some key industries. It had a talented staff and the university affiliation proved useful in providing graduate students as competent research assistants. Its publications are impressive and have been of great benefit to NARUC agencies.

The New York Mercantile Exchange

One day in 1980, I received a call from Dick Leone, the President of the New York Mercantile Exchange. I had know Leone while he was a Capitol Hill staffer, but more particularly when he was the State Treasurer of New Jersey. My very good friend Bill Hyland, who I had known when he was the head of the New Jersey Board of Public Utility Commissioners, had been appointed Attorney General of New Jersey by the newly elected Democratic Governor Brendan Byrne. I was retained by the state as an energy consultant to the governor. As a consequence, I knew many of the players in the state, including Leone. He asked whether I would be willing to be a public governor on the Board of Governors of the Exchange. I told him I didn't know diddley squat about commodity exchanges. He said there were plenty of folks up there in New York who did, but there really wasn't anyone who knew anything about federal governmental regulatory agencies. Congress had recently created the Commodity Futures Trading Commission to oversee the nation's commodity exchanges, and he thought it would be helpful to have someone on his Board who was familiar with the world of regulatory agencies. He thought that the great mass of the membership of the Exchange not only didn't understand how the CFTC worked, they also didn't believe it had any right to get involved in their business. Additionally, one of the contracts traded by the Exchange was heating oil, which clearly involved energy policy issues. He arranged for me to go to New York and meet with the chairman of the Exchange and a few other key members.

The Exchange's charter provided for three public governors and there was a vacancy. Michel Marks, the twenty-nine-year-old chairman, proposed me and the Board acquiesced. The Exchange had its trading floor and offices in the World Trade Center Building Number Four. Thus, I started monthly trips to New York.

It did not take long for me to get thrown into the midst of a major problem facing the Exchange. About a year before I arrived on the scene, the Exchange suffered an experience that all exchanges dread. A commodity traded on the Exchange was Maine potatoes. Because of disastrous weather conditions, the Exchange defaulted on the contract; that is to say, there was an inadequate supply of potatoes to meet the demands of those who were entitled to receive them under the terms of the contracts they had properly bought through the Exchange. The prior Board had resolved the claims against the Exchange by making decisions and cash settlements in a manner that protected the Board members who were potato traders to the detriment of other parties trading on the Exchange. After a detailed investigation and in a formal proceeding, the CFTC advised the Exchange that it was considering decommissioning its charter and throwing it out of business. After engaging in some strenuous negotiations, the Exchange and the Commission entered into a consent agreement. It was quite an agreement. The CFTC agreed to settle the case in return for the Exchange agreeing to establish a Compliance Review Committee comprised of three individuals by name (Horace de Podwin, a public governor and the head of the Rutgers University Business School; Hugh Cadden, a consultant and former head of the CFTC Compliance Division; and me) and further agreeing to accept and implement the reforms and changes the Committee proposed. These were not recommendations by the Committee but mandates that had to be implemented. Additionally, the Exchange was fined $250,000, the heaviest fine ever levied to that time. Thus, the future viability of the Exchange was at stake. The scuttlebutt was that the CFTC chairman Jimmy Stone, appointed by President Carter, wanted to eliminate the Exchange to show how tough a regulator he was, but that my participation in the Review Committee resulted in a reprieve.

Horace also had an economic consulting firm and thus our meetings were held in his offices in the Empire State Building. We produced a series of changes in procedures the exchange would have to make. Our toughest requirement was that NYMEX beef up its electronic capability by installing new equipment costing well over a million dollars. The Board had no choice and despite some low-grade grumbling, the deed was done. Two years later, the CFTC cited NYMEX for having the best compliance program of all exchanges.

Someone at the Exchange suggested that the idea of a commodity contract for crude oil was worth considering. It was a time when many new types of contracts were being offered, including such non-commodity items as international currency fluctuations. Michel Marks asked me to chair the advisory committee to the board that would look into the possibilities and, if it seemed feasible, prepare a contract for submission to the CFTC for its approval. Basically, a contract on an exchange is an agreement on the part of one party to sell and another party to purchase an item at an agreed upon price in the future. In the case of agricultural products, the concept is fairly easy to grasp, but where the product was to be crude oil, there were many wrinkles that had to be dealt with. Most contracts are in effect cashed out at the end of the trading month, but for those that are not, arrangements for delivery must be spelled out in the contract. In essence, the futures contract should replicate the manner in which the cash market functions. This was the challenge for our committee. Members of the committee were representatives of the various industrial and commercial aspects of the industry. The crafting of a contract that would meet the needs of those who would use the exchange was difficult and complex, but one industry member of the committee, Francis Oliver of Sun Oil Company, knew the industry thoroughly and guided us to produce a contract that was successfully submitted to the CFTC and has proved to be among the outstanding successes in commodity exchange history.

Later the board authorized the exploration of the possibility of a contract dealing with natural gas. Again, I was the chairman of the advisory committee. Because of the unique handling and storage of natural gas, it was extremely difficult to come up with a satisfactory contract, but again using the input from the different elements of the industry and after more that a year's effort, success was achieved. It is now the means by which parties know the current and future value of gas arrived at by willing buyers and sellers.

Allegations of improper conduct by the Chairman of the Board William Bradt and the Exchange's Vice President for Compliance created a furor in the Board, and a Special Committee of Inquiry was established. I was designated chairman and the other two committee members were Cathleen

Douglas Stone, a public governor, and Ira Schein, an Exchange trader and a former elected board member. The committee's detailed report based on testimony from twenty-three witnesses and a thorough examination and evaluation of documentary materials resulted in the resignation of the Chairman and the firing of the Compliance Vice President. The committee's report was submitted to the CFTC and was deemed to have fully and fairly investigated the allegations of improper conduct and no further action was required.

My two separate tours of duty on the Board totaling about eight years were special. I learned a whole new field and had the opportunity to get to know a group of extraordinary people. They may not have been the most profound or intellectual individuals on the planet, but there was a natural shrewdness and quickness about them. I left with a good feeling of having participated in rescuing an exchange that was on the ropes and seeing it evolve into one of the strongest exchanges in the country. When I first joined the Board, seats on the Exchange sold for a few thousand dollars; in 2005, the going price was over $2 million.

MY CAREER CHOICES

By and large, my government career and legal practice have been in the public sphere. As a law student, I preferred courses in legislation, labor law, and regulation of business, rather than property law, contracts and torts. As a government lawyer and in private practice, I found that, generally, my clients' motivations and objectives were relatively straightforward and laudable. For me, working on behalf of government and in the public sphere doesn't mean you are a better lawyer. It means, in most cases, that you can enjoy it more and have a good feeling about using your abilities in those directions. I have been able to engage in a wide variety of activities that have made my life happier and livelier.

Over the last fifteen or twenty years, there has been a pronounced shift in how law is practiced, especially in larger cities and in larger firms. The former loyalty to a firm that gave incoming lawyers the opportunity to develop a reputation and a practice, in many instances, has been discarded or at least greatly weakened, especially with the wholesale transferring of major specialty sections from one law firm to another because there is more money to be made. This may not be true of every transfer, especially when the new affiliation results in greater synergy between specialized areas of legal practice; but, in general, it is my observation that too often loyalty loses out to prospects of greater wealth.

There is nothing like having a happy and pleasant environment where you spend most of your working hours accomplishing something worthwhile for your clients. Like most people, I would prefer to have more money than less money; but I can truly say that money was not a driving factor in my career and I am better off for it. Besides, I like to tease my children by telling them that I am sparing them the burdens of inherited wealth.

Part Five

MY PERSONAL LIFE

Chapter Seventeen

Family, Friends, and Heritage

My life is a testament to how significant it is to having the fates smile upon one. I'm aware of the old adage that says that the harder one works, the luckier he or she becomes. However, I believe that luck, being in the right place at the right time, seems to fall more frequently on some than on others. In the great balancing that occurs in a lifetime, luck is not weighed quantifiably: obviously, luck at the slot machines in a casino does not equate to the great good fortune of having five healthy children, just as waking up to a rainy day on the day of your wedding is not in the same league as a spouse contracting cancer.

My glass has always been at least half full. Even when two of my wives died of cancer, I focused on the fact that in each case we had had a very good life: it made the grieving process much more manageable. Insofar as my professional life was concerned, I had no pre-set career goals, unlike some of my classmates who knew what they wanted to be; but gentle winds blew me in favorable directions. Life is a great deal easier going if you see and stress the positive.

THE WOMEN IN MY LIFE

When it came to wives, I was very lucky. But I was struck with catastrophic bad luck with the death of the last two, each dying of ovarian cancer thirteen years apart. Dorothy Cohn, my first wife, was my college sweetheart and the mother of my children. We married during World War II, and shared a happy life in Fort Monmouth, New Jersey; Lincoln, Nebraska; Knoxville, Tennessee; and Washington, DC. With the many full days in my various jobs, the heavier burden of running the household and raising the children fell on her, and she did an admirable job. We lived comfortably on my government salary, with Dorothy having only limited outside help. After more than thirty years of marriage, we divorced in February 1978. We remained on good terms until her death in August 1995.

My second wife was Bernice Shurman of South Carolina. She had two sons and a daughter from her first marriage, and a daughter from her second marriage, Lori, whom I adopted. Bernice was a sexy high-spirited, beautiful redhead with a strong sense of humor.—When Bernice told me that some of my sewer bunch buddies had made passes at her, I said I admired their taste.— During a trip to Las Vegas in the fall of 1979, we claimed to have gotten married. In fact, we did not marry because she would have had to forfeit her widow's government pension if she married before reaching the age of sixty. We actually got married in December 1981 in the county clerk's office in Rockville, Maryland.

Bernice was generally a healthy woman, but when the pain in her stomach did not go away, she went to a number of doctors who were unable to tell her what the problem was. By the time Dr. Michael Gold at the Washington Hospital Center diagnosed her illness as ovarian cancer, it was too late. The operation to remove the cancer was unsuccessful, and she died in September 1983.

I knew Cecile "Cece" Zorinsky as the wife of Senator Eddie Zorinsky of Nebraska, who was a fraternity brother. Cece was also a very good friend of my sister and mother. When Eddie died of a heart attack, Cece decided to run for Congress from the Omaha District. She came to my office to discuss her campaign. I wasn't very helpful, and she lost in the Democratic primary, despite having led in all pre-election polls.

We were married in Omaha in November 1989, and *The Washington Post* quoted her observation that she was moving up in the alphabet. We enjoyed a good life until the fateful day her surgeon confirmed his (and our) worst fears that she had ovarian cancer. She died in April 1996.

Subsequently, Cece's daughter Suzy and Suzy's friend Nancy Kutler thought it would be a good, or at least interesting, idea if Nancy's mother, who had been twice widowed, and I got together. It was better than a good idea: it was a superb idea. Bea Karp, the lady in the plot, and I hit it off immediately. That was in 1997, and we continue to cavort like elderly teenagers. Bea, who is beautiful and bright, was characterized by one of my friends as a "dainty charmer." By the long arm of coincidence, she, too, had two spouses who died of cancer.

Bea is a survivor of the Holocaust. As a little girl about eight years old, she and her family, including her younger sister, were uprooted from their home in western Germany by Nazis, and sent to a French concentration camp in 1940. Her parents were sent to Auschwitz, where they perished. The girls led a harrowing existence until the war ended, when they traveled to London to stay with relatives, and then to the United States. Bea has committed herself to telling her personal experiences to school and church groups and various community organizations. It is one thing to study the Holocaust as a school subject (if it is taught) and quite another to hear firsthand from one who participated in that nearly unbelievable cataclysmic undertaking by the Nazis.

With our children and grandchildren in Massachusetts, North Carolina, Illinois, Nebraska, Maryland, Nevada, California, Bea and I help sustain the airlines. In September 2006, we took it in stride to go together to Israel to visit Bea's sister and my cousin.

MY CHILDREN

When children come into your life, everything changes. My son Bruce was born in Lincoln, Nebraska in 1948, arriving while I was attending the University of Nebraska, and, like his siblings, grew up in Washington, DC. After graduating from the Capitol Page School, he attended the University of Nebraska Law School. He joined a law firm in Lincoln, and then moved to St. Louis, Missouri, where he became an Assistant U.S. Attorney. He later practiced real estate law in San Diego, but when the bottom fell out of the real estate business, he became a bankruptcy lawyer. He and his wife have a two-lawyer firm.

My daughter Rosalyn, who was born in Knoxville, Tennessee in 1951, is an artist who traveled through the turbulent 1960s. She graduated with honors from the California College of Arts and Crafts in Oakland, and went on to the University of California at Berkeley, where she was certified to teach art in California schools. After graduating, she took a job as an artist and art teacher with a charismatic Tibetan Buddhist teacher who had come to northern California to establish a Buddhist center. In her thirty years with the organization, she has been the art director of their publishing company, creating over one hundred paintings, illustrating hundreds of books, including seven children's books, and also serving as executive director of the publishing company. The Buddhist community and its school have flourished, and Rosalyn is a calm, serene and satisfied soul.

My son Murray was also born in Knoxville in 1954. He attended Oberlin College and the University of Chicago, studying art history. He writes on many subjects with an emphasis on art, and his work has appeared in publications, including *The Washington Post, The Baltimore Sun, The New Yorker*, and *The Legal Times* of Washington, DC. He frequently took the former director of the National Gallery of Art to task for deficiencies in the operation of the Gallery, including testimony before a U.S. Senate Committee. He also created and developed an art gallery in Montgomery County, Maryland, which specialized in the work of Jewish artists.

My son Sheldon was born in Washington, DC in 1955, and is the jokester in the family. After graduating from high school, he did not at first intend to go on to college. A few years later, on his own, he later decided to attend Montgomery County (Maryland) Community College, and then transferred to the University of Delaware, where he received a Business Administration degree. He went to work for Nationwide Paper Company in Los Angeles, and because he was a whiz at games, he mastered the company's new computer system and with two other fellows went around the country instructing regional and district offices in its use. Sheldon is a terrific game player, having won a number of pinball machine contests, including an international championship, so computers came naturally to him; but he now works as a poker dealer in Las Vegas. He and his wife have two precocious children, Emily and Trevor (all grandchildren are precocious).

My daughter Laura was born in Washington, DC in 1963. Laura is especially sharp in mathematics. During high school, she had enough confidence to abandon an honors program because she wanted to spend her time in artistic pursuits. She, too, graduated from Oberlin, and after a year of work in a DC bookstore, enrolled in the Bank Street School in New York City, a school that prepares students for teaching positions. After receiving her Master's degree, she landed an assignment teaching fourth and fifth graders at a private school in Manhattan. She then joined a friend of hers in Atlanta at a think-tank whose mission it was to better prepare teachers to teach math and science, and from there, to Durham, North Carolina, where she kept Duke University's computer system for faculty and administrators in operating condition. Her current job is with a publishing house that has a unit devoted to technical publications. Laura takes descriptive materials provided by scientists and technicians and converts them into understandable English. She and her husband have two sons, Clay and Noah.

My daughter Lori, who I adopted, attended the Capitol Page School and graduated from the University of Tennessee. Lori worked in the office of Congressman Charlie Wilson of Texas, one of the wildest and most uninhibited members serving in Congress at the time, who was noted for having very attractive female staff members, known as "Charlie's Angels." When he left Congress, Lori turned to lobbying in Washington, DC, and has been quite successful. She is married and has one son, Stephen.

MY FRIENDS

In the friends category, I really scored high. My friends are from high school, college, fraternity pledge brothers, Army buddies, my poker gang, and the many different assignments I had in Washington, DC, including former law partners and my current affiliation.

Annie and Don Farber go back to 1948, and Don to 1941. (Our fathers were even together in Camp Dodge, Iowa, during World War I.) Don is a distinguished entertainment lawyer and Annie is a retired Professor of Mathematics.

Murray Comarow and I date back to 1954, when we met at a Hadassah couples discussion club and the lovely Donna Comarow, his wife, joined the team in the 1980s. Murray has been involved with the postal service since the late 1960s and is deemed the most knowledgeable analyst of the system. Donna is a psychologist who authored an important book on the practice.

Alex Radin has been a friend since I first got to Washington, DC in 1954. Over the years, our lives touched frequently because of his role in building the American Public Power Association in to a formidable advocate for the municipally owned power systems of this country. His wife, Carol, is a creative artist who paints "outside the box."

Stan and Selma Cohen also go back to 1954. I met Stan in 1950, while I was job-hunting in Washington, DC. Stan is now deceased, but Selma, his widow, is a widely known artist.

I am aware of the risk involved in listing a handful of friends, but I really have to stop. A small telephone book of names of friends and relatives just won't fit.

My Poker Gang

As the offspring of two poker players and the father of a professional poker dealer, I remain an enthusiastic member of a poker gang. Grady Poulard, whom I have know for over twenty years, first as my next-door neighbor in Southwest Washington, DC, and as the sparkplug for our twice a month bloodletting, is the glue that keeps our gang together. The members of my poker gang have changed through the years and the stakes have escalated, but the game still holds fascination for me and provides camaraderie.

The Jury is Out

One happy band of warriors I meet with three or four times a year includes three former jurors whom I served with on a jury panel in a criminal case in the District of Columba Superior Court in the year 2000. As the jury was concluding its deliberations, one juror, the mâitre'd of a downtown restaurant, invited the jury to have brunch at his restaurant one Sunday. Four of us who sat at one table had a pleasant and stimulating conversation. As we were departing, we agreed it would be a good idea to meet again. So, the jury group was born. One of our members is a lawyer who works in a federal regulatory agency; another is a partner in a big-time Washington, DC law firm; the third is a Department of Justice employee in a specialized field; and I round out the gang. Occasionally, spouses or significant others join us at lunch. We have no plans to discontinue meeting.

The ROMEOs

Another *ad hoc* group of friends in my own age group is an informal gang that meets monthly for lunch, conversation, occasional debate, and general good fellowship. We have no by-laws, no dues, no officers, and, until a few years ago, no name; that is, until one of our creative members dubbed us the "ROMEOs," short for "Retired Old Men Eating Out." One of our gang is the former Provost and Acting President of American University. Another served as the Executive Director of two Presidential Commissions and as a senior Postal Service official. A third was a high ranking official of the Labor Department. Another is a former distinguished *New York Times* reporter. Yet another was a college professor and Dean of an academic department at American University.

As described in a June 12, 2006 article in *The Washington Post*, the ROMEOs hardly ever discuss sports, sex, war stories (although most of us are veterans), grandchildren, or personal matters, although occasionally health matters may be touched upon because we are all in our eighties or nearly so. Our standard topics include politics (we veer a little left and a little right); the state of the world; hot scientific or business issues; and Supreme Court decisions. Our humor is a little better than the food at the delicatessen that is our meeting ground.

MY HERITAGE

This is a good place to say a few words about my heritage. My father was born in a *shtetl* (a small rural village) in Russia, which at one time was part of Poland, but today is the Ukraine. According to my dad's Uncle Morris, the family had lived for four or five generations in the village of Schimsk (the village in "Fiddler on the Roof" provides the flavor). The family had a grain mill, but life was hard with lots of mouths to feed and a desire to escape military service. My father was the oldest child. In 1910, when he was twelve or thirteen, his parents let him go to the United States with two fifteen-year old cousins. My father ended up in Omaha, where his Uncle Gershon had arrived around the turn of the century.

My mother's parents came to the United States in 1905 from a little town called Yampola, in the same area as Schimsk. My mother was one and a-half years old when her family came through Ellis Island. They headed for Omaha for the same reason that Uncle Gershon had; namely, they had relatives there. My grandparents had a little clothing store in the low rent district of downtown Omaha. They had two children born in the United States: Frank, about seven years younger than my mother; and Mollie, six and a-half years younger than Frank. My mother always complained that, as the oldest, she was required to speak English, so her parents could learn the language. Thus, although her Yiddish was rather weak, her sense of humor was intact.

I was born on September 1, 1923. As the story was later told to me, upon hearing the nurse's announcement that my mother had just delivered a baby boy, my mother responded by saying, "We'll have to call him 'Bill,' because he came on the first of the month." Perhaps a defining incident took place while my mother was pregnant with me. According to the legend, she was playing poker with the girls one Sunday evening, and an angel appeared to her and whispered, "Annie, this is your first, so you get a choice." My mother said, "You mean a boy or a girl?" "No," said the angel, "I mean smart or lucky." My mother quickly said, "Lucky." When I heard this story at about twelve or thirteen years of age, I teased my mother by saying, "Ma, why didn't you say 'both?'" She, of course, replied, "It never occurred to me."

Apparently, I knew I was Jewish at an early age. The story goes that, at about age four, I was playing in the yard one day wearing a little sailor suit when a man walked by and asked if I was "a little marine." I answered, "No, I'm a little Jew."—The guy cracked up and went to the front door to tell my mother.—Living in a predominately gentile neighborhood, I experienced a few anti-Semitic jibes and a mild skirmish or two; but, in general, I had very little trouble and was a buddy of the only black kid in our grade from the only black family with children in the school.

My folks owned a grocery store with a two-bedroom house connected to the rear of the store, so our family was pretty close. Like many first-born children, I had ruled the roost until my sister Shirley came along. Shirley was born six and a-half years after I was, and I kept reminding her that it's always going to be that way. She was a zippy little kid with a positive outgoing personality.

Shirley's quick thinking probably saved our folks' lives and maybe hers. Our house in North Omaha behind my father's grocery store was a very comfortable and pleasant home that was heated with natural gas. One warm day, our delivery boy had driven me to high school and returned to the store to find my dad slumped over on the butcher block. Shirley who was seven or eight at the time had seen her dad unconscious in the store and her mother collapsed in the bedroom of the house. She called our Aunt Nena, and told her that something scary was going on. Nena who lived only a mile and a half away immediately called the fire department (911 would not be invented for decades). Firemen arrived and said that in another ten or fifteen minutes one or both would have died. Cold weather had frozen the ground, but the thawing action had damaged the pipe leading into the property, with gas escaping into the house and store. At that time natural gas was odorless. Whether it was due to my folks' experience or others, I don't know; but thereafter, an odor was added to natural gas to provide a warning.

Shirley was married to Earl Levy for nearly thirty years and they had three children. When her husband died in 1983, she became a single working mother raising children. Shirley's three children now live across the country, and she, too, has discovered the pleasures of being a grandparent.

On reflection, how a little Jewish kid from Omaha, Nebraska, the son of immigrant parents, wound up on the Kennedy and Johnson White House staffs is just one more illustration of the opportunities that exist in this country— especially if one happens to be born "lucky."

Part Six

REFLECTIONS OF A
WHITE HOUSE COUNSEL

Chapter Eighteen

Reflections on the Role of White House Staff

There may be better staff jobs than the White House staff, but I've never heard of one. Before I got there, knowledgeable people had told me of the terrible hours and the pressures of the job. They were correct, but the benefits are so tremendous that I've counseled many who were uncertain whether to take the assignment to do so if at all possible.

The White House is a highly stimulating place to work, and although you are using the reflected authority of the President, there is so much power concentrated in the modern presidency that you do have a chance to do some good and, above all, you have a ringside seat at the significant events that affect the nation. Exercising some of this authority on behalf of the President can make one feel more important than is appropriate. In my view, the staff role is more difficult than that of the principal. When you are using someone else's spilled over authority, you are also affecting that person's reputation. For me, that tended to make me more cautious and circumspect than situations might have called for, but I never wanted to err at the other extreme.

THE WAY THINGS WORK

When a White House staff member calls somebody in government or out of government and asks that some thing or other be done, the receiving party isn't sure whether that individual just came out of the President's office with instructions, whether it's the staff's own idea, or whether his grandmother in Omaha suggested it. The tendency, assuming a fair reputation, is not to question. That's a pretty big burden to bear.

One incident in the JFK White House had a heavy Nebraska flavor. Not too long after the administration got going, reporters in Nebraska questioned

Governor Frank Morrison, a fairly liberal Democrat, about reports that he was being pressured by the White House to do its bidding in large part because of the prominence of Ted Sorensen in the administration. Frank was a folksy sort of fellow and said, "Yeah, that's right. Just about every other morning, President Kennedy calls me up and says, 'Frank, how's construction on I-80 coming along out in the western part of the state?'" That was the perfect answer, and it was quoted in *Time*.

Some time later, Ted Sorensen and I were in the President's office when Evelyn Lincoln, whose father had been a one-term Democratic congressman from western Nebraska, came into the office. She told the President that Governor Morrison was calling from Lincoln. I hurriedly told the President about the *Time* report. The President picked up the phone and said, "Frank, how's construction on I-80 coming along out in the western part of the state?"

The Vice President

Aides to a President will put almost everyone else in a subordinate position, with the possible exceptions of their spouse and children, which makes the Vice Presidency a very tough job. The Trinity River project in Texas was one example. I had a call from Vice President Lyndon Johnson who said, "Lee, the BOB fellers tell me the Trinity River project papers are on yore desk." I admitted that they were, and LBJ proceeded to give me the history of that project from its earliest beginnings in excruciating detail. He had a great memory and the project had a long and complicated history. Also, it was intimately involved in his political career. All of a sudden, I had to figure out how to tell the Vice President of the United States that I had to interrupt his conversation because I had to prepare a memorandum for the President of the United States. And I did.

Some White House staff took every opportunity to belittle LBJ and to treat him rudely. I've already indicated that I was never disrespectful of LBJ, but I admit that I forgot to invite him to one of President Kennedy's meetings with leadership groups on civil rights and to provide him copies of the meeting memos prepared for JFK. At Bobby Kennedy's request, I evaluated his performance as Chairman of the Committee on Equal Opportunity in Employment. I believed then and now that, as President, LBJ wiped the slate clean insofar as I was concerned.

Cabinet Members

Quite sticky is the relationship between cabinet members and independent agency heads and White House staff. Cabinet members do not have equal access to the President. In general, the heads of State, Defense, Treasury, and Justice will be able to get through to the President by telephone or a personal meeting without delay. If it's the way it used to be, most others will have to filter through a gatekeeper. For some in the outer rings, especially former governors, it's not easy to hear, "The President is tied up but we'll get back to you when we can."

Abe Ribicoff, the very popular Governor of Connecticut, was the first major elected office holder to come out in support of Senator Kennedy when he was seeking the Democratic Party's nomination for president, and his appointment to be Secretary of Health, Education and Welfare was the first one to be announced by the new President-elect. As a proud member of the Cabinet, too frequently, his calls to the President were answered by Ted Sorensen, who had begun his government career in the Federal Security Agency, a predecessor agency to HEW. When Sorensen wasn't available, Mike Feldman would return the call and, so help me, I once did so. Abe didn't think that was the greatest arrangement, and there were probably other factors involved; but in any event, he resigned. He ran successfully for the Senate from Connecticut, and served with great distinction for many years.

There's a cute story about Abe that is also instructive. As secretary, he had hired and was swearing in a new assistant. In administering the oath of office, he said, "Repeat after me, 'I, Boisfeuillet Jones, do solemnly swear. . . .'" Now, that is one tough name to pronounce, and Abe had mispronounced it. "Bo" (his nickname) faced a dilemma. He could pronounce it the way he had all of his life with the *Boo* sound and possibly embarrass his new boss, or he could do it the way Ribicoff had and mispronounce his own name. Like the true polite southerner that he was, Bo did it Abe's way.

The Media

A key principle is that the President is the good guy and staff takes the rap if there's a screw-up. Paul Scott, a syndicated columnist and, incidentally, a Nebraskan, called to say that he had talked with a fellow named Jack Stack, who was proposing that Bolling Air Force base in the Washington, DC area be converted to an international trade center. Stack said that President Kennedy had some interest in the proposal, but I was holding it up. Scott said he was planning to write about it and was letting me know as a courtesy. I told him I'd worry if he wrote that I thought it was a great idea but that the President couldn't be persuaded. I didn't tell Scott that I had run it by the President, who was not enchanted by the idea. He didn't write about it. Of course, the President can always take responsibility, but usually a staff member will be the bearer of bad news.

Gratuities and Gifts

Staff should act responsibly and avoid actions that could embarrass the President. General Harry Vaughn, President Truman's wartime buddy and White House staff, created grief for the President by accepting a food freezer as a gift. Governor Sherman Adams, President Eisenhower's Chief of Staff, was forced to resign over accepting a vicuna coat from a New Hampshire business man. The prize winner in this category was, of course, Vice President Spiro Agnew, who accepted cash from Maryland contractors in his vice presidential office and was permitted to resign. Once, when a District of Columbia group of businessmen were developing a new bank to operate in the District, one of the promoters offered to sell me some shares of stock at the promoters' price. That was not hard for me to turn down. Even easier to reject was a suggestion from an old friend from senate staff days that there was money to be made if I joined in a proposal to convert some abandoned federally-owned salt mines in Kansas to storage facilities for helium.

When John Macy, Chairman of the Civil Service Commission, and LBJ's major appointment headhunter, came to me and said some of his people thought it would be very helpful if there were an executive order defining what acceptable behavior was for federal personnel in terms of what gifts and entertainment, including meals, was alright to accept, I agreed and we went to President Johnson with the idea. The President's immediate reaction was that any such order would stir up all sorts of questions about the Bobby Baker days when LBJ was Majority Leader of the Senate. There had been some rather juicy stories about gifts and women. We responded, saying that such an order could be very helpful and he ought to take a look at a draft. He told us to go ahead, and we developed a formulation about the value of gifts (nominal) that could be received. We ruled out acceptance of meals, except where they were part of normal governmental activity such as an inspection of a plant or where commercial facilities were not available. The order prohibited the use of company-provided transportation and payment of transportation charges except where commercial alternatives were not available.

We knew that with the vastness of the federal establishment, there would be those who would ignore any prescribed rules, but most would appreciate knowing what was deemed acceptable and what was not. An additional benefit was the ability of the federal official or employee to explain his or her refusal to accept such items by pointing to the prohibited policy, thereby avoiding the appearance that he or she necessarily thought such actions were improperly offered, possibly offending the would-be givers. When we presented the proposed order, the President said to me, "Did you check this with Abe Fortas and Clark Clifford?" I hadn't and so I did. Neither had a problem and LBJ signed it. Not one word was written about Bobby Baker, and the executive order was regarded as appropriate and constructive. With modifications, the order is still in effect.

Much later, as Chairman of the Federal Power Commission, I participated in a seminar and, like all other participants, was to be given a gold watch. I told the program manager that I couldn't accept the watch, that he could either give it to me and I'd return it immediately, or he could simply not give me one when the others were presented theirs. He asked me if I was crazy since the $250 watch was already engraved and had my name on it. I told him with tears in my eyes that some pointy-headed bureaucrat had dreamed up the ban on such gifts. Of course, I didn't tell him who that bureaucrat was.

Working Behind the Scenes

The question of staff anonymity is quite interesting. It was said that FDR's staff had a "passion for anonymity;" however, over time, as the interest of the media in White House operations has expanded, increasing attention has been given to White House aides. As we know, people have various styles and characteristics. Some shine and are modest or even shy about pushing themselves forward; some shine and will find a way to let the world learn about it. There are even those who don't shine, but would have the world believe they do. And there's the category in which people aren't modest and never had a passion for anonymity, but are virtually anonymous anyhow. I was in that group.

Increasingly, White House staffs are known to the public and speak out in support of the administration. President Kennedy had some real stars on his staff and let them be seen. I remember Ted Sorensen being on "Meet the Press," which, I believe, was a first.

Speechwriters and Promises

When LBJ was considering asking Dick Goodwin to join his staff and write some speeches for him, he wanted to know what I had to say about Dick, because I had worked with him on the Kennedy staff. I said Dick was one of the smartest guys I knew, that he wrote beautifully and fast, and could make a real contribution. I added that he probably would rub some staff the wrong way. But, all in all, he was on balance an excellent bet. Personalities and modes of behavior are pretty well set by the time one is in a White House staff position, and I remember my predictions on Goodwin turned out right. Dick produced some of LBJ's most memorable and important speeches, including his defining "Great Society" speech on May 22, 1964; the riveting "American Promise" voting rights address on March 15, 1965, before a joint session of Congress; and LBJ's triumphant remarks in the Capitol Rotunda at the signing of the Voting Rights Act on August 6, 1965.

An interesting aspect of LBJ's voting rights legislation is the tendency of speechwriters to want to present a three-point program or a four-point program in the signing speech, even if they really don't have that many points. It just sounds better and is suitable for media coverage. In LBJ's signing speech on August 6, 1965, the speechwriter threw in a fourth item: "I have already called a White House conference to meet here in the Nation's Capital this fall." It was simple enough, but I knew the inherent difficulties in committing to such a conference so far in advance and urged that the promise be deleted. It wasn't. We managed to stall until the next year and, by that time, I was on my way to the Federal Power Commission. So, we asked two very distinguished civil rights advocates to serve as co-chairmen: Morris Abrams, the Georgia lawyer who had won the "one man - one vote" landmark Supreme Court case and who was then the President of Brandeis University; and William Coleman, a highly respected black Republican lawyer who later served as Secretary of Transportation. Framing the agenda, the structure, and those to be invited to participate was a tough job, and I was asked to slide away from my new job at the FPC to lend a hand. It's always nice to be asked, and I was pleased to do so, although my recollection is that not much was accomplished by the conference, but the speechwriter did get that fourth point into the speech.

Presidential Pardons

In the case of presidential pardons, the procedures used by Presidents Kennedy and Johnson worked the following way. Basically, the recommendations of the Justice Department lawyer who handled applications for presidential pardons, the late Harold Reis, were reviewed by me and generally accepted. If there were questions, the specific case would go back to the Justice Department for more information or clarification. So far as I was aware, no special appeals were made to the White House, and I would surmise that, if there were such efforts, they would have been referred to Justice for normal handling. The one special case I recall involved a former Democratic National Committee official (I believe a Treasurer) by the name of Marc Connolly. He had met the standards that Justice used in its evaluations for pardons, but because of the potential newspaper examination, President Kennedy gave it special attention and probably discussed it with Attorney General Bobby Kennedy, and signed the pardon. I was surprised at how many medical doctors were granted pardons after many years of rehabilitation. Almost all of them had been convicted of income tax evasion.

Later, the pardoning power got a lot of attention in specific cases: President Ford and the pardon of Richard M. Nixon; President George H. M. Bush and the pardon of Defense Secretary Casper Weinberger; and President Clinton's pardon of Marc Rich, the fugitive financier living abroad whose wife contributed to the Clinton Presidential Library.

Knowing Your Limits

It is a basic requirement for staff members to know for sure how the President or any other principal would respond to a situation, so you can act with confidence and save wear and tear on the boss. But you are expected to know when you don't know and to seek his or her guidance.

About six o'clock one evening, Adam Yarmolinsky, an assistant to Secretary McNamara who served on my informal interagency civil rights panel, called to tell me that there was a small problem at an air force base in Rapid City, South Dakota. A group of airmen wanted to engage with others in a demonstration against a federal governmental policy not involving military matters, and the Department had no policy, written or oral, covering such situations. We went over the issues. They would not be in uniform and the demonstration would take place after working hours. When I asked when was this going to take place, Adam said, "In an hour and a half." We agreed that an answer was needed on the spot. So, I said, "Well, Adam, go ahead if you think it's the right thing to do." This was one of maybe forty calls I would receive every day, and I promptly forgot about it and went on about my business.

About a week later, I had a call from President Kennedy. The conversation started, "Did you . . . ?" I thought, "Uh-oh." He went on, ". . . tell Defense that it was OK for soldiers to demonstrate against the government?" Now I wanted to explain that the call came late, that I thought that we (Adam and I) were talking about one situation in which there was no time to establish a governmental policy, and we were not establishing such a policy. But as I was groping for the best way to put my answer, he said, "Why didn't you ask me?" That, of course, was the clincher.

I had access to the President and, obviously, should have called him, because, clearly, he didn't think my handling of the question was correct. Happily, that was the only such incident in which I was involved. The President was not angry, just annoyed. I rarely saw President Kennedy angry.

President Johnson appreciated the fact that I told him what I believed, not what I thought he believed or wanted to hear, as may be gleaned from Photo 18.1 and Photo 18.2. On three important occasions, he was open to challenges to decisions he had made: first, setting up a panel to review regulatory appointments; second, meeting with the parents of the missing civil rights workers in Mississippi; and, third, closing Camp David.

But he didn't always heed my recommendations. For nearly a year after the assassination of President Kennedy, President Johnson had not returned to

Photo 18.1. On occasions such as this meeting on the highway Beautification Bill, it was Lee White's practice in his role as Special Counsel to tell the President what he believed, not what he thought the President believed or wanted to hear. Cabinet Room, October 4, 1965. L-R, background: obscured; Speechwriter Robert Hardesty; Congressional Liaison Larry O'Brien; Assistant to the President Ralph Dungan; Special Counsel Lee C. White; Peter LiBassi; Secretary of Transportation Alan Boyd; Assistant to the President Chuck Roche; Senate Congressional Liaison Mike Manatos; L-R foreground: Assistant to the President Jake Jacobsen; President Lyndon Johnson; Assistant to the President Joseph A. Califano, Jr. (obscured). (In attendance but not pictured: Liz Carpenter; Paul Southwick; Jack Valenti; Clifton Carter; Vice President Hubert Humphrey) Photo Credit: Yoichi R. Okamoto. (Personal Collection of Lee C. White)

Dallas. When I learned that the NRECA annual meeting was to be held in Dallas with approximately 10,000 people in attendance, I suggested to the President that he would have to go to Dallas sometime and that this was an appropriate occasion. He had been instrumental in the creation of the Pedernales Rural Electric Cooperative, which served his home town of Johnson City, and had been a strong supporter of the rural electrification program. That was a piece of advice that didn't score a touchdown.

THE LAST WORD

It's inevitable that disagreements will arise between a President and his cabinet and staff, but there is no question about who has the last word. I'm sure

Photo 18.2.   President Johnson didn't always heed the recommendations of Special Counsel Lee C. White, but, on occasion, the President was open to challenges to decisions he had made. Lee C. White and President Lyndon Johnson are pictured in a discussion prior to a meeting on transportation policy in the Cabinet Room on May 5, 1965. (In attendance but not pictured: Secretary of Commerce John T. Connor; Director of Bureau of the Budget Kermit Gordon; Undersecretary of Commerce Dan Martin; Secretary of Transportation Alan Boyd; Assistant to the President Bill Moyers) Photo Credit: Yoichi R. Okamoto. (Personal Collection of Lee C. White)

it is handled differently by different individuals, but I believe, in general, it goes something like this: The disgruntled party thinks to himself or herself, I know I was right, but the President is the boss and if I resign, I'll probably be replaced by someone who will not be as knowledgeable and effective as I am. What I'm doing is important and I'd hate to see it screwed up. And perhaps not stated but subliminally, I really enjoy the assignment and the perquisites that go with it. That chauffer-driven car is easy to get used to. There may even be some who might fear recriminations. For those who elect to leave, there is the choice of whether to leave with a blast or simply slide away.

One example involved the Johnson administration's handling of the Florida Department of Agriculture's request for the right to bring more *braceros* (foreign workers) into the state to help harvest crops. Secretary of Labor Willard Wirtz, after careful examination of the issues, denied the request. Bill Wirtz was an exceptionally bright lawyer and effective Labor Secretary. But his decision was challenged by the senior senator from Florida, Spessard Holland, a conservative Democrat and an old friend of LBJ. When Senator Holland complained to the President, I was asked to look into it and wrote a memorandum on the issue. After discussing it with the Senator Holland and Secretary Wirtz, I reported that I thought the secretary was correct. LBJ decided otherwise and reversed Wirtz, who was livid. Secretary Wirtz called me late in the afternoon and told me he would not take that from Johnson, and that I should "tell that son-of-a-bitch, 'I resign.'" I told Wirtz that it wasn't my place to pass on such a message and "You tell that son-of-a-bitch, 'I resign.'" I suggested he take some time to think it over and tomorrow would be time enough. Secretary Wirtz obviously thought it over because he never called back and did not resign.

Undersecretary of State George Ball disagreed vigorously with LBJ over Vietnam policy, but chose to stay and be a strong voice in opposition. Secretary of State Cyrus Vance in the Carter administration believed he could not remain because of his strong opposition to President Carter's handling of the Iranian hostage crisis and resigned as quietly as he could. It's pretty hard for so prominent an official to simply slink away.

THE ROLE OF RELIGION

During the Kennedy and Johnson administrations, religion was a neutral factor both in the selection of staff and in public policy positions and programs. There were a number of Jews in prominent positions in the Kennedy and Johnson administrations, including Wilbur Cohen, Undersecretary and later

Secretary of Health, Education and Welfare; Manuel "Manny" Cohen, Chairman of the Securities and Exchange Commission; and Sheldon Cohen, the Commissioner of Internal Revenue. Once, when Ted Sorensen mentioned to JFK that we four in the Special Counsel's office—Ted, Mike Feldman, Dick Goodwin, and I—were Jewish, the President responded with the equivalent of "So what?" Our service during this period was relatively free of discrimination and controversy.

Early in the Kennedy period, someone sent me a small article from the Washington Jewish newspaper with a headline reading, "Lee White Not a Member of Temple Sinai." This was true but there were, of course, millions of organizations of which I was not a member and millions of people who were not members of Temple Sinai. Apparently, there had been an earlier article listing members of Temple Sinai who worked in the Kennedy administration, which included my name, and someone wanted to straighten out the record. I was a member of Tifereth Israel, a Conservative congregation.

Mike Feldman occupied what was in essence the "Jewish desk" in the White House, serving as liaison with the various Jewish and Israeli organizations. Where relations with the Israeli government were involved, the National Security staff under McGeorge Bundy also advised the President. When Mike left the White House in 1965, Mac Bundy and I talked about whether I should take over Mike's role. For a number of reasons, we decided against my doing so. That did not prevent the Lubavitchers, a zealous Hasidic Jewish sect, from finding their way to my office.

Also, President Johnson sent me as his representative to the annual meeting of the Association of Conservative Congregations at the Concord Hotel in the Catskills. My wife, the rabbi and two other members of the congregation drove to the meeting. When we checked in at the gate, we gave our names: White, Brown (Sidney) and Wine (Harvey). When the rabbi gave his name, Abramowitz, the fellow at the gate said, "Thank goodness." The meeting was fairly uneventful and my remarks were brief and non-controversial. Simply showing up at such events normally constitutes a minor plus, or as we used to say, "It can't hurt." In this case, the excitement came on the way home.— It was the night of the colossal New York City and Northeast power failure, November 9, 1965.

It was eerie passing by New York City and heavily populated New Jersey in darkness, listening to the reports on the radio. The next day, I learned that the White House staff had not been aware of the blackout until LBJ learned of it from radio while riding around on his ranch and called the White House to tell the staff to get in touch with the Federal Power Commission. I doubt that any other President would have known that the FPC was the right place to contact. When the media got on the story, almost every reporter had to ask where the FPC was located, because it did not normally appear in the breaking news. Driving home that night I had no idea that I would wind up there one day.

A MISSED OPPORTUNITY

Although I'm not enthusiastic about admitting mistakes, I would have to say that I blew one golden opportunity. Wisconsin's Senator Gaylord Nelson came to the White House with a couple of newspaper-sized albums filled with favorable articles and editorials he had received as Governor, promoting environmental protection and preservation of green space. I failed to catch his enthusiasm and vision, as apparently did others in the administration. It was not until 1970 that the Environmental Protection Agency was created during the Nixon administration, and Congress under the leadership of Senator Edmund Muskie, Democrat of Maine, enacted the Clean Water Act and then the Clean Air Act.

THE PERKS OF WHITE HOUSE STAFF SERVICE

Having talked about some of the burdens of staff duty at the White House, the many benefits and perquisites of that particular assignment deserve to be mentioned for they are significant. First was the simple thrill of being there. If the White House is the center of the Executive Branch of government, the West Wing is the heart. As shown in Photo 18.3, there I was in that happy spot.

The hours were long, including Saturdays and even Sundays on occasion. This can take a toll on families, especially those with young children. Thus, it was most welcome when Kenny O'Donnell would call and say that the presidential yacht, the *Sequoia*, would be available on Saturday afternoon at the Navy dock. Boarding that handsome boat with your wife and kids and relaxing with a drink as it traveled down the Potomac to the Chesapeake Bay helped offset a lot of late nights and weekends. The Navy crew that served as the White House mess cooking staff knew how to fix hamburgers and hot dogs as well as more substantial dishes. The *Sequoia*'s normal use was for the President and his family and friends, but its most significant role was as a lobbying and persuading device for the President when legislation needed some help. The beauty of it was that, once aboard, you couldn't decide to leave early. It also had a prestige factor—any senator or congressman who had been on a cruise with the President let everyone know about it soon and often. I believe President Carter made a major mistake when he got rid of it.

Photo 18.3.   Despite the burdens of White House staff duty, Lee C. White shared a happy interlude with Johnson administration staff following a meeting on transportation policy in the Cabinet Room on May 5, 1965. L-R: Chairman of the Council on Economic Advisors Arthur Okun; Maritime Administrator Nick Johnson; Secretary of Transportation Alan Boyd; Special Counsel Lee C. White; President Lyndon B. Johnson; Director of the Bureau of the Budget Kermit Gordon. (In attendance but not pictured: Secretary of Commerce John T. Connor) Photo Credit: Yoichi R. Okamoto. (Personal Collection of Lee C. White)

Equally helpful in sharing some of the benefits of the job with family was spending time at Camp David. A weekend there wasn't heaven but mighty close. With well appointed cottages, the same Navy mess boys, movies, pool, skeet shooting, a bowling alley, and just beautiful scenery for walks made it a real treat for the family. I never knew where the cut-off for these special benefits occurred, but happily I was on the right side of the divide. I believe O'Donnell probably used his own judgment, but I'm not completely sure.

State dinners at the White House were special, as were the cultural events scheduled and staged by the Department of the Interior, such as a cello concert by the gifted Pablo Casals. The National Park Service's jurisdiction is sweeping. One Christmas vacation, our family spent a couple of days at the lighthouse at Cape Hatteras, North Carolina, an historic facility which memorializes the remarkable life saving corps of volunteers who rescued victims of the many shipwrecks at that treacherous spot in the Atlantic Ocean. There were special productions at Ford Theater, also under Park Service jurisdiction. The chance to ride on Air Force One and trips to the Virgin Islands and Puerto Rico for my wife and me made life a lot more enjoyable. We also were VIP guests at the launching of the aircraft carrier *John F. Kennedy* at Newport News, Virginia. Being part of the delegation to examine the hydroelectric projects in the Soviet Union was a very special benefit. One personal perk resulted from President Kennedy's fondness for relatively skinny cigars. Evelyn Lincoln passed on to me the fat ones that had been given to JFK.

The ability to eat in the White House mess and to bring guests was another special benefit, and many of my friends and relatives were able to share in that happy environment. LBJ was quite a raconteur and many of his stories were uproarious, the only trouble being that frequently he'd start telling them about 3:30 or 4:00 o'clock on Saturday afternoon when everyone wanted to go home.

Although it did not happen often, seats in the Presidential Box at the Kennedy Center came our way on occasion. I recall the time that Don and Annie Farber, our closest friends over the years, asked if we could get tickets to the play "Amadeus" at the National Theater. Don is a very successful New York City entertainment lawyer and had been quite generous in treating us to New York plays, so the request was a reasonable one. The problem was that the house was sold out for the entire performance. It dawned on me that a fellow I knew who had done some work for the Chicago Sanitary District, Maurice Tobin, had become the president of the National Theater. In desperation, I called his office to see if it could help out, throwing around the fact that I knew Maurie. Well, lo and behold, his presidential box was not being used the night we were interested in and he said we were welcome to use it without charge. For the Farbers, this demonstrated two of my characteristics: I'm lucky, and I'm cheap.

Christmas gifts from the boss are not uncommon, but when the boss is the President, those gifts can be somewhat special. The Johnsons gave beautiful prints of paintings of White House rooms and, in some cases, venison. The Kennedys gave paintings also, but books as well signed by both President and Mrs. Kennedy. The most poignant was the gift at Christmas 1963 in which Mrs. Kennedy wrote that they had both intended to join in presenting the book.

The greatest perk of all came when I made the cutoff for a chauffer-driven car to pick me up at home and return me, as well as take me to the Capitol and any other reasonable location. To be able to relax and read a couple of newspapers in comfort and not have to fight traffic was a special luxury. As stingy as I was with government funds, I could even justify in my own mind the benefits to the job. Frequently, I would find items on the front page of the newspaper and know that I would be working on them that day. The time was usefully spent, the nerves were calm and I could be reached by radio (this was long before cell phones and pagers). The biggest jolt in leaving the White House for the Federal Power Commission, besides a cut in salary, was the loss of that car. It's very easy to get used to that piece of luxury.

There was also a benefit for the kids. On the occasion of Bruce's Bar Mitzvah, President Kennedy sent him an autographed copy of *Profiles in Courage*. When Bess Abell, Mrs. Johnson's social secretary, asked if I knew any young Jewish kid who could play the role of a Bar Mitzvah boy in a playlet starring the great actor Fredrick March to be presented at a White House dinner, I just happened to know one, my son Murray.

In addition to the governmental side of the perk ledger, there was the outside segment. Although nobody would characterize my wife and me as social butterflies, lots of invitations came our way—for example, embassy receptions, dinners, and movie premiers. As far as I can recall, I only attended one lunchtime affair; it was at the Belgian Embassy honoring the departing Secretary of Commerce Jack Connor. LBJ happened to call while I was away and told me when I got back to the office, "Not you, too. I didn't think you did things like that." There were two, however, that did not materialize. A white-tie dinner for some head of state (I forget which one) was scheduled at the State Department. I owned a tuxedo, but not tails. As I was about to rent the suit, some significant event occurred at the honoree's home country and the dinner had to be cancelled, but at least I didn't have to pay for the rental.

The other situation was far more solemn. I'm not sure how people get on invitation lists, but after a couple of years, my wife and I were invited to a reception at the home of Mr. and Mrs. Phil Graham, the publisher of *The Washington Post*. We accepted. Shortly before the scheduled event, we received a black bordered notice of the cancellation due to the death of Mr. Graham. Tragically, he had committed suicide.

There were, sad to say, some missed opportunities. Ed Welch, the executive director of the Vice President's Space Committee kept after me to go to Cape Canaveral to view a space launching. I kept putting him off and never did get to the Cape. I was to participate in the opening of the World's Fair in Seattle, but had to cancel when things started popping on the civil rights front in Alabama.

Finally, I have to face up to the fact that with my degrees in Electrical Engineering and Law and a pretty good work record probably my greatest contribution to civil rights progress was my suggestion to schedule the joint session. Years later, after President Johnson had died, I was participating on a panel at the LBJ Library in Austin, Texas, and Mrs. Johnson was sitting in the first row. As I told the story and, looking right at her, I said I knew I had really scored with LBJ, because that Christmas, when gifts were passed out to the staff, I got a big venison steak, not the usual ground stuff I previously got. Mrs. Johnson got a big charge out of that because insiders knew that the President decided what each member of the staff got depending on how the President was feeling about his or her performance at the time.

The White House days were long and frequently tense, but the assignment was a terrific place to be. For most of us, it was the highlight of our careers.

Epilogue

I have often visualized the Republic as a tremendous battleship that would move forward steadily with relatively minor adjustments to the left or the right. But more recently, and particularly since 9/11, I have felt our great ship of state has lost its bearings, veered off-course, and steadily gone astray in increasingly dangerous waters, while it's admiral rigidly adheres to an uncertain course, denies we are lost, defiantly defends his vice admiral and crew, and dismisses legitimate protest as unpatriotic acts.

Thus, in the course of writing about my experiences in the two administrations in which I served, namely, the John F. Kennedy and the Lyndon B. Johnson Presidencies, I have found it compelling (really irresistible) to compare these administrations with the George W. Bush administration, as the latter rounds out its last two years. I have previously mentioned how the passage of time tends to enhance the positive events of the past in one's memory, whereas the negatives or failures tend to diminish or even disappear. That observation, and the fact that I regard myself as a left-leaning liberal Democrat (even though my patriotic immigrant parents gave me the middle name of Calvin because I was born eight days after John Calvin Coolidge, a Republican, took office on the occasion of President Warren G. Harding's death) make it tough to be objective. But I'll try, at least, to be civil.

To be blunt, the George W. Bush administration combines some of the worst characteristics of bad governance. It is super-secretive, with a penchant for "losing" key documents and misapplying the doctrine of executive privilege, which badly damages its credibility. It is unduly and blindly partisan and has spawned divisiveness rather than unity. It is profligate in its spending, disdaining budgetary discipline and amassing enormous national indebtedness. It favors the wealthiest in tax cuts and is guided heavily by the influence of big business. It attempts to transform the nation into a theocracy through its

213

policies and spending. It cooperates with unscrupulous lobbyists. In the name of national security, it violates constitutional and statutory provisions designed to protect the rights of citizens. Its appointments to administrative and especially judicial positions are almost exclusively from conservative, not mainstream, quarters, and a staggering number of its nominees are grossly incompetent. Its actions have been responsible for the nation's plummeting standing in world opinion to a level never before known. The Bush administration did not invent scandals, but it has broken all national and probably international records, both in sheer numbers and in the broad scope of its scandals. If left to its own devices, this "perfect storm" of considerations could lead to a national calamity, and I fear for the nation's future.

THE EXECUTIVE BRANCH AND CONGRESS

One striking difference is in the relationship between the Executive Branch and the Congress. In the JFK years, even though both Houses of Congress were controlled by Democrats (just as the Bush administration dealt with Republican control for most of the first six years), we sometimes groused that the committee chairmen were so accustomed to pounding the Eisenhower people that we had to remind them that we were Democrats, too. JFK met one-on-one with every committee chairman in both Houses. My assignment was to prepare a memorandum, based on consultation with appropriate department and agency people, advising the President of the issues each committee had before it. He personally knew all of the Senate chairmen and most of the House chairmen, but the goal was to demonstrate respect and stress cooperation. Even powerful chairmen welcomed a personal conversation with the President.

LBJ reveled in dealing with (or outmaneuvering) congressional leaders. He frequently invited chairmen to dine with him to discuss what was going on in their committees, and he enjoyed gossiping about his old haunts. Congressional relations were a top priority for both JFK and LBJ, and nobody ever filled that role better for both presidents than the late Larry O'Brien.

Both JFK and LBJ, unlike President Bush, had served in the House of Representatives and in the Senate; but even though Vice-President "Dick" Cheney had served in the House in a leadership position and presumably had many friends among his former colleagues, the Bush people, from where I sit, treat the legislature almost with disdain.

Without strong personal relationships and for whatever reason or reasons, President Bush appears to regard legislative leaders as implementers of administration policies and programs, not collaborators. To an outsider, it seems as though someone (probably the Vice-President) told him the powers of the Executive Branch had been weakened through the years and that he should reclaim those lost authorities. It isn't hard to label him a unilateralist, as he calls himself "the Decider." Now that he has to deal with a democratic-controlled Congress, we'll see if that bravado weakens somewhat.

EXECUTIVE PRIVILEGE

The doctrine of executive privilege existed from the beginnings of our government as a matter of comity between the legislative and executive branches. It was President Richard Nixon who broke the pattern by claiming that the Watergate tapes did not have to be disclosed because of executive privilege. The Supreme Court unanimously rejected the Nixon claim. The Bush administration's attempt to deny testimony before Congressional committees by White House staff, if pursued, is likely to have the same result and should.

JFK and LBJ each treated the privilege as one to be exercised with restraint. Both of them formally advised Congress that only they, personally, would exercise or authorize executive privilege. The only incident I recall was Secretary of Defense McNamara's refusal to reveal the names of his speech writers on the ground that McNamara's speech was his own and he alone could be questioned on it. As was well known, LBJ on occasion chased leaks. When his policy of refusing to make appointments to his administration if the name of the would-be nominee appeared in the press became widely understood, he was a bit surprised to learn that some opponents of the nominee would plant a story to get rid of that particular candidate.

In contrast, another pillar of the Bush crowd's approach to governing appears to be secrecy. The almost obsessive secrecy boggles the mind. It is inconceivable that JFK or LBJ would refuse to make known the participants of an energy policy task force, as did the Bush administration, even taking the case to the Supreme Court. Undoubtedly, the events of September 11, 2001 justified some beefed up secrecy; but the energy policy task force predated 9/11.

WHITHER CONSERVATISM?

Favoring the wealthier segment of the nation's population in proposing tax cuts and opposing an increase in minimum wages may be Republican theology, but the current administration plays that game to the extreme. Its casual concern about increasing the national debt by trillions and the President's failure to veto a single appropriations bill loaded with thousands of "earmarks" seems, to this Democrat, to belie Republican orthodoxy. His threatened veto (at this writing) of the Iraq War appropriations bill is no exception. It continues the trend in spending taxpayers' dollars for a war with a highly uncertain outcome. If the Iraq War appropriations bill is vetoed, it won't be because of massive expenditures for war or earmarks by a Democratic Congress, but rather the President's determined opposition to a timetable for troop withdrawals.

BREAKING DOWN THE WALL BETWEEN CHURCH AND STATE

Speaking of theology, the great push by the Bush administration to bring religion into governmental activities is simply appalling. In commentary on the matter, John Kennedy, as a presidential candidate, addressed a large group of religious leaders in Houston, clearly and forcefully declaring that his religious beliefs would not impact his decisions on public policy issues. And they did not. The Bush administration's establishment of a White House Office promoting faith-based institutions (funded with taxpayers' dollars) to assume responsibility for governmental programs aiding the poor and disadvantaged breaches the nation's tradition of a wall between government and religion. The Bush folks misunderstood President Reagan: he said tear down the wall in Berlin, not the wall between church and state.

Finagling with scientific findings for political purposes is beyond the pale. Contrast the Bush Food and Drug Administration's handling of the day-after birth control pill with the Kennedy administration's gutsy, politically painful support of Surgeon General Luther Terry's recommendation to label cigarettes as dangerous to health. But, I concede, it, at least, looks as if the reality of global warming has finally been acknowledged by the Bush political arm.

ENVIRONMENTAL POLICIES

The Kennedy-Johnson years saw great strides in making this nation a more livable and environmentally safer country. Under the leadership of Secretary of the Interior Stewart Udall, the Land and Conservation Fund Act was passed to provide a funding mechanism for adding to and protecting our national parks, national forests and other public lands. The Bureau of Outdoor Recreation was created. The Wilderness Act provided for designating parks, rivers, seashores and lakeshores as wilderness areas to be protected against encroachments. Numerous new national seashores and lakeshores were created.

Let us not forget that conservation of this nation's wonderful natural resources was initially promoted by a Republican president, Theodore Roosevelt, and aided by another Republican, Gifford Pinchot, the Governor of Pennsylvania and first chief of the United States Forest Service. Contrast those accomplishments with the Bush administration's efforts to permit logging in national forests, drilling for oil in environmentally sensitive areas, and easing of anti-pollution controls on coal-burning electric utilities.

On issues involving regulation of business and industry, the Bush people invariably favor the industry position on such matters, most notably on environmental policies and practices. When pushed by electric utilities, the Bush EPA eased the requirement for anti-pollution measures when old plants were modified, a position repudiated by the Supreme Court of the United States.

PRESIDENTIAL APPOINTMENTS

Presidents have the unquestioned right to appoint individuals to lifetime terms in the federal courts, and the Senate has the right and obligation to confirm or deny those appointments. Presidents JFK and LBJ each appointed Democrats to the Supreme Court, but they were mainstream appointments. The George W. Bush appointments have, in too many instances, been candidates who are outside the mainstream. It's as if the Bush thrust is to ensure a heavily conservative federal judiciary for decades. As a lawyer and a citizen, this gives me great pain.

Both George W. Bush and JFK had very narrow election victories. President Kennedy reached out to Republicans, appointing Ford Motor Company CEO Robert McNamara as Secretary of Defense, and Wall Street investment banker Douglas Dillon as Secretary of the Treasury. LBJ appointed John Gardner, a Republican, and then President of the Carnegie Corporation and the Chairman of the Carnegie Foundation for the Advancement of Teaching, to be Secretary of Health, Education and Welfare. President Bush's initial cabinet had one Democrat, Norman Mineta, the Secretary of Transportation who was retained from the Clinton administration, and now he's gone. Quite a contrast.

Although difficult to quantify, it is my impression that the administrations I served in included individuals who had considerable governmental experience, as opposed to the Bush appointees. Experience is not an absolute assurance of stellar performance in presidentially appointed positions, but the odds are better that there will be smoother and more effective operation than is true of a team with too many who have no prior government service. On-the-job training can be very costly. (It was widely joked that Vice President

Cheney and Defense Secretary Rumsfeld gave experience a bad name.) As to the quality of the talent brought to the job, because comparisons are tricky, it may not be fair to say ours were better than the Bush appointees, but I believe it's true.

QUESTIONS OF GOVERNING

These contrasts and criticisms are not nit-picking political griping. They are among the basic elements of national governance, and the Bush administration does not fare well in the comparisons. Of course, not every action taken by the Bush administration is unacceptable. And I do not claim that the JFK and LBJ presidencies were without some errors and major goof-ups.

Very early in the JFK term, the disastrous Bay of Pigs invasion of Castro's Cuba was a big black eye for the United States. President Kennedy assumed full responsibility for the disaster, rather than point fingers at the Eisenhower advisors who had hatched and planned the idea, which was the right course for him to take because he had approved the venture. President Kennedy also knew instinctively that although he could legitimately talk about the role of his advisers, the wiser course was to assume full responsibility for the fiasco. His assumption of the blame resulted in a significant jump in his approval rating. Admission of mistakes comes harder for the Bush team.

How a president governs is, of course, of great consequence, and I have laid out some significant differences between the JFK and LBJ Presidencies and the George W. Bush administration. But more important, is the fundamental thrust of each administration that comes into power. In the Kennedy presidency, its goals were to move the nation forward and build military strength. Thus, the space race with Russia was undertaken with a goal of putting "a man on the moon" and returning him safely to earth; and it was accomplished. Mass transit and urban renewal programs were initiated. The environmental breakthroughs, mentioned above, have made this country a better place to live. And the showdown with Russia over the Cuban missile crisis was successfully met.

The LBJ presidency mounted the most vigorous attack on reducing poverty in this country that was ever undertaken. Civil Rights and Voting Rights legislation were enacted. Federal support for education was enacted for the first time in the nation's history. Not every undertaking bore fruit and, certainly, there were missteps; but what a record of achievements.

Contrast this record not only with Bush's tax cuts for the very wealthy and its opposition to an increase in the minimum wage, but also the stealthy move, at the end of 2006, by the Bush-appointed Securities and Exchange

Commission to change its rules requiring transparency in the public reporting of compensation of corporate executives in such a way that is likely to result in misleading information for shareholders and the public. And consider the effort to weaken, if not remove, the separation of church and state. The heavy influence of corporate America in the programs and polices supported by the Bush administration has, in my view, tipped the scales far too heavily in their favor. The Occupational Safety and Health Administration has been run by some former officials of companies that are to be regulated by OSHA. It's no wonder the Bush record is one of cutbacks in enforcement and relaxing of regulations. The foxes are in the chicken coop.

Spying on U.S. citizens without court approval and the excesses and abuses of the FBI in ignoring legal requisites in information gathering sound like the Cold War tactics of the former Soviet Union. Even where the Bush proposal for education—"No Child Left Behind"—held considerable promise, it was grossly underfunded, poorly executed, and marred by scandals. The total lack of concern for massive deficits and a staggering national debt (together with tax cuts) will burden our children and their children for a very long time.

GOVERNMENT "FOR THE PEOPLE"

I am a Democrat, and a proud one. I believe that government "for the people" can and should strive to improve the lot of its citizens and provide for the nation's security. As a dyed-in-the-wool optimist and a native Nebraskan, I even believe it is possible that there could be a Republican administration that would espouse and try to achieve those goals. Regardless of political parties or affiliation, we as a nation need to reaffirm and adhere to the guiding principles of our Constitution.

A Chronology of
My Life, Work, and Times

1923 September 1	Born in Omaha, Nebraska to Ann Ruth Ackerman White and Herman Henry White
1930 March 23	Birth of Shirley Joyce White, my sister and only sibling
1936 – 1938	Began my first job at age twelve delivering newspapers on foot and by sled during one of the coldest winters on record in Omaha; transferred from Saunders Grade School to Central Grade School when my family moved from our house in central Omaha into a multi-unit apartment building owned by my maternal grandparents, after my father was seriously injured by a hit-and-run driver and his grocery business went bankrupt
1941 January	Chosen Commander, ROTC Unit, Omaha North High School
1941 September	Enrolled on a scholarship at University of Nebraska College of Engineering in Lincoln
1941 December 8	United States declared war on Japan
1942 August	Hitchhiked to California with Rodney Franklin, my closest high school friend, after a summer job shoveling salt in refrigerator cars at Omaha's Cudahy Packing Plant
1943 March 31	Enlisted in the Army Reserve; called to active duty in the U.S. Army, Fort Leavenworth, Kansas
1943 July	Sent to basic training in the Army Air Corps, Clearwater, Florida; entered the Army Specialized Training Program and attended the electrical

	engineering program at Lehigh University, Bethlehem, Pennsylvania
1944 August	Assigned to the Signal Corps School, Camp Crowder, Missouri
1944 December 28	Graduated from Signal Corps Officer Candidate School in Fort Monmouth, New Jersey, as a Second Lieutenant
1944 December 31	Married my college sweetheart, Dorothy Cohn of Harlan, Iowa
1945 January	Moved to Red Bank, New Jersey, to enter the Signal Corps Officers School at Fort Monmouth
1945 July	Assigned to a Signal Unit to be staged in China for the planned ground invasion of Japan; departed the 48 States in a troop ship that broke down in the Hawaiian Islands, where I was forced to spend two weeks awaiting another ship
1945 August 6–14	United States bombed Hiroshima and Nagasaki; Japan surrendered
1945 September	Reassigned to an officer pool at Camp Clark, near Manila, Philippine Islands, when the U.S. Army changed its plans for a ground invasion of Japan to mobilize troops for the Occupation
1945 November	Joined the 62nd Signal Battalion of the Tenth Corps as Battalion Adjutant, in Kure, Japan, the site of the Japanese Naval Academy in southern Honshu
1946 July	Departed for the United States from Eighth Army Headquarters in Yokohama, after the Australians took over responsibility for southern Honshu from the U.S. Army Tenth Corps
1946 August 12	Returned to Fort Lewis, Washington; discharged from the U.S. Army as a First Lieutenant after three and one-half years of service
1946 September	Re-entered the University of Nebraska College of Engineering with the benefits of the GI Bill and credit for engineering courses taken at Lehigh University
1947 May	Chosen Treasurer of the Innocents, the University's senior mens' honorary society
1947 September	Elected to take courses in law during my last year of college at the urging of my friend Don Farber

1948 June	Awarded a Bachelor's degree in Electrical Engineering
1948 July	Accepted and then declined a job with Sylvania Electric Products in Emporium, Pennsylvania; returned to Lincoln, Nebraska and attended law school at the University of Nebraska, with the benefits of the GI Bill
1948 November 13	Birth of our son Bruce David
1949 May	Elected Editor-in-Chief of the Nebraska Law Review
1950 June	Graduated from University of Nebraska Law School
1950 July	Accepted a position with the Tennessee Valley Authority Division of Law, Knoxville, Tennessee
1951 November 23	Birth of our daughter Rosalyn Adele
1953 May	Introduced to Senator John Fitzgerald Kennedy by Ted Sorensen, the Senator's Legislative Assistant and my friend from law school
1954 January 4	Birth of our son Murray Lewis
1954 January 8	Moved to Washington, DC and joined the staff of Senator John F. Kennedy as a Legislative Assistant
1954 November	Served as Assistant to Joseph P. Kennedy, a member of the second Hoover Commission established to review policies and programs of the Executive Branch, while Senator John Kennedy, his son, convalesced from back surgery
1955 June	Returned to work in Senator Kennedy's office after the Hoover Commission completed its mission
1955 December 14	Birth of our son Sheldon Richard
1956 August	Senator Kennedy captured national attention at the Democratic National Convention, Chicago, by graciously endorsing the Vice Presidential nomination of Estes Kefauver of Tennessee, who defeated Kennedy by a narrow margin
1957 January	Served as Counsel, Senate Small Business Committee
1958 January	Served as Administrative Assistant to Senator John Sherman Cooper, a Republican from Kentucky
1960 March 23	Death of my father, Herman Henry White
1961 January 21	Joined the White House staff as Assistant Special Counsel to President John Fitzgerald Kennedy

1963 July 11	Birth of our daughter Laura Helene
1963 November 22	Assassination of President Kennedy, Dallas, Texas
1963 November	Appointed Assistant Special Counsel to President Lyndon Baines Johnson
1965 March 1	Appointed Special Counsel to President Johnson
1966 March 2	Appointed Chairman, Federal Power Commission, by President Johnson
1968 June 2	Granted Honorary Doctor of Laws degree by the University of Nebraska
1969 August 1	Joined the law firm of Semer, White & Jacobsen
1970	Became counsel to the Association of Metropolitan Sewerage Agencies, a collection of major city waste treatment agencies, which later became the National Association of Clean Water Agencies
1970 July	Appointed to the Board of the Environmental Defense Fund; served on a three-member Litigation Review Committee whose approval was required before litigation could be initiated
1970 October	Founded the Utilities Housing Council, later reorganized as the Utilities Council on Community Development
1972 July	Served as campaign manager for R. Sargent Shriver, Democratic candidate for Vice-President, running with presidential candidate Senator George McGovern of South Dakota
1973 June	Appointed Chairman, Energy Policy Task Force of the Consumer Federation of America; subsequently selected as President of the Consumers Energy Council of America
1973 August	Co-founded the law firm of White, Fine & Verville after Semer, White & Jacobsen dissolved
1977 September	Elected to a three-year term on the Board of Governors of the District of Columbia Bar
1977 October	Appointed to the Board of Directors of the National Regulatory Research Institute, the "think tank" of the National Association of Regulatory Utility Commissioners, at Ohio State University
1978 February	Marriage to Dorothy White ended in divorce
1980 June	Appointed to the Board of Governors of the New York Mercantile Exchange as a representative of the public

1981 December 30	Married Bernice Shurman and adopted her daughter, Lori Jeanne
1983 September 8	Death of Bernice Shurman White
1984 February	Elected to the Board of Directors of the Central Hudson Gas & Electric Corporation
1984 November 8	Birth of grandson Miguel White
1985 November 25	Birth of grandson Stephen White
1989 October 19	Served as a Board Member of the Hemisphere Initiatives and monitored voter registration for the upcoming Nicaraguan presidential election
1989 November 19	Married Cecile "Cece" Rottman Zorinsky
1990 May	Served on a blue ribbon committee established by the Generic Pharmaceutical Industry Association and charged with inquiring into problems of the industry and making recommendations to restore public confidence in generic drugs in response to abuses by some generic drug manufacturers and the Food and Drug Administration
1993	Appointed and subsequently elected to the Board of the Yenkin-Majestic Paint Corporation
1993 November 28	Birth of granddaughter Emily White
1994 February	Joined Linton, Mields, Reisler & Cottone, a consulting firm, as General Counsel, when White, Verville, Fulton & Saner dissolved
1995 August 29	Death of Dorothy White
1996 January	Joined the law firm of Spiegel & McDiarmid as Of Counsel
1996 April 15	Death of "Cece" White
1997 February 28	Death of my mother, Ann Ruth Ackerman White
1999 May 22	Birth of grandson Trevor White
2001 December 29	Birth of grandson Clay Weeks-White
2005	Founding member of the ROMEOs
2006 July 16	Birth of grandson Noah Weeks-White

Abbreviations and Acronyms

9/11	September 11, 2001
ΣAM	Sigma Alpha Mu
AEC	Atomic Energy Commission
AFL-CIO	American Federation of Labor—Congress of Industrial Organizations
AG	Attorney General of the United States
AID	Agency for International Development
AMSA	Association of Metropolitan Sewerage Agencies
AP	Associated Press
APPA	American Public Power Association
AT&T	American Telephone & Telegraph Corporation
BOB	Bureau of the Budget (established in 1921 as part the Department of Treasury; reorganized in 1970 as the Office of Management and Budget within the Executive Office of the President)
CECA	Consumer Energy Council of America
CEO	Chief Executive Officer
CFA	Consumer Federation of America
CFTC	Commodity Futures Trading Commission
DC	District of Columbia
DNC	Democratic National Committee
Ds	Democrats
EPA	Environmental Protection Agency
ESP	Extra-Sensory Perception
FBI	Federal Bureau of Investigation
FCC	Federal Communications Commission

FDR	Franklin Delano Roosevelt (1882–1945; 32nd President, 1933–1945)
FOGCO	Federal Oil and Gas Corporation
FPC	Federal Power Commission (established as an independent agency by the U.S. Congress in 1935; reorganized in 1977 as the Federal Energy Regulatory Commission)
GI Bill (of Rights)	The Servicemen's Readjustment Act of 1944, which, as originally enacted, enabled World War II veterans to participate in education and training in lieu of entering the job market and to obtain home loan guarantees between 1944 and 1956
GM	General Manager
HEW	Department of Health, Education and Welfare (established in 1953 as the successor agency to the National Security Agency, which was created in 1939; reorganized as the Department of Health and Human Services in 1979)
HHFA	Housing and Home Finance Agency (established in 1943 as the successor to the National Housing Agency; reorganized by the U.S. Congress in 1965 as the Department of Housing and Urban Development)
HUD	Department of Housing and Urban Development
JFK	John Fitzgerald Kennedy (1917–1963; 35th President, 1961–1963)
K-P	Kennedy-Paiewonsky
LBJ	Lyndon Baines Johnson (1908–1973; 36th President, 1963–1969)
NARUC	National Association of Regulatory Utility Commissioners
NBC	National Broadcasting Corporation
NRECA	National Rural Electric Cooperatives Association
NRRI	National Regulatory Research Institute
NSC	National Security Council
NW	Northwest
NYMEX	New York Mercantile Exchange
OEP	Office of Emergency Preparedness
OK	Satisfactory
OSHA	Occupational Safety and Health Administration
RFK	Robert Francis Kennedy ("Bobby") (1925–1968)

ROMEOs	Retired Old Men Eating Out
ROTC	Reserve Officers' Training Corps
Rs	Republicans
SBA	Small Business Administration
SEC	Securities and Exchange Commission
SNCC	Student Non-Violent Coordinating Committee
SOB	Son of a Bitch
TIPRO	Texas Independent Petroleum and Royalty Owners
TV	Television
TvA	Television Agency (or Television Authority)
TVA	Tennessee Valley Authority (established by the U.S. Congress in 1933)
UAW	United Automobile Workers Union
U.S.	United States
UT	University of Tennessee
VA	Veterans Administration
VIP	Very Important Person
WPCF	Water Pollution Control Federation
YMCA	Young Men's Christian Association

Index

disagreements, 127, 203, 204, 206; limits of, 89, 203; media, 127, 134, 199; perks of, 128, 208–12; reflected authority, 72, 140, 197. *See also* religion, role of
White, Laura Helene, 190, 224
White, Lori Jeanne Shurman, 167, 188, 190, 225
White, Lee C., ii; as FPC Chairman, 140, 143, 149, 160, 173–74, 224; as TVA lawyer, 5–9; career choices, 4–5, 10–11, 36, 43, 51, 111, 137, 138–39, 140, 144, 162–64, 166, 173–74, 183–84, 187; family heritage of, iii, 192–93, 213; introduction to JFK, xx, xxi, 223; Jewish identity of, 25, 41, 80, 193, 194, 207, 211; military service of, 221–22; on luck, 94, 95, 72, 108, 128, 152, 187, 193, 194, 210; on practice of law, 170–71, 183; on memory, xii, xiii, 105, 118, 213; photos, *60, 102, 113, 121, 129, 135, 149, 204, 205, 209;* political identification of, 40–41, 52–53, 164, 171, 178, 213, 219; Senate staff assignments, 12, 18, 38–39, 40; White House assignments, 64, 69–70, 71–72, 79, 81, 84, 86, 89, 93,

94–95, 118–19, 125–26, 127–28, 131. *See also* civil rights; Federal Power Commission; Moyers, Bill; Nebraska, University of; Sorensen, Ted; Tennessee Valley Authority
White, Miguel, 225
White, Morris, xi, xii, 192
White, Murray Lewis, xxi, 89, 189, 211, 223
White, Rosalyn Adele, xxi, 10, 125–26, 189, 223
White, Sheldon Richard, 89, 190, 223
White, Shirley Joyce. *See* Levy, Shirley Joyce White
White, Stephen, 190, 225
White, Trevor, 190, 225
Wilderness Bill, 71–72
Wilkins, Roy, 95; photo, *129*
Wirtz, Willard, 206
Wofford, Harris, 94
WPCF. *See* Water Pollution Control Federation

Yenkin-Majestic Paint Corporation, 225
Young, Whitney, 95, 133; photo, *129*

Zorinsky, Cecile "Cece" Rottman. *See* White, Cecile "Cece"
Zorinsky, Eddie, 188

About The Editor

Zabelle Zakarian is an editor with an interest in history and autobiography pertaining to public policies and institutions. Her publications include *Medic: The Mission of an American Military Doctor in Occupied Japan and Wartorn Korea*, published by M.E. Sharpe, Inc. She earned a Doctor of Science degree at The Johns Hopkins University and holds a B.F.A. in Humanities from the California Institute of the Arts. She resides in Washington, DC.